Working in the Cloud

Using Web-Based Applications and Tools to Collaborate Online

Jason R. Rich

PEARSON

800 East 96th Street, Indianapolis, Indiana 46240 USA

Working in the Cloud: Using Web-Based Applications and Tools to Collaborate Online

Copyright © 2018 by Pearson Education, Inc.

ISBN-13: 978-0-7897-5902-3
ISBN-10: 0-7897-5902-0

Library of Congress Control Number: 2017945176

1 17

Trademarks

All terms mentioned in this book that are known to be trademarks or service marks have been appropriately capitalized. Que Publishing cannot attest to the accuracy of this information. Use of a term in this book should not be regarded as affecting the validity of any trademark or service mark.

Microsoft® and Windows® are registered trademarks of the Microsoft Corporation in the U.S.A. and other countries. Screenshots and icons reprinted with permission from the Microsoft Corporation. This book is not sponsored or endorsed by or affiliated with the Microsoft Corporation.

Warning and Disclaimer

Every effort has been made to make this book as complete and as accurate as possible, but no warranty or fitness is implied. The information provided is on an "as is" basis. The author(s) and the publisher shall have neither liability nor responsibility to any person or entity with respect to any loss or damages arising from the information contained in this book.

Microsoft and/or its respective suppliers make no representations about the suitability of the information contained in the documents and related graphics published as part of the services for any purpose. All such documents and related graphics are provided "as is" without warranty of any kind. Microsoft and/or its respective suppliers hereby disclaim all warranties and conditions with regard to this information, including all warranties and conditions of merchantability, whether express, implied or statutory, fitness for a particular purpose, title, and non-infringement. In no event shall Microsoft and/or its respective suppliers be liable for any special, indirect, or consequential damages or any damages whatsoever resulting from loss of use, data, or profits, whether in an action of contract, negligence, or other tortious action, arising out of or in connection with the use or performance of information available from the services.

The documents and related graphics contained herein could include technical inaccuracies or typographical errors. Changes are periodically added to the information herein. Microsoft and/or its respective suppliers may make improvements and/or changes in the product(s) and/or the program(s) described herein at any time. Partial screenshots may be viewed in full within the software version specified.

Special Sales

For information about buying this title in bulk quantities, or for special sales opportunities (which may include electronic versions; custom cover designs; and content particular to your business, training goals, marketing focus, or branding interests), please contact our corporate sales department at corpsales@pearsoned.com or (800) 382-3419.

For government sales inquiries, please contact governmentsales@pearsoned.com.

For questions about sales outside the U.S., please contact intlcs@pearson.com.

Editor-in-Chief
Greg Wiegand

Senior Acquisitions Editor
Laura Norman

Editorial Services
The Wordsmithery LLC

Managing Editor
Sandra Schroeder

Indexer
Cheryl Lenser

Proofreader
The Wordsmithery LLC

Technical Editor
Karen Weinstein

Editorial Assistant
Cindy J. Teeters

Designer
Chuti Praserstith

Compositor
Bronkella Publishing LLC

Graphics
TJ Graham Art

Contents at a Glance

Table of Contents

About the Author

Jason R. Rich (www.jasonrich.com) is an accomplished author, journalist, and photographer. Some of his recently published books include *iPad and iPhone Tips and Tricks,* 7th Edition (Que), *My Digital Entertainment for Seniors* (Que), *Ultimate Guide to YouTube for Business* (Entrepreneur Press), *How to Do Everything iCloud,* 2nd Edition (McGraw-Hill), and *The Crowd Funding Services Handbook* (Wiley).

Through his work as an enrichment lecturer, he often offers technology-related workshops and classes aboard cruise ships operated by Royal Caribbean, Princess Cruises Lines, Norwegian Cruise Lines, and Celebrity Cruise Lines, as well as through Adult Education programs in the New England area. Please follow Jason R. Rich on Twitter (@JasonRich7), LinkedIn (www.linkedin.com/in/jasonrich7), and Instagram (@JasonRich7).

Dedication

This book is dedicated to my family and friends, including my niece Natalie, my nephew Parker, and my Yorkshire Terrier, named Rusty, who is always by my side as I'm writing.

Acknowledgments

Thanks once again to Laura Norman and Greg Wiegand at Pearson Education for inviting me to work on this project and for their ongoing support. I'd also like to thank Charlotte Kughen and everyone else at Que whose talents helped to make this book a reality.

We Want to Hear from You!

As the reader of this book, *you* are our most important critic and commentator. We value your opinion and want to know what we're doing right, what we could do better, what areas you'd like to see us publish in, and any other words of wisdom you're willing to pass our way.

We welcome your comments. You can email or write to let us know what you did or didn't like about this book—as well as what we can do to make our books better.

Please note that we cannot help you with technical problems related to the topic of this book.

When you write, please be sure to include this book's title and author as well as your name and email address. We will carefully review your comments and share them with the author and editors who worked on the book.

Email: feedback@quepublishing.com

Mail: Que Publishing
          ATTN: Reader Feedback
          800 East 96th Street
          Indianapolis, IN 46240 USA

Reader Services

Register your copy of *Working in the Cloud* at quepublishing.com for convenient access to downloads, updates, and corrections as they become available. To start the registration process, go to quepublishing.com/register and log in or create an account*. Enter the product ISBN, 9780789759023, and click Submit. Once the process is complete, you will find any available bonus content under Registered Products.

*Be sure to check the box that you would like to hear from us in order to receive exclusive discounts on future editions of this product.

Chapter | **1**

Introducing Cloud-Based Computing and Collaborating

This chapter introduces you to cloud-based computing and covers the following topics:

- What "the cloud" is and which cloud services and tools are discussed within this book
- What the differences are between cloud file sharing and online collaboration tools and services
- What equipment you need to begin using cloud-based computing tools and services
- What you should know before you start working in the cloud

Anyone who uses computers has probably heard the terms "cloud computing," "cloud-based file sharing," and "online collaboration." Perhaps you've even used your PC or Mac computer (or your Internet-connected smartphone or tablet) to take advantage of some of the cloud-based tools currently available to you.

After all, manufacturers certainly are making it convenient for their users to use cloud services. Microsoft has integrated the Microsoft OneDrive service into its Windows 10 operating system, Apple has incorporated functionality for the Apple iCloud service into its macOS and iOS operating systems, and Google has integrated Google Drive functionality into the Android operating system.

Each of these popular cloud-based services is designed to handle a wide range of functions, many of which are fully automated. Here are just a few examples of what you can do in the cloud:

- Online file sharing
- Syncing data, documents, photos, music, videos, and files between computers and mobile devices that are linked to the same account
- Backing up and archiving important information

In addition to OneDrive, iCloud, and Google Drive, there are many cloud-based services designed specifically for business professionals and teams. Some of these services offer specialized functionality; others combine a collection of online-based tools and services that make it easy for people to collaborate and share information (data, documents, photos, files, and multimedia content), as well as store and easily access information online, regardless of what type of computer or mobile device is being used.

The goals of any cloud-based computing or online collaboration service are to improve organization, enhance productivity, increase employee or collaborator engagement, improve communication, save time, and help to ensure data security. In addition, these tools can decrease the carbon footprint of a company, group, or individual by replacing paper-based content with digital files and reducing the need for people to travel in order to work together.

Working in the Cloud: Using Web-Based Applications and Tools to Collaborate Online is all about using the latest cloud-based services and tools for file sharing, storing content online, and collaborating with other people. From this book, you will find out what you can do using cloud-based computing tools and services and acquire the knowledge you need to make intelligent decisions when it comes to choosing the most suitable tools and services for your work habits and budget.

Before I get into all the ways cloud-based tools can be used in the workplace and explain what's possible when it comes to online-based collaboration, I'm going to introduce the core concepts associated with working within cloud-based environments.

What Is the Cloud?

In a nutshell, cloud computing refers to storing and accessing data, documents, files, photos, and other content online on remote servers rather than in local storage on your computer's hard drive, storage that's physically connected to your computer, or the internal storage within your smartphone or tablet. The remote and secure server is accessible to you via the Internet. So "the cloud" is just another way to refer to Internet-based or online storage. When you're storing, accessing or syncing data online, running online-based applications from your computer or mobile device, or collaborating with other people via the Internet, you're engaging in what we call *cloud computing*.

In Practice

Internet Required

To be able to work the cloud or do any form of cloud-based computing (including real-time online collaboration), you must have continuous Internet access for your computer or mobile device. As long as you're connected to the Internet, your content is readily accessible to you anytime from anywhere.

For example, if you create a document on your PC at work and you store it in the cloud, that document is immediately accessible to your other computers and mobile devices that are linked with the same cloud-based account.

FYI: Cloud Computing Is Growing in Popularity

In 2012, cloud-based computing represented a $100 billion industry. By 2017, it had grown to be a $127 billion industry. With more and more individuals, teams, companies, and organizations relying heavily on cloud-based computing for so many different tasks, by 2020 the industry is expected to reach $500 billion!

Individuals, teams, and companies in all types of industries have discovered many ways to use cloud-based computing. The main reason for the widespread use is that when content is securely stored in the cloud, it becomes accessible to authorized users anywhere, anytime, and from any computer or mobile device they're using.

One of the drawbacks to working the cloud is that there are now many different cloud-based services available, and many people and companies wind up using several different services. This can result in some confusion: Whereas you once knew that all of your data was stored locally on the hard drive of your primary computer, now you might need to remember in which service your data is stored.

For example, you might store your photos within your personal iCloud Photo Library account but keep your Microsoft Word documents in your Microsoft OneDrive account. To add to the problem, you might store and sync your work-related files with a Dropbox account and upload your Adobe Photoshop files in your online-based Adobe Creative Cloud account. That's four different accounts to keep track of!

FYI: Virtual Private Clouds

Some cloud-based services are readily available to all computer users, including small to mid-size businesses. In addition, some larger corporations rely heavily on cloud services that they operate themselves. Private cloud-based computing services are referred to as *Virtual Private Clouds (VPCs)*.

According to IBM (https://www.ibm.com/cloud-computing/learn-more/what-is-virtual-private-cloud), "A virtual private cloud (VPC) is an implementation of cloud computing hosted behind a corporate firewall. VPCs are managed by a cloud provider [such as IBM]. Some offerings include automated features to allow for minimal intervention. Unlike a traditional public cloud, the provider provisions a portion of its infrastructure for a single user. This keeps that user's data separate from others."

Although VPCs are a viable solution for larger corporations, the primary focus of this book is on "public" cloud-based computing services and online platforms that are readily available to individuals, small groups, teams, and small to mid-size companies.

The Mechanics of Cloud Storage

You might be wondering how information is stored in the cloud and when it gets stored there. When you use a cloud-based service, one of several things can happen:

- You use software or a mobile app installed on the equipment you're using to create, edit, or review data, a document, or a file. After you've created the content, you save locally and also sync it to the cloud via the cloud-based integration that's built into the software or app you're using. That content is then available to all of your other computers and mobile devices that are connected to the Internet and linked to the same cloud-based account.

- You create content on your computer or mobile device that is stored in the cloud and then share it with specific other people who are invited to access that content via a cloud-based service (using their own accounts for that service). This is an example of *cloud-based file sharing*.

- You use your computer or mobile device's web browser to access an online service that offers web-based applications. These applications store your created or edited content online. You can access that content from any computer or mobile device, and you can also share the content with specific other people.

- You use a cloud-based collaboration service to work with other people in real time. This can include sharing a computer screen (or a collaborative virtual workspace), simultaneously working with the same content files, and communicating via text messages, voice calls, or video calls. This is what's referred to as *real-time online collaboration*.

FYI: Businesses That Use the Cloud Realize Definite Benefits

In 2016, Skyhigh Networks (www.skyhighnetworks.com/cloud-computing-trends-2016) reported the following: "Studies have shown that businesses taking advantage of productivity-enhancing cloud services grow 19.6% faster than their counterparts that don't."

Security Concerns in the Cloud

With so many individuals and companies continuously uploading and storing information in the cloud, security concerns with cloud-based tools are very real. According to research published in 2016 by Skyhigh Networks (www.skyhighnetworks.com/cloud-computing-trends-2016), "18.1 percent of all documents uploaded to cloud-based file sharing and collaboration services contain sensitive information. Of that, 4.4 percent is confidential data (e.g. financial records, business plans, source code, etc.), and 3.9 percent contains personally identifiable information (Social Security numbers, tax ID numbers, etc.). Another 2.3 percent contains payment information (e.g. credit card or debit card numbers), and 1.6 percent contains personal health information (e.g. medical record IDs, patient diagnoses, etc.)."

If you'll be using cloud-based file sharing or online file storage to handle these types of important data, security should definitely be a concern that you should not take lightly. After all, you want to make sure the appropriate people have access only to data, documents, and files they should be privy to. You don't want to accidently grant the wrong person access to confidential content that they shouldn't see.

All of the services and tools discussed throughout this book have their own cutting-edge security measures in place, but there are some additional steps you can take to protect your privacy and data when working in the cloud.

It's important to understand that even when using the latest online security tools, some hackers and tech-savvy, unscrupulous people can find ways to gain access to private content that's stored in the cloud.

The following are some of the most common security-related concerns:

- **Insider threats:** When "authorized" employees access and use information for unauthorized purposes or accidently access information to which they should not be privy.

- **Compromised accounts:** When account usernames and passwords are stolen and used by unauthorized people to access content stored in the cloud.

- **Privileged user threats:** When senior company employees use their privileged access or social engineering to obtain access to content that is beyond their role of responsibility within their organization. This access can be for the sake of personal curiosity or for more malicious purposes.

- **Data exfiltration:** The unauthorized copying or transferring of data from the cloud (that is, stealing data), typically done by hackers and cybercriminals.

CAUTION

How to Deal with Security Threats

Chapter 4, "Understanding Cloud-Based Security Concerns," covers more about the security issues related to cloud-based computing. However, throughout this book, services like Box, Cisco's WebEx, Dropbox, Microsoft Office 365, Microsoft OneDrive, Microsoft SharePoint, Salesforce, and Skype for Business, which are among the most trusted services being embraced by corporate IT departments around the world, are discussed.

Considerations When Selecting Services

In the early days of cloud computing, it was necessary to use different tools and services to handle specific tasks because there weren't many tools that integrated multiple functions. These days, however, many of the cloud-based computing services offer a collection of tools, features, and functions that allow most or all of your cloud-based computing needs to be handled by one service. When you do have to use more than one service, some are designed to work seamlessly together to create a more cohesive user experience and virtual work environment.

With so many cloud-based services and tools to choose from, which are the best ones for your specific needs? There are literally hundreds of cloud-based file sharing and collaboration tools available. All these tools allow people to share content and exchange information, and they enable businesses to enhance productivity and communication while maintaining security and keeping IT-related costs down. How do you choose which service is best for you?

As you investigate services and tools and make your decision about which to use, you need to

- Understand and keep tabs on where online your data, documents, files, and content are stored

- Know how to find and access what you need, when you need it

- Be able to share specific files, with specific other people, in a secure way

- Easily collaborate and communicate with others in real time using cloud-based tools, use text messaging, voice calling, video calling, computer screen sharing, webinars, software demos, interactive training tools, and digital slide presentations as needed

- Ensure you can access your content from any computer or mobile device you'll be using, whether it's a Windows PC, Mac, iOS mobile device, and/or an Android-based mobile device.

Cloud-based services and tools aren't without their problems, though. Some problems hindering success with cloud-based services and tools include the following:

- There are many cloud-based computing services and tools to choose from, many of which offer overlapping functionality but not necessarily the same functionality. Thus, you might need to use more than one cloud-based service to get all the features you need; in that case, you'll have to switch between services as you work because they might not integrate with one another.

- You need to keep track of which cloud-based services and platforms you're using for specific tasks and then keep track of where your related data, documents, files, and content are stored.

- Cloud-based computing technologies are changing and evolving very rapidly. As a result, users need to stay proficient using the latest functionality available in order to avoid errors related to storing, managing, or sharing content.

- Not all of the cloud-based computing platforms are easy to use or designed to work seamlessly across all computer hardware and mobile device platforms.

- Not all of the cloud-based computing options offer comprehensive solutions that are cost effective to implement.

- Some cloud-based computing solutions require a significant change in your everyday work habits, whereas others integrate almost seamlessly into the software, mobile apps, tools, and resources you already use.

- A learning curve is typically required for all users to become proficient with using the online-based tools adopted by a company or team.

- Users have concerns about security issues related to storing important, classified, or sensitive information in the cloud.

- Users worry that productivity could be seriously impeded if the cloud service goes offline—even if the outage lasts only a few minutes.

Throughout this book I discuss ways you can navigate around the pitfalls associated with cloud-based computing and help you choose the very best tools for your needs.

How to Use Cloud-Based Computing

Almost every week, cloud computing-related services are introducing new tools and features that enable you to use these technologies in more interesting ways. This book focuses on the three areas:

- Using a cloud-based service to back up and sync your data, documents, files, photos, videos, and content between your computers and mobile devices

- Sharing data, documents, files, photos, videos, and content that you store in the cloud with specific other people while keeping the rest of your information and content private

- Using cloud-based tools to collaborate and communicate with other people in your company or on your team, potentially in real time

---

FYI: Online Collaboration

Many software applications and mobile apps—for word processing, spreadsheet management, database management, bookkeeping, digital slide presentations, note taking, and project management, for example—now allow for real-time and secure online collaboration with others via a cloud-based service.

In other words, two or more people can work together from remote locations on a Microsoft Word document, and all collaborators can see changes and additions as they're being made—in real time. At the same time, the collaborators can brainstorm and communicate with their fellow collaborators using text messaging, voice calls, or video calls via the Internet.

The great thing about online collaboration is that as long as all parties are using the same tools and have access to the Internet, it doesn't matter where the collaborators are. They can be sitting in their respective offices within the same building, or each person can be working miles apart from each other—potentially anywhere in the world.

What You Need to Get Started

What you need to get started using cloud-based computing and the online collaboration tools that are available to you depends on what you're trying to accomplish. At the very least, you'll need the following things:

- A PC or Mac computer and/or a smartphone or tablet

- Internet access

- An account with at least one cloud-based computing service

- Specialized software or mobile apps for handling specific tasks that are compatible with the service(s) you opt to use

- A basic understanding of how to use your chosen tools and how you want to collaborate with other people via the Internet

In Practice

Additional Equipment Might Be Required

If you plan to use Internet-based voice or video calling features to communicate with collaborators, you need to make sure your computer is equipped with a webcam (camera), microphone, and speakers. Most recent model computers have this equipment built in.

If the service you opt to use requires that you install specialized software on your computer, or you have to have a special mobile app on your smartphone or tablet, make sure you download the most current version of the software or mobile app. Cloud computing and online collaboration services continuously update their respective software and apps with new features, functions, and security enhancements, so it's important that you use the most current version of the required software or mobile app.

However, if you're using a web-based service that you access via a standard Internet web browser, make sure you're using the latest version of your favorite web browser, and that it's compatible with the selected service. For example, you might find that some video-calling or file-sharing tools work better with one specific web browser than with others.

Likewise, some services might be accessible from an iPhone or iPad but not from an Android smartphone or tablet. Each cloud service outlines the minimum hardware requirements and specific types of equipment that are required to use it. This is also covered in later chapters of this book.

CAUTION

Internet Access Is Always Needed

Without Internet access, you can work "locally" on your computer or mobile device, but the content you create or edit isn't uploaded or synced to your online account—and you aren't able to collaborate with other people in real time—until an Internet connection is reestablished. Once the computer, smartphone, or tablet you are working with re-connects to the Internet, your files automatically sync to the account and are available to your other computers, mobile devices, and collaborators.

Likewise, if you're somewhere where an Internet connection is not available, you will not be able to access any data, documents, files, or content that is stored in the cloud until you're able to acquire an Internet connection. So if you're about to take a trip on an airplane that doesn't offer in-flight Wi-Fi, before you leave you need to download the files and content you want to work with to the computer or mobile device you plan to use during the flight.

If you plan to collaborate with others, you'll maximize productivity and avoid confusion and miscommunication if everyone on your team uses the same cloud-based tools. All content (files, documents, and so on) should be accessible from a common online-based location or service.

Make sure the people you're working with become familiar with how to use the online collaboration tools you've selected to use. You might need to set up training sessions with your collaborators to make sure everyone knows how to access and use the tools at their disposal. By training everyone on the tools, you minimize the chance that someone will accidently delete or alter important data, files, or content.

You should also establish online etiquette and procedures in terms of how the communication and collaboration tools should be utilized. If team members do not follow pre-established collaboration guidelines, you might easily lose important information, have miscommunications become commonplace, and waste a lot of time with irrelevant messages, emails, and calls.

The focus of Chapter 3, "Becoming a More Efficient Collaborator," focuses on helping you make sure all of your collaborators understand how and when to use the selected tools to accomplish tasks and achieve goals. Keep in mind that starting to work with a new cloud-based tool might require that people adopt new work styles and habits.

In Practice

Only One Account Required

It's important to understand that each person using a cloud-based service only needs *one account* with each service, even if they'll be using several different computers and mobile devices to access the account. Each of your devices (such as your desktop or laptop computer and your smartphone or tablet) must be linked to and signed in to the same account information to automatically sync and become accessible across all your equipment.

If you opt to collaborate with other people via the cloud, each person needs to sign in to the same service using their own account information. The designated team leader will need to invite the collaborators to share specific files, information, and/or content. The details about sending invitations and sharing files are explained later in the book.

What You Should Know Before Getting Started

With cloud-based services and tools, you can accomplish a lot or work in new and innovative ways, especially when it comes to making your content easily accessible. To select appropriate tools, you need to assess your needs and existing work habits. After you start using the new tools, it's essential that you use them in an appropriate manner. In other words, you have to make sure your content is securely stored and readily available only to the people who need access to it, without compromising security.

CAUTION

Backups Are Still Required

When you use a specific operating system, software package, or mobile app that offers integration with the cloud, your content (data, documents, files, photos, and so on) can automatically sync with your cloud account, which means the most current versions of your content are always accessible to you. However, if you delete or alter a file locally from your computer, for example, in many cases, the synced file that was stored in the cloud is also deleted or updated, often within seconds.

As a result, relying solely on the cloud account might not be a viable backup solution for your important content. Make sure you understand what content is stored online and how local changes affect the files stored in the cloud. You might need to consider using a dedicated backup solution in addition to the cloud services you use for specific tasks.

Starting with Chapter 2, "Determining Your Needs for Cloud-Based Solutions," I explain more about the specific services and tools that are covered in this book. You'll begin to develop a better understanding of the types of file syncing, backup, and collaboration tools available to you.

Determining Your Needs for Cloud-Based Solutions

This chapter introduces you to popular cloud-based tools and services and offers

- An overview of online file storage, file-sharing, and online collaboration tools, and ways you can use them for work-related purposes
- A summary of the cloud-based services and tools at your disposal

As explained in the previous chapter, "Introducing Cloud-Based Computing and Collaborating," *cloud computing* is a catch-all phrase that covers pretty much anything you do on your computer or mobile device, where content is stored on or retrieved from the Internet, shared with others via the Internet, or collaborated on via the Internet.

If you're like most people, cloud computing has probably become part of your personal computing activities as you use your computer and mobile device. Many of the cloud-based tools can also be used to help you save time, become more organized, boost your productivity, improve your communication, and streamline your collaboration efforts when you're handling work-related tasks. And the list of available tools for working in the cloud is growing all the time!

Common Business Uses for Cloud-Based Tools

As mentioned in Chapter 1, you can use cloud computing in a number of ways to improve your efficiency:

- Enables you to store data, documents, files, and content in the cloud for backup or archival purposes.
- Helps you sync and share content among your computers and mobile devices.

- Enables you to share specific data, documents, and files with specific other people via the Internet.

- Facilitates collaborating on the creating, reviewing, or editing content in real time using the collaboration tools built into popular software and mobile apps. You can also use screen sharing, Internet-based voice calling, Internet-based video conferencing, messaging, and virtual white boards to interact with your collaborators.

Not all of the cloud-based services discussed within this book offer each of the features or tools listed here. If you haven't already selected the tools you'll be using, it's important that you choose a service that offers the functionality you and your team can make the most use of right away—and sometimes that might mean that you need more than one service.

The following sections take a closer look at some of the types of file storage, file sharing, and collaboration tools available to you right now.

FYI: Online Security Takes Many Forms

All the cloud-based services discussed throughout this book offer at least some security and privacy tools and features. That security comes in different forms, including encrypting data, documents, and files that are stored in the cloud; requiring a username and password to access information stored on the cloud; enforcing two-factor authentication; and integrating with existing firewalls. Security is covered in more detail in Chapter 4, "Understanding Cloud-Based Security Concerns."

Managing Customer Relationships

Customer Relationship Management (CRM) tools are designed to handle the needs of sales teams, customer service departments, and marketing teams for organizations in a variety of industries—financial services, retail, healthcare, manufacturing, and other service-oriented businesses. CRM tools provide easy access to comprehensive prospect or customer information. Customer service agents, for example, can better manage cases, look up customer histories, address problems, and implement solutions more efficiently. Furthermore, these tools streamline how information is collected, managed, retrieved, and analyzed.

What sets cloud-based CRM solutions apart from other CRM solutions is that a team of information technology (IT) experts isn't required to set up and manage the tool. Once an account is set up, employees are provided with interactive tools to help them find more leads, close more deals, and become more productive when interacting with prospects and clients. With information at their fingertips, employees can more accurately predict customer wants and needs based on past behavior.

Companies that implement a cloud-based CRM solution are able to increase sales, enhance customer loyalty, and improve the real-time, up-to-date accessibility of important information among its employees. This leads to improved productivity, regardless of company size or type of industry. Because information is cloud-based, employees can access and share it, throughout and between departments. A sales or customer service team member who is on the road can access the same information from their mobile device or Internet-connected laptop that's available to the rest of the team back at the office.

FYI: What Is CRM?

Customer Relationship Management (CRM) involves the practices and tools a company uses to intelligently and efficiently manage customer and prospect information. The more you know about your customers and prospects, the easier it is to build and then manage long-term and positive relationships.

By ensuring all of your appropriate employees or team members have the same up-to-date and accurate information, you can eliminate redundancies in efforts, improve communication, and enhance your customer interactions. When using a cloud-based CRM tool, all your customer data is stored online in one centralized and remote location, which allows organizations of any size to streamline the sales or customer service process.

A cloud-based CRM tool collects much more than basic contact information. It enables companies to collect and track call logs, call notes, deal conversations, and price quotes and also share files that are relevant to a customer's needs. This type of tool can also generate daily to-do lists, schedule call alerts, trigger emails, and automate a wide range of otherwise time-consuming tasks—all of which prevent details from falling through the cracks.

As you'll discover, cloud-based CRM applications are much more efficient and interactive than traditional contact management solutions for building and managing professional relationships with customers and prospective customers.

Syncing and Storing Files Across Devices

One of the most common uses of a cloud-based service is to store files in the cloud and be able to sync them across a variety of devices. Today, many people work on multiple devices: a desktop computer at work, a desktop computer at home, a laptop computer that travels with them, a smartphone, and a tablet, for example. With the appropriate cloud-based tool, you can set up app- or software-specific content to automatically back up and sync to a single and secure cloud-based account so that you can access it from any device that's connected to that account.

FYI: A Cloud-Based Account Serves as Remote Storage

When a cloud-based service is used for remote file storage and data syncing, all content is stored on an online server (not locally), but the computer or mobile device treats that online storage the same way it treats a local hard drive. However, what's stored in the cloud is accessible (via the Internet) to all other computers and mobile devices that are linked to the same account.

For example, if a user creates a Microsoft Word document on her desktop computer at work, that document can automatically be uploaded to a cloud-based account, such as a Microsoft OneDrive account. The document is then almost instantly accessible from all of that user's other computers and mobile devices that are linked to the same cloud-based account.

If the computer or mobile device the document was created on gets lost, stolen, or damaged, loss of productivity is minimized because all of the user's important data, documents, and files are already stored online. The information can be retrieved from anywhere using any other computer or mobile device that is linked to the same cloud-based account.

Typically, after a cloud-based file storage or data syncing is set up and activated on a user's computers and mobile devices, the backup and syncing functionality works automatically in the background. This ensures that data, documents, files, and content are always available to a user, whenever and wherever it's needed, regardless of which of their computers or mobile devices are being used. As long as Internet connectivity is available, the most current version of a user's work is accessible.

In Practice

Use Search Tools to Quickly Locate Content

When important data, documents, files, and content are stored online, it's essential that you and your team members be able to locate that information quickly and efficiently. Cloud-based file storage solutions offer integrated tools for organizing, searching for, and quickly accessing what you need, when you need it to make it easy for you to quickly retrieve what's stored in the cloud.

For example, the file-sharing services typically allow you to create custom-named folders and subfolders and then sort those folders by name, date, file size, file type, or other criteria that you specify. You can use a search tool to quickly locate content based on your search criteria, which might include a keyword, date, or file type.

Sharing Files

Cloud-based file sharing enables different users to each have their own cloud-based account with a specific service so that they can share data, documents, files, or content with specific other users in a secure way. All of the user's other files and content remains private.

> **CAUTION**
>
> ## File Sharing Is Different from Collaboration
>
> When a file, such as a Microsoft Word document, is shared among multiple people, each user can view, edit, print, and share that document. If the various users make changes, multiple versions of the document are created and in play, and those changes might later need to be merged into a single document. Essentially, each user is modifying his or her own copy of the file. Changes cannot be seen by the other users in real time if you're only using cloud-based file sharing.
>
> Alternatively, two or more people can use the real-time collaboration tools to work on the same document at the same time. All users see all changes and edits as they're being made. Only one version document is continuously updated and shared with all collaborators. While this collaboration is happening, team members can communicate through group messaging and other forms of online communication.

Communicating with Group Messaging

You're probably familiar with text messaging and instant messaging from using your smartphone or almost any social media service to interact with your friends and family. All smartphone cellular service providers offer text messaging as a component of their service plans, and Facebook and most other social media services offer instant messaging, group messaging, or direct messaging as ways for users to communicate using primarily text-based messages and emojis.

> **FYI: The Different Forms of Messaging**
>
> *Text messaging* typically refers to text-based messages being sent from one user to another. In the past, text messaging occurred on smartphones and tablets via a cellular service provider's cellular network. Responses can be generated in real time or at the recipient's convenience. *Instant messaging* is just like text messaging, but traditionally it's done via the Internet through a social media or messaging service. *Group messaging* allows for more than two people to participate in the same text-based message conversation.
>
> These days, the lines have blurred between the types of messaging services offered by Internet-based services and cellular services. For example, text messaging from a smartphone can now include group messages, and instant messages can be sent or received from an Internet-connected smartphone or tablet.
>
> *Direct messaging* is a type of text messaging that happens through a social network. Instead of communicating via public posts, the communicators send direct messages that can only be seen by the sender and recipient.
>
> For security and compliance purposes, many companies permit work-related text, instant messaging, or group messaging between employees using only approved services—not through an employee's personal social media account or personal mobile device.

Group messaging can be handled through an employer-sanctioned service that allows collaborators, co-workers, or team members to exchange text-based massages as an efficient way to communicate from their computers and/or mobile devices. Group messaging can be used to allow two people to communicate with each other, but these conversations can also be opened up to larger groups of people so everyone in the group can see everyone else's messages as they're composed and sent. Each person has the ability to respond as needed. Group messages are a convenient way for project teams to communicate quickly and efficiently—even when they're miles apart.

Many of the cloud-based collaboration tools discussed within this book offer integrated group messaging and direct messaging functionality that allows two or more people to communicate using text-based massages in a secure way. Typically, these services keep a record of all conversations, so they can be referred to easily.

Depending on the group messaging service being used, in most cases, you can create and manage different chat rooms or message groups with conversations that are happening simultaneously, and you can quickly switch between conversations. A wide range of privacy options and productivity tools are offered by the various group messaging services.

Conducting Interactive Polling and Q&A Sessions

Sometimes, when a large group of people is interacting online, it becomes cumbersome to have everyone chime in with their thoughts on a decision. An alternative is for a group or team leader to initiate a poll that can help everyone reach a consensus quickly. A poll is also a convenient way for differing opinions to be documented and tracked.

Many of the online collaboration tools that offer group messaging tools, video conferencing, and voice calling (conference calling) also provide the ability for a moderator or group leader to compose and conduct a poll. Some tools also make it possible for you to host a Q&A session where attendees can pose questions for the host or group in an organized and moderated way.

This type of interaction works particularly well when online collaboration tools are being used for teaching. The tools can typically be adapted to meet the needs of teams or groups of any size that are using cloud-based communication tools to interact.

Integrating Services with Microsoft Office 365

Among the world's most popular tools for word processing, spreadsheet management, digital slide presentations, note taking, contact management, and scheduling are the applications in the Microsoft Office suite (https://products.office.com).

Office 365 is a cloud-based and cloud integrated version of the Office suite that allows for data, documents, and files to be stored in the cloud; shared; and created, edited, or reviewed in a real-time collaborative environment.

The Office 365 applications are compatible with the software and mobile app versions of Word, Excel, PowerPoint, Outlook, OneNote, and Access, as well as the online-based versions of these applications. However, instead of having to purchase the entire Office suite or individual applications within it, Office 365 uses a monthly subscription model. You can choose from several different price plans so that you get one that meets your or your organization's needs.

Many of the online collaboration services—such as Dropbox (and Dropbox Paper), Slack, and Trello, which are covered in chapters later in this book—fully integrate with Office 365. If your team or company already uses Office applications, be sure to seek out a file-sharing, file-storage, or online collaboration service that easily and securely integrates with Office 365. There are plenty to choose from.

FYI: More About Office 365 and Other Options

The focus of Chapter 11, "Using Microsoft Office 365 for Collaboration and File Sharing," is on how individuals, groups, and companies can use Office 365's collaboration and file-sharing tools. Chapter 11 also explores some of the other online collaboration services that fully integrate with Office 365.

An alternative to the Microsoft Office suite of applications is Google's G Suite (which is the focus of Chapter 10, "Working in Google's G Suite"), which includes the cloud-based and cloud-integrated applications offered by Google, including Docs, Sheets, Forms, Slides, Sites, Drive, Calendar, Hangouts, and Gmail. Another option is Apple's iWork applications (Pages, Numbers, and Keynote), which also offer online-based collaboration tools, file storage, and file sharing.

Collaborating in Real Time

Depending on which service or toolset you utilize, real-time online collaboration can take many forms, allowing collaborators to

- Use real-time screen sharing and virtual whiteboards

- Work simultaneously on creating, editing, or reviewing data, documents, and files

- Take advantage of group messaging, Internet-based conference (voice) calling, or Internet-based video conferencing

- Share data, documents, or files that are stored in the cloud

Perhaps the most useful thing about online collaboration is that collaborators can be located almost anywhere (as long as Internet access is available) and, in most cases, can actively participate in a collaboration session using a Windows PC, Mac, smartphone, or tablet.

Sharing Screens and Virtual Whiteboards

Real-time screen sharing allows one person to use almost any software on his computer while other people watch their respective screens to see exactly what the host is doing. This allows the host to demonstrate something or present a digital slide presentation, for example.

Some software also enables the host to create a virtual whiteboard during a collaboration session, which allows the meeting participants to use their devices to type, write, draw, or add content to the same virtual white board that everyone is viewing on their respective screens. Instead of everyone sitting in the same conference room, participants can be in disparate locations but still see a virtual whiteboard as they interact with other meeting participants using voice or video conferencing.

FYI: Cross-Platform Compatibility Is a Must

When you're working with others in a company or project team, the service you use needs to be compatible with a variety of platforms. In other words, users should be able to use the tool whether they're using an Internet-connected Windows PC or Mac desktop or laptop computer, an Apple iPhone or iPad, or an Android-based smartphone or tablet.

Recording and Playing Back Virtual Meetings

Among the useful benefits of many cloud-based collaboration tools is that everything that happens during the meeting can be recorded and stored in the cloud so it can be retrieved and reviewed at a later time.

This functionality is particularly useful for participants in a meeting who want to refer to specific conversations or ideas that were discussed, or to allow people who missed a meeting to see and hear exactly what was discussed at their convenience.

Voice Calling and Video Conferencing

In addition to text-based messaging, two of the primary ways people can communicate when using online collaboration tools are via Internet-based voice calling or video conferencing.

Internet-based voice calling and conferencing allows people to have a live conversation without using a traditional phone service.

Regardless of where the participants are located, no long distance phone charges are incurred because the calls are handled via the Internet.

This type of conferencing is integrated into many cloud-based collaboration services. You can often use the camera and microphone built into the computer or mobile device to have real-time video calls between two or more people.

FYI: Virtual Meetings Are Cost Effective

In today's fast-paced business world, playing phone tag is commonplace, and scheduling an in-person meeting with two or more people can prove extremely challenging. When people who have to meet are located in different offices, in different states, or in different countries, in-person meetings become costly and extremely time-consuming to conduct.

In most major cities, simply traveling across town can waste several hours because of traffic; finding and paying for parking is an additional time- and money-waster. For meetings that need to bring people together from distant locations, the cost of airfares, rental cars, and hotel accommodations make the cost of those meetings hard to justify.

Virtual meeting functionality, video conferencing, and online collaboration tools bridge the space between people who work in separate locations and allow them to work together or meet as if they're in the same room. The ability to use technology to bring people together is one of the biggest appeals of cloud-based computing. It reduces time wasted traveling to and from meetings, lowers costs, and dramatically improves productivity and communication.

Understanding how to utilize technology to communicate in the most cost-effective and efficient way possible can give you a tremendous advantage over your competitors.

Overview of Online File-Sharing and Collaboration Services

This section provides a brief overview of the online-based file sharing and collaboration services that are covered within this book. Chapters 5 through 16 each cover one of these services in much more detail.

In Practice

Services from Microsoft, Apple, and Google

Many individuals rely on services like Microsoft OneDrive, Apple iCloud, and the cloud-based services offered by Google to handle their personal computing needs. Which service is utilized is typically based on the type of equipment someone is using, as well as personal preference. Windows 10 PCs integrate seamlessly with Microsoft OneDrive; Macs, iPhones, and iPads integrate seamlessly with Apple iCloud; and Android-based mobile devices integrate seamlessly with Google Drive and other online-based Google services, such as Google Docs.

You can also install specialized software (or an app) to make that equipment fully compatible with another cloud-based service:

- If you're a Windows 10 PC user who wants to utilize Apple iCloud, download and install the free iCloud for Windows software to your PC (https://support.apple.com/en-us/HT204283).

- Mac and iOS users can use OneDrive by downloading the appropriate software (https://onedrive.live.com/about/en-us/download) or mobile app (https://itunes.apple.com/us/app/microsoft-onedrive-file-photo-cloud-storage/id477537958).

- PC, Mac, and iOS mobile device users who want to use Google Drive first need to download the appropriate software or mobile app (https://www.google.com/drive/download).

FYI: Understanding the Cost of Cloud Computing

When it comes to calculating the true cost of cloud computing, things can be a bit convoluted. You can typically sign up for and use most cloud-computing services for free. Your account will include a certain amount of online storage space and a basic collection of features and functions. For a monthly or annual fee you can unlock more online storage space and additional functionality.

Cloud-computing services for business users are seldom free. Most involve a monthly or annual subscription fee for each user. When evaluating which service, pay attention to the per-user and per month fee, as well as the cost of additional add-on fees that might be required.

Most services offer a free trial period. Take advantage of this to determine whether what's offered actually meets your needs. During your trial period, don't implement the service across your entire organization. Instead, assign a small team or group to analyze the toolset and be sure to maintain a backup of all data, documents, files, messaging conversation transcripts, and so on that are created during the trial period. Otherwise, you might not have access to this information later if you end up opting to use a different service.

Box

Box (www.box.com) is a cutting-edge yet surprisingly easy-to-use and scalable cloud-computing platform that offers secure file-storage (with file management capabilities), file-sharing, and collaboration tools that are compatible with Windows PCs, Macs, iOS mobile devices, and Android mobile devices.

Box works with hundreds of software and mobile app developers to facilitate integration between Box and thousands of popular applications. When you work with software or an app that's compatible with Box, your content will automatically sync with your Box account.

Services that are somewhat similar to Box (although each offers additional features and functions that are unique) include

- Apple iCloud (www.apple.com/icloud)

- Dropbox (www.dropbox.com)

- Google Drive (www.google.com/drive)

- iDrive (www.idrive.com)

- Microsoft OneDrive (https://onedrive.live.com/about/en-us)

FYI: Box Integrates with Apps You Likely Already Use

Box fully integrates with Microsoft's Office 365, combining its collaboration and security tools with those built into the Office 365 applications. This allows users in different locations to easily collaborate when using Word, Excel, PowerPoint, Outlook, or OneNote.

Similar functionality is also built into most of Google's apps, including those within G Suite. This integration supports more than 100 document and file formats. Plus, you'll find seamless Box integration built into Salesforce, DocuSign, Cisco WebEx, and Slack.

In Practice

Box Add-Ons Expand the Service's Functionality

Beyond the Business and Enterprise subscription plans offered to businesses and organizations (read Chapter 5, "Collaborating with Box," for more information about the different subscription plans), important service add-ons you should consider investing in include Box KeySafe, which grants users control of encryption keys for protecting their content; Box Governance, which allows companies using Box to implement data retention rules, support defensible eDiscovery, and enforce content security policies; and Customer Support Services, which offers full-service support to Box users. Additional fees apply for these add-on services.

Cisco WebEx

First and foremost, Cisco WebEx (www.webex.com) is a video-conferencing tool designed for business users. It offers the resources to host virtual meetings (via Internet-based video conferencing), online-based training sessions, and online events. The service is entirely cloud based, meaning that all conference or meeting attendees need to participate is a web browser running on their computer or mobile device (and Internet access). Any phone line can also be used to experience clearer audio. As a standalone platform, Cisco WebEx meets or exceeds the video-conferencing needs of most teams, small groups, organizations, and companies.

FYI: WebEx Adoption

As of mid-2017, 93 percent of Fortune 500 companies already use WebEx. The service hosts more than 26.5 million virtual meetings and video conferences per month.

Cisco Spark is an accessory program for WebEx that transforms a video conference into an interactive virtual meeting space that includes group messaging, an interactive whiteboard, file sharing, and integration with many popular software packages and mobile apps.

In Practice

WebEx Offers Plenty of Security

Built into the WebEx platform is end-to-end encryption and what the company calls "locking meeting spaces." These security tools protect the video-based meetings as well as the messaging and file sharing that transpires during the meeting within the WebEx platform. Using tools built into the service, meetings can be recorded and later shared with people who could not attend. The available Admin controls give the person in charge added tools for managing the virtual meetings and video conferences. This includes integration with Outlook, Exchange, or your organization's own employee directory.

If your organization's needs go beyond video conferencing and virtual meetings, add-on services offered by Cisco include Cisco WebEx Event Center (used to host events and webinars), Cisco WebEx Training Center (used to produce and host online training or courses), and Cisco WebEx Support Center (used to provide remote support to your customers or prospects).

Other cloud-based services that offer video conferencing and virtual meeting functionality include

- Any Meeting (www.anymeeting.com)
- Free Conference Call (www.freeconferencecall.com/video-conferencing)
- Google Hangouts (https://gsuite.google.com/products/meet)
- GoToMeeting (www.gotomeeting.com)
- Polycom (www.polycom.com)
- Skype for Business (https://www.skype.com/en/business/skype-for-business/)
- Zoom (http://zoom.us)

CAUTION

Security Issues with Video Conferencing

To learn more about potential security issues related to video conferencing via a cloud-based service such as WebEx, see Chapter 4. Cisco has also published a white paper on this topic, *Web Conferencing: Unleash the Power of Secure Real-Time Collaboration,* which you can download for free by visiting www.cisco.com/c/dam/en/us/products/collateral/conferencing/webex-meeting-center/white-paper-c11-737588.pdf.

FYI: More Info About Cisco WebEx

The focus of Chapter 6, "Using Cisco WebEx for Large-Group Collaboration," is on how to use WebEx to handle virtual meetings and video conferences.

DocuSign

Many cloud-based computing services offer file-sharing and real-time collaboration tools. Far fewer offer secure tools for reviewing business correspondence and contracts, allow users to add annotations, and make it possible to insert a legally binding virtual signature in a document. That's where DocuSign (www.docusign.com) comes in.

DocuSign is a cloud-based *eSignature* service that can be used on its own or in conjunction with some other file-sharing or collaboration tools. You can embed the electronic signing functionality offered by DocuSign into an existing website, portal, or application.

FYI: What's an eSignature?

An eSignature is a virtual and legally binding signature that can be created in seconds by a user and placed within almost any document or contract.

DocuSign enables one party to send a document or contract to a recipient for review. The recipient can securely review, annotate, and/or sign that document on their computer or mobile device. With a few mouse clicks or on-screen taps, the annotated and signed document is returned to the sender. Either party can view the status of the document or access the fully executed, signed document via the cloud.

Other services that offer eSignature functionality include

- ApproveMe (www.approveme.com)
- eSign Systems (www.esignsystems.com)
- eSignatures.com (www.esignatures.com)
- SignNow (www.signnow.com)

In Practice

DocuSign Integration with Other Services

Through partnerships with software and app developers, DocuSign can quickly and easily integrate with Microsoft applications (including Outlook, Word, and SharePoint), Salesforce, several of Google's G Suite applications, Box, and thousands of other software packages and mobile apps. The eSignature and annotation tools offered by DocuSign allow many companies to streamline transactions that would otherwise require sending hardcopies of paperwork to be reviewed and signed by other parties.

FYI: More Info About DocuSign

Read more about DocuSign in Chapter 7, "Using DocuSign to Review, Edit, Sign, and Share Documents."

Dropbox and Dropbox Paper

Dropbox (www.dropbox.com) has become one of the most popular cloud-based file-storage and file-sharing services in the world, with more than 500 million users and 200,000 businesses relying on this service for file storage and management.

Beyond simple online file storage and sharing, Dropbox offers file syncing between all of a user's computers and mobile devices that are linked to the same Dropbox account, plus offers two-factor authentication and password-protected and expiring shared links. Dropbox Business expands upon the core functionality of Dropbox, with added security, file versioning and recovery, and plenty of available online storage space.

FYI: File Versioning and File Recovery

When multiple people are working with the same document, *file versioning* allows for various versions of that same document to be saved separately, so it's possible to go back to previous versions. Without this feature in place, new additions or changes to a document overwrite the old versions.

File recovery allows for accidently deleted or overwritten documents or files to be recovered with ease, typically within a specific amount of time, such as 7, 14, or 30 days.

Dropbox integrates seamlessly with 300,000 popular software packages, mobile apps, and other collaboration tools. In 2017, Dropbox introduced Dropbox Paper, which is an online collaboration toolset that integrates seamlessly with Dropbox.

Services that are somewhat similar to Dropbox include

- Apple iCloud (www.apple.com/icloud)

- Box (www.box.com)

- Google Drive (www.google.com/drive)

- iDrive (www.idrive.com)

- Microsoft OneDrive (https://onedrive.live.com/about/en-us)

FYI: More Info About Dropbox and Dropbox Paper

Read Chapter 8, "Managing Collaboration with Dropbox," for more information on how to use Dropbox.

Evernote

Evernote (www.evernote.com)—which started out as a single-user note-taking application for computers and mobile devices—has evolved into a note-taking, information-gathering, cloud-based file-storage, file-sharing, and interactive collaboration tool that supports all popular hardware platforms, including Windows PCs, Macs, iOS mobile devices, and Android mobile devices. Plus, there's an online edition of Evernote that's accessible from any web browser.

In addition to allowing users to create, view, edit, and collaborate on text-based notes, Evernote allows information, documents, images, web research, and other types of content to be collected and easily imported into an Evernote file. You can store files in custom notebooks (folders), which can sync automatically so all your notes and information are accessible via Evernote from anywhere that you can log in.

Individual notes or entire notebooks can be shared securely with other people, or two or more people located in different places can use Evernote's real-time and secure collaboration tools to create, review, or edit content together.

Other note-taking and information-gathering applications that are cloud-based include

- Apple's iCloud Notes (www.icloud.com)

- Google Keep (www.google.com/keep)

- Microsoft OneNote (www.onenote.com)

- SimpleNote (https://simplenote.com)

- Zoho Notebook (www.zoho.com/notebook)

FYI: More Info About Evernote

Read Chapter 9, "Taking Notes and Staying Organized with Evernote," for more information on Evernote.

Google G Suite

Google has evolved into much more than the world's most popular Internet search engine. Online-based tools and services offered by Google now include email, scheduling, contact management, instant messaging, group messaging, and a suite of business tools that offer cloud-based collaboration. These services all work in conjunction with Google Drive, which is Google's cloud-based file-storage and file-sharing service.

All of Google's most popular tools for business are offered together as G Suite (https://gsuite.google. com). When businesses use G Suite, applications including Docs (word processing), Sheets (spreadsheet management), Forms (interactive forms, surveys, and questionnaires), Slides (digital slide presentations), and Sites (webpage design) integrate with Gmail, Hangouts, Calendar, and Google+ to create a scalable, customizable, and user-friendly way for businesspeople to create, edit, view, store, sync, and share documents.

G Suite includes custom Gmail email addresses for all users (email@*yourcompany*.com), as well as at least 30GB of online storage space for each user. Advanced security and admin controls allow companies to properly manage everything related to G Suite and its users, and migration tools make it easy to import and export data, documents, files, and content between G Suite applications and other popular applications and cloud-based services.

Other popular office suites that utilize the cloud include

- Apache OpenOffice (www.openoffice.org)

- Apple iWork (www.apple.com/iwork)

- Microsoft Office 365 (www.office.com)

- Zoho Workplace (www.zoho.com/workplace)

FYI: More Info About Google's G Suite

Read Chapter 10 to learn more about Google's tools.

Microsoft Exchange and SharePoint

Microsoft Exchange, which is designed specifically for businesses, is an email service that also offers secure messaging and calendar (personal and group scheduling) functionality. Microsoft Exchange operates using the Windows Server operating system. It's designed to enhance and streamline communications within a mid- to large-sized company. SharePoint is Microsoft's solution for collaborative project management in a work environment.

Both Exchange and SharePoint are cloud-based systems that allow for secure information exchange and collaboration. Although these services are offered by Microsoft and were originally designed for Windows-based computer users, they're now fully compatible with Macs and virtually all smartphones and tablets.

Because Microsoft Exchange and SharePoint Server editions cater to the needs of larger businesses and use a company-owned server, they are scalable and customizable. Smaller organizations can use Exchange Online, which has services hosted and managed by Microsoft (on Microsoft's servers). This, however, is a more complex and costly option to implement than Office 365 (see the next section).

In Practice

Microsoft Bundles Its Services

For small to mid-sized companies, Microsoft Exchange Online is a standalone hosted service from Microsoft that includes Office 365, SharePoint, and Skype for Business.

FYI: More Info About Microsoft Exchange and SharePoint

Read Chapter 12, "Handling Large-Group Collaboration with Microsoft Exchange," for more information on how to utilize Microsoft's premium cloud-based tools.

Microsoft Office 365

Microsoft Office (www.office.com) continues to be the most widely used suite of work-related applications in the world. This suite includes Word (word processing), Excel (spreadsheet management), PowerPoint (digital slide presentations), Outlook (scheduling and contact management), OneNote (note taking), Publisher (desktop publishing), and Access (database management).

All these applications are available separately or as a suite of applications, called Microsoft Office, which you can purchase and install on your computer. However, you can also get a subscription to a cloud-based version of Office, called Office 365. File-sharing and online collaboration tools are built into Office 365 to allow multiple people to collaborate when creating, editing, or reviewing any Office-related document or file.

FYI: More About OneDrive for Business

Microsoft OneDrive for Business (https://products.office.com/en-us/onedrive-for-business/online-cloud-storage) is a standalone, cloud-based, file-storage, data-syncing, and file-sharing tool that offers similar functionality to Box and Dropbox. It also integrates seamlessly with Office 365.

Although OneDrive compatibility is built into the latest versions of the Windows operating system for PCs, as well as into the Office 365 applications, it's also compatible with Macs, iOS mobile devices, and Android mobile devices when special OneDrive software (or the OneDrive mobile app) is installed on non-Windows-based systems.

FYI: More Info About Office 365

Read Chapter 11 for more information on Microsoft Office 365.

Salesforce

Salesforce (www.salesforce.com) is an example of a popular, cloud-based, customer relationship management application that is customizable and scalable to meet the needs of companies and organizations working in a variety of different industries. By making customer or prospect information readily available, Salesforce allows companies to improve their sales and customer service efforts, while streamlining and automating many otherwise time consuming tasks.

Other CRM options include

- Accelo's Capterra (http://grow.accelo.com/capterra-crm)
- Act! (www.act.com)
- Infusionsoft (www.infusionsoft.com)
- Insightly (www.insightly.com)
- Netsuite CRM (www.netsuite.com/portal/products/crm.shtml)
- Pipedrive (www.pipedrive.com)
- Zoho CRM (www.zoho.com/crm)

FYI: More Info About Salesforce

Read Chapter 13, "Bringing Teams Together with Salesforce," for more information on Salesforce.

Skype

Skype for Business is a tool for making and receiving Internet-based (Voice-Over-IP) phone calls and group conference calls. It also offers text messaging, group messaging, and video conferencing from any Internet-enabled device.

With Skype, you can record and share phone calls and video conferences, and you can host meetings with up to 250 participants. In the meetings, you can use screen sharing, interactive whiteboards, and PowerPoint presentations. Skype for Business also integrates with Office applications.

Companies already using Outlook to manage contacts and scheduling can schedule Skype for Business phone or video conferences from within Outlook.

Other cloud-based services that offer video conferencing and virtual meeting functionality include

- Any Meeting (www.anymeeting.com)
- Cisco WebEx (www.webex.com)
- Free Conference Call (www.freeconferencecall.com/video-conferencing)
- Google Hangouts (https://gsuite.google.com/products/meet)
- GoToMeeting (www.gotomeeting.com)
- Polycom (www.polycom.com)
- Zoom (http://zoom.us)

FYI: More Info About Skype for Business

Read Chapter 14, "Communicating via Skype," for more information about Skype.

Slack

Think of Slack (www.slack.com) as a group messaging service on steroids, but it also includes a comprehensive collection of cloud-based file-storage, file-sharing, and online collaboration tools. This service works with PCs, Macs, and all smartphones and tablets. It is designed to promote and improve on team communication and collaboration.

Slack works seamlessly with thousands of popular applications and other cloud-based file-sharing, file-storage, and collaboration tools, making is easy to find information quickly and efficiently whether information is stored within the transcript of a messaging session; or within PDF files, Word documents, Google Docs documents, or other types of compatible files.

FYI: More Info About Slack

Read Chapter 15, "Discovering Slack," for more information on how to use Slack.

Trello

Trello (www.trello.com) is a cloud-based collaboration tool for groups or teams that allows for whiteboards, lists, virtual index cards, and other content to be shared using a highly visual user interface. Team members work with a virtual bulletin board by creating, editing, and collaborating using virtual color-coded cards. Information and comments can be displayed, checklists and to-do lists can be created and used, file attachments can be shared, and projects can be managed from beginning to end. The Trello service integrates with a wide range of popular software packages, mobile apps, and cloud-based storage and file-sharing services.

In Practice

Use Trello with Other Services

Many teams and groups use Trello to share information on an ongoing basis, but during virtual meetings (which happen in real time) they use video-conference tools offered by another company.

FYI: More Info About Trello

Read Chapter 16, "Maximizing Communication Efficiency with Trello," for more information on using Trello.

FYI: Other Specialized Applications

You can find a cloud-based tool for many different kinds of specialized purpose that you or your organization might need. For example, if you use any of Adobe's applications, such as Photoshop, Illustrator, InDesign, or Premiere, you can use Adobe's cloud-based service, called Adobe Creative Cloud, to store, sync, share, and manage your work.

The world's most popular bookkeeping application, Intuit's QuickBooks—as well as other Intuit applications that businesses rely on—has a cloud-based component that enables people to access and work with relevant data from virtually anywhere. This is also the case with the popular ADP Payroll application, MailChimp (an email marketing application), Shopify (an e-commerce solution), Workday (a human resources application), and SAP's Concur (a travel and expense report application), to name just a few.

Virtually all commonly used and specialty software applications and mobile apps have been integrated with the cloud. Just as with all of the other cloud-based platforms and services discussed throughout *Working in the Cloud,* each software application that somehow relies on the cloud has its own security tools built in to protects your data, documents, files, and content once it's stored online.

FYI: The New Files Mobile App

Built into iOS 11 for all iPhone and iPad models is a new app called Files, which replaces the iCloud Drive app. After you set up the app (which takes just minutes), you can use it to access, view, annotate, share, print, and move many types of files that are stored within compatible cloud-based services, including iCloud Drive, Dropbox, and Box.

The Files app is great because it works with many of your existing cloud-based accounts. As long as your iPhone or iPad has Internet access, you can keep files, documents, and photos stored within the cloud and then easily access them when you need them; this means you don't need to occupy internal storage space on your mobile device.

You can use the app's Search tool to quickly locate files so you can preview and annotate content directly from the Files app. Tap the app's Share icon share the file with other people; transfer the file to a different folder, subfolder, or cloud-based service; export the file to a compatible app that's installed on your iPhone or iPad; or print the file using an AirPrint-compatible printer that's wirelessly linked with your mobile device.

In a nutshell, the Files app makes it easier to access, store, and manage files stored in the cloud from virtually anywhere your mobile device has an Internet connection.

Chapter | **3**

Becoming a More Efficient Collaborator

This chapter offers a handful of useful strategies to help you become more efficient using cloud computing for a variety of tasks. This chapter introduces you to the following:

- Strategies for using cloud-based file-storage and data-syncing services
- Tips for protecting your data, documents, and files when using file sharing via a cloud service
- Suggestions for achieving the best possible results when using real-time collaboration tools to work with others in a virtual workspace

The majority of cloud computing services offer a vast and ever-expanding collection of tools to help you become more efficient when working with data, documents, files, and content.

When you work in a company, which services and tools you use might be dictated to you; your managers and IT department might decide which services the company as a whole will use. This will require you to adopt the service and modify your current work habits while taking the steps necessary to protect the content you're working with. If you have previously stored files locally on your computer, for example, and worked with collaborators face-to-face in a conference room, you now need to get into the habit of storing your content online and interacting efficiently with your collaborators in virtual workspaces.

If you're the decision-maker within your team or business, the burden of choosing the best cloud-based tools becomes your responsibility. Before you make any decisions, however, it's essential that you develop a clear understanding of your company's current operation and needs, as well as the work habits of everyone who will ultimately be using the services you choose. When you have that knowledge, you properly evaluate each service from a functionality perspective and choose one or more ways to use cloud computing that will ultimately be beneficial to your organization. Other important considerations include cost, employee training, and data security and compliance issues.

Working Efficiently with File-Storage and Data-Syncing Services

There are several benefits to using a cloud-based file-storage and data-syncing service. First, your data, documents, files, and content aren't stored locally, where it's accessible only to a single computer or mobile device; it's stored in the cloud, so it's accessible to any computers and mobile devices to which you can connect the account. This accessibility provides convenience, but it also serves as a secure remote backup. If a computer is lost, stolen, or damaged, for example, you can still access your important content by using other equipment with virtually no downtime.

You should treat cloud-based file storage just like local storage when it comes to organizing and managing files. Create folders and subfolders and give them descriptive names that relate directly to the content you're storing in them. Also, keep filenames short and relevant. Because files are automatically stored based on date and time, you typically don't need to include this information in the filename. If you're working with a group of people who will be sharing files and folders, establish a clear policy for naming and organizing the files and folders in a way that everyone will easily understand.

In Practice

Incorporate Tags, When Applicable

Based on the service you're using to store your content in the cloud, it's often possible to associate tags, or keywords, with each file and folder. Tags make it even easier to find, sort, or organize relevant content when using a Search tool.

You and your collaborators should be consistently diligent in storing only appropriate and related content within each folder or subfolder so that everything stays well organized. Try to avoid going more than three to five levels deep when using subfolders. In other words, maintaining an easy-to-navigate file structure is important. Any files or folders that are mislabeled or stored incorrectly need to be fixed.

In Practice

Keep Certain Files Together

If you work with files related to a specific subject matter that needs to be managed with extra care because of compliance regulations, you should group these files into aptly named folders so they're easy to locate.

If you use more than one cloud service, it can be hard to track what things are stored in which location. When possible, it's important to rely on a single cloud-based file-storage solution for all of your needs. By keeping files in one central service, you won't waste valuable time keeping track of on which service specific data, documents, and files are stored; you also won't need to switch between two or three separate services to gather all the content you need for a specific project and then remember where revised versions of files were later stored.

To simplify data syncing between all of your computers and mobile devices, make sure that the service works with the software, mobile apps, and equipment you'll be using. If necessary, download and install the service's proprietary software or mobile app onto each of your computers and mobile devices. The only way for content stored in the cloud to automatically sync with all of your computers and mobile devices is if you use the same account information to log in to each service from each of your computers and mobile devices. Also, all of the service's setup and configuration settings typically need to be set exactly the same on each computer and mobile device.

As you transition to working with a cloud service and toolset where everything is stored online and none of your data, documents, or files are stored locally, remember that if you don't have continuous Internet access, you won't have access to your content. Common situations when you might not have Internet access include

- You opt to work from home, but your home's Internet connection stops working.

- You're on the road and travel to an area where there's no cellular data service, and you can't find a public Wi-Fi hotspot.

- You're traveling by airplane, but the aircraft is not equipped with Wi-Fi during the flight.

- The Internet in the hotel where you're staying during a business trip is unreliable.

- You're traveling abroad, and you want to avoid costly international cellular data roaming charges.

These and other situations require that you plan ahead. Before leaving your office, for example, anticipate what content you'll need from the cloud and download those files to your laptop computer's internal hard drive, a portable hard drive, or the internal storage of your mobile device. Otherwise, you'll have to wait until you can once again establish a secure Internet connection before you can access your content.

> **CAUTION**
>
> ## A Secure Internet Connection Is Desirable
>
> Especially if you need to access private, classified, or sensitive content stored in the cloud, you want to ensure that you use only secure Internet connections when you're working outside of your office. You might need to install additional security software onto your laptop computer or mobile device so that you have an additional layer of protection if you attempt to access your cloud account from an unsecure public Wi-Fi hotspot.
>
> Chapter 4, "Understanding Cloud-Based Security Concerns," suggests that you might need to establish a virtual private network (VPN) via your computer or mobile device when accessing any public Wi-Fi hotspot. A VPN can easily be established using your existing equipment. It provides online privacy and anonymity by creating an encrypted connection when sending and receiving data between your computer or mobile device and the public (unsecured) Wi-Fi hotspots you connect to from coffee shops, Internet cafes, airports, hotels, public libraries, or your home. This encrypted connection protects your credit card information, banking information, emails, and everything else from snooping strangers.
>
> Norton Wi-Fi Privacy (https://us.norton.com/wifi-privacy) is one option that individuals or groups can use to establish a VPN. A per-user fee of between $4.99 and $9.99 per month applies, based on the number of computers and devices a user needs to protect.
>
> If you work for a company that manages its own network, your IT administrator might provide you with other security software that caters specifically to the needs of your company or organization.

Tips for Effective File-Sharing

With many cloud services, you have the option to share specific files or entire folders with other people or groups of other people. When you do this, the person or people you opt to share content with can share content in your account. Everything else that's stored within your account theoretically remains private and inaccessible by those other users.

Maintain Control of the Files You Share

File-sharing management is the owner's responsibility. A simple user error could easily lead to the wrong content being shared with the wrong people, or content being made available to your entire team or organization when it was only meant to be shared with a single individual. Before taking advantage of the file-sharing capabilities of any service, make sure you understand how the functionality works and that you know how to manage the sharing privileges and permissions associated with your files and folders. Based on the type of content being shared, consider putting additional (optional) security measures in place, such as password-protecting the shared files or folders. Some services also allow owners to set up a two-step verification process, which helps ensure that only the invited people can gain access to shared content.

FYI: Owners Versus Invitees

The *owner* is the person who controls a cloud account, selects the files and/or folders to be shared, and then determines specifically with whom the content will be shared. The owner might be a project manager or team leader, or the person who initially created or composed the content.

Invitees are the people who are granted permission to access specific files or folders that are stored within the owner's cloud-based account.

As the owner, you always maintain the ability to invite additional people to share the content with or revoke someone's access to the content later. It is your responsibility to ensure that your content is properly organized and that you invite only the appropriate people to access the content that they should become privy to. When necessary, you may need to revoke access to people who no longer need access to the content.

In Practice

File Downloading

When you're sharing files and folders or collaborating on files, it's a good idea to deactivate the ability for collaborators or team members to download the files (at least until the document is finalized). By preventing others from downloading, all necessary people always have access to the latest version of a document, but you're preventing unauthorized people from accessing it (because people can't download and share the file). All work done to the document is automatically logged as part of a document history, which is typically created by the cloud-based service, so you have an audit trail that might be needed for compliance purposes.

If work-in-progress files need to be shared with people outside of the cloud, activate password protection to that document or file, and try to avoid sharing it via email.

In Practice

Understand What Can Happen with Shared Files

Every time you opt to share any content with other people via any sharing service, it's up to you (the owner) to set permissions for each file and folder as well as for each person you're sharing with. The permissions determine what the invitees are able to do with the content you're sharing.

Don't rely only on default settings when sharing files, especially if you're working with sensitive or confidential content.

Manage Permissions for Shared Content

All file-sharing services allow the content owner to determine what exactly can be done with the content being shared. For example, permission options might include the following:

- **Read Only**—The invitees can open and read the files on screen, but they can't alter or store the files locally.

- **Read and Edit**—The invitees can freely read and edit the shared files.

- **Read and Comment**—The invitees can read these files, but they can only add comments, not edit or alter the files directly.

- **Download**—The invitees can view (and potentially edit) the content and download it to their own computer(s) or mobile device(s). This setting gives the invitees, as well as the owner, control over the content. Whether or not the invitee can edit a shared document is based on the security settings the sender has applied to the file.

- **Share with Others**—The invitees are able to share the content with others at their discretion.

- **Printing Options**—The owner can determine if others are able to print the content locally or just view it on their screen.

- **Expiration Date for Shared Content Links**—The owner can make the link active for a pre-defined time period, ranging from several minutes, to several hours, days, weeks, or months. After the link expires, the invitees no longer have access to it.

> **In Practice**
>
> ## Get Into the Habit of Checking Your Settings
>
> The easiest way to avoid mistakes is to diligently manage your account. On a daily or weekly basis, get into the habit of accessing your account and check the status of each file and folder that you're sharing. Make sure the settings and permissions are correctly adjusted based on the sensitivity of the content, and verify that you're sharing only with the proper individuals.
>
> Common errors to check for include
>
> - Accidently selecting the wrong file(s) or folder(s)
> - Choosing the wrong people to share the selected file(s) and folder(s) with
> - Incorrectly adjusting the permission options, which gives the invitees the ability to edit, share, print, or otherwise work with the content in ways they're not authorized to do
> - Failing to revoke access to content that other people no longer require access to—for example, if someone has left the team or company but their access to the cloud-based content remains in place
>
> When a file-sharing service is adopted by a group of people or company, one person is typically given administrator control. The administrator can activate security features and manage all account settings for everyone, which can override individual user settings. What the administrator can do is based on the service being used. I discuss more about administrator capabilities throughout this book.

Understand How You Can Lose Control of Content

When you invite people to collaborate on a file or document, or you grant them permission to view and edit the document as well as download it to their computers or mobile devices, you lose significant control over that content. Even if an invitee's ability to download and print content that they're working with in the cloud is disabled and they're only able to view it on their screen, that invitee could theoretically use his computer or mobile device's screen capture functionality (or screen recording software) to later duplicate and reproduce that content.

A more common occurrence relating to when a content owner loses control over their file(s) is when permission is granted for others to download the content. After the content leaves the secure cloud-based workspace, the invitee can typically do with it as she pleases—editing it, printing it, and distributing it at her discretion.

If the owner later revokes someone's access to the cloud-based version of the file, the invitee is prevented from obtaining file updates (as the owner or authorized collaborators edit the content), but any files the invitee has already downloaded are still at large and possibly being edited by the invitee.

In Practice

Locking Down Files

You can use built-in features of some software to protect files, including Microsoft Word documents, before you store them in the cloud. From the Microsoft Word Security window, you're able to protect a document against modifications related to Track Changes and Comments, or you can strip the document of any personal information upon saving it.

After a document or file has been secured or protected using tools built into the software you're using, it can then be uploaded and shared using a cloud-based service. Then, even if an unauthorized person manages to download to the document by hacking into your cloud-based account, for example, they still won't be able to open that document file if its password protected using a different password than the one used to gain access to your cloud account.

Maintain a Version History for Important Documents and Files

Most cloud-based services automatically store older versions of a file or document as it's being edited. This version history allows users to access older versions of files for reference (for example, to determine when a change was introduced) and allows the cloud-based service to maintain a detailed audit trail for each document or file.

You have to make sure this feature is turned on in the service you're using; also make sure that older versions of a file or document are protected against deletion by individual users. Then you determine how long file or document histories are maintained and stored by the service.

If version history functionality is important to your team or organization for compliance purposes, or just for peace of mind (to protect against accidental deletion of important information, for example), look for services that maintain a complete file history forever rather than for only 30, 60, or 120 days. For this feature, you might need to subscribe to a premium version of the service.

When working with files and documents that have a version history (a copy of every version of that file or document is kept as changes or revisions are made), pay attention to the file's date and time to ensure you're always working with the most up-to-date version. Some services make only the latest file or document version readily available to all users and store the older versions of that file or document in a safe folder that's not as easily accessible.

Etiquette and Strategies for Real-Time Collaboration

Whether you're relying on virtual whiteboards, group messaging, video conferencing, or real-time collaboration tools that allow multiple people to work with the same file or document simultaneously, all collaborators need to be proficient using the tools and understand how and when it's appropriate to interact with their team members and collaborators. You need to make sure everyone understands why the online collaboration tools are being used and what the expected outcome should be. Some goals for online collaboration within a team or organization include the following:

- Reducing reliance on email

- Reducing the need for in-person meetings

- Reducing occurrences of phone tag and time spent on the phone reiterating what was already discussed with other team members or collaborators

- Improving group communication

- Increasing transparency and maintaining a detailed log, transcription, recording, or history of all conversations, chats, and work done on files

- Ensuring that the latest version of all relevant files, documents, data, and content is readily available to all team members and collaborators and that everything is stored within a single, secure, cloud-based location

- Making sensitive content only available to authorized people in a secure way

- Providing all team members and collaborators with the same set of tools to ensure file and data compatibility and accessibility, regardless of what hardware each person is using

- Providing a way for people to communicate, exchange information, share content, and collaborate in real time from any location

Real-time collaboration works the best when a virtual workspace is available to a group of people who are assigned to work on a specific project or task. The content and communication within each virtual workspace should be related only to that project or task. In addition, don't start a group discussion within a cloud service's group chat and then continue the same conversation with only some of the collaborators on the phone, in person, or via email.

Communication that occurs outside the virtual workspace means that the cloud-based collaboration tools are not able to track and store a transcript and log of what's transpired, which could result in a breach in compliance regulations. It can also lead to miscommunication or the loss of important information that hasn't been properly documented and shared with everyone involved.

15 Tips for Getting the Most from Using Collaboration Tools

Use the following strategies to ensure online collaboration happens in an organized and productive way:

- Define your team or group of collaborators and make sure everyone has access to the same online collaboration tools from their accounts.

- Define the scope or overall goal of the collaborative efforts.

- Get everyone up to speed using the collaboration tools that have been selected by the team leader. If someone doesn't know how to access a video conference, share a file, or utilize group messaging, this could waste everyone's time or result in easily avoidable user error that will make using the cloud-based collaboration tools less secure.

- Set deadlines or milestones that everyone needs to work together to achieve. If necessary set a virtual meeting schedule as a new project or task gets underway. Use the collaboration tool's ability to generate, manage, and share task or to-do lists for this purpose.

- Set specific security guidelines, by defining what can and can't be discussed or distributed outside of the collaboration team.

- Have everyone agree to use the selected tool (or tools) to manage the designated task or project.

- Set restrictions relating to what topics should or should not be shared with the entire team, and develop procedures for how individual team members should interact with each other within the virtual workspace. For example, instead of suggesting two team members converse privately on the phone, have them communicate via the cloud-based platform's text messaging service, which helps maintain a transcript of all discussions.

- Don't waste people's time. When a conversation between two team members needs to take place, don't hold that conversation in a forum where everyone is present or has to participate (such as a group video conference, virtual meeting, or group text message session). Instead, converse one-on-one in a private virtual workspace, or send private messages to each other using the collaboration tool's direct messaging feature.

- When interacting using any real-time collaboration tools (using group messaging, voice conference calls, video conferences, or collaboration tools to work on a document, for example), instruct everyone to stay on topic. If one or more people bring up lunch plans, upcoming vacation plans, or what happened the previous night on their favorite television show, everyone will be distracted, and the workspace will be cluttered with information and content unrelated to the task or project at hand.

- Assign a team leader or admin person to oversee how the cloud-based tools are being used, manage user accounts, and keep everyone focused. Define the role and responsibilities of the team leader or admin person, as well as the responsibilities of each team member or collaborator.

- Have each user customize his or her account profile so it includes and displays their full names, job titles, profile photos, and any other important details that team members or collaborators need to identify with whom they're working. Refrain from using a cute or funny nickname for yourself; that's acceptable when using social media but not appropriate for a work environment. Account profiles are particularly important for large teams or entire companies that are using cloud-based tools to communicate and exchange information.

■ Have each user turn on notifications related to the collaboration tools so that everyone is alerted when a new group message is posted, something requires a user's attention, a new file is uploaded, or when content is edited, for example. With notifications turned on, team members do not need to constantly monitor the workspace to make sure they don't miss anything important. Instead, when something requires a particular person's attention or the whole group needs to be brought up to date on something, the appropriate people receive an email or text message that prompts them to access their accounts.

■ Agree to a method for team members to share new ideas, comments, and constructive feedback in a way that allows everyone to be heard but that does not hinder progress. All team members and collaborators should be invited to participate and share, and feel comfortable doing so, without receiving harsh, unprofessional, or negative feedback or criticism.

■ Take advantage of a group scheduling or time-management tool when planning and coordinating schedules and virtual meeting times.

■ Have the team leader post daily, weekly, and monthly progress reports to keep everyone apprised of how far along the group is toward achieving desired goals or milestones. When it becomes necessary to tweak or re-evaluate a goal, deadline, or objective, everyone involved should be kept up to speed using the communication tools provided by the cloud-based collaboration service.

In Practice

Evaluate What Works and What Doesn't

As each video conference, virtual meeting, or real-time collaboration session comes to an end, the project or team leader should carefully evaluate the tools and process to determine what could be handled better in the future, or what alternative (or additional) communication or collaboration tools could be used to further enhance productivity.

Workflow bottlenecks, human errors, security issues, incidents of miscommunication, or scheduling problems should be identified and evaluated so improvements can be made or fixes can be implemented in the future. Whenever possible, request feedback from collaborators and team members.

Develop a Meeting Plan

Virtual meetings, video conferences, and real-time collaboration sessions (where multiple people work together simultaneously) provide forums for people to exchange information, brainstorm ideas, and work as a cohesive group, even when everyone is in a different location.

To maximize the use of any virtual meeting or video conference tool, it's important for the meeting host to create a detailed plan in advance of the meeting. Use these steps to create a plan:

1. Put someone in charge of the meeting.

2. Define meeting objectives.

3. Determine who needs to attend the meeting, conference, or virtual gathering, and what each person's responsibilities or role will be. Convey this information to the participants in the meeting invitations or using a direct email message, for example.

4. Determine a date and time when you know most or all invitees will be available. This task is made easier if the company or team uses a group scheduling program.

5. Set a date and time for the meeting and send out invitations using the tools offered by the tool you'll be using. Put someone in charge of managing RSVP's and reassigning meeting responsibilities if one or more people can't attend.

6. Create a detailed meeting agenda that includes time estimates for each phase of the meeting.

7. Determine which meeting tools (white board, screen sharing, group chat, and so on) are necessary and outline how each will be used during each phase of the meeting.

8. Prepare and gather all documents or files that will be presented or used during the meeting. This might include PowerPoint slides, spreadsheets, or relevant documents.

9. Just prior to the scheduled meeting, make sure all documents and files are ready to present, and test out the technology to be used.

10. At the designated meeting time, have someone take attendance and make sure all invited participants are signed in and ready to go before the formal meeting starts. Work out any connection issues to the meeting platform.

11. If necessary, set ground rules for who can speak and when, or how and when the platform's group messaging or file-sharing tools should be used.

12. Follow the meeting agenda as closely as possible, which allows everyone to stay on schedule for the rest of their day.

13. Invite questions or feedback at a designated time during or at the end of the meeting.

14. At the conclusion of a meeting, define what needs to be done next by participants. If necessary, set up the next meeting or a detailed plan of action for moving forward.

15. Follow up after the meeting with a summary of what transpired, distribute copies of relevant notes and files, and provide a link for participants to re-watch the video conference (if applicable). Make sure all participants understand how and where to access data, documents, files, and notes that were created or referenced during the meeting. The conference's link can also be provided to invitees who could not attend the live meeting or conference but who need to catch up on what was covered.

Strategies for Effectively Using Chat or Group Messaging

When people use text messaging, instant messaging, or group messaging in conjunction with social media to interact with friends and family, there really are no rules. This applies to Facebook Messenger, Twitter, Instagram, SnapChat, and countless other social media services, as well as text messaging from any smartphone. In other words, you're free to say whatever you want, whenever you want, with few or no consequences. You're also free to use sentence fragments, slang, sexual innuendos, nicknames for people, all sorts of abbreviations, and emoji characters to help you communicate.

The text message, instant message, or group messaging service you use at work function pretty much the same way as the messaging tools offered by popular social media services, but the way you're expected to communicate is very different. When you use these communication tools in a work setting, even if the people you're communicating with are also your friends, it's important to always maintain a professional demeanor.

It is the responsibility of the administrator or team leader to establish specific rules, policies, or guidelines for users to follow when engaged in work-related conversations using the designated text message, instant message, or group messaging service adopted by the company or team.

The following are strategies to use while using any type of messaging tool in a work environment:

- Always stay on topic.
- Create separate chats or message threads for specific subjects or projects.
- Refer to people within messages using their full usernames, not nicknames.
- Make sure everyone using the messaging service has completed their account profiles. Profiles should display full names, positions, and photos along with other relevant information. This is particularly important within large organizations where not everyone knows everyone else by name.
- Use complete sentences that do not include abbreviations or inappropriate emoji characters.
- If whatever you want to say would not be appropriate to say in person, on the phone, or via email with the person you're communicating with in a work setting, don't say it in a text message, instant message, or group message.
- Avoid discussing any highly personal or controversial topics that are outside the realm of what's work related.
- Only include people in group message threads that need to be included and who are authorized to have access to whatever information will be discussed.
- Remember that the messaging service you're using for work automatically maintains a complete transcript of all conversations, which is readily available to the account administrator and your superiors. Avoid saying nasty, discriminatory, or racist comments about your employer or coworkers.

- For communication of something that only one other person within that chat needs to know, use the application's direct message feature. Don't share the message with the entire group.

- If the messaging service permits, create descriptive chat room names or titles that are relevant to the topic being discussed.

- Keep all conversations on one designated messaging service. When it comes to work-related conversations, avoid using social media platforms that aren't company sanctioned or your personal social media accounts to communicate with co-workers or clients.

- Avoid incorporating inside jokes or references that only select people in a group would understand or relate to.

- Keep in mind that with most services, once a group message is posted or someone receives a direct message, the recipient is alerted immediately on their computer or mobile device. If you're working with a group spread out over multiple time zones, or one person is working late into the night, refrain from posting messages that could disturb or wake people, unless it's extremely important.

- Ask each user to customize the notification settings in their accounts to prevent unimportant message notification messages from disturbing them when they're busy with other tasks during the day or when they're trying to sleep at night.

- Never have arguments or unprofessional disagreements in a group forum.

- Remember the age-old saying that goes "Think before you speak." This guideline also applies when communicating through a messaging service. Before clicking Send, determine if your outgoing message could be misconstrued or misinterpreted in anyway.

CAUTION

Proofread All Messages!

Before sending any message to anyone in a work environment, always proofread what you've typed *before* clicking the Send button. This is particularly important if the autocorrect or spell-check feature is turned on. Especially if you're typing a message quickly, while focusing on something else, it's easy to make typos that could result in you sending an inappropriate or error-filled message.

Chapter | **4**

Understanding Cloud-Based Security Concerns

This chapter focuses on many of the security-related issues individual users of cloud computing platforms and services will need to contend with to protect their content. This chapter covers the following:

- What security and compliance features and tools you should use from a cloud-based computing platform or service
- Common security-related problems resulting from human error
- Basic strategies users can implement to protect their cloud-based accounts and content

Each cloud-based computing service uses its own security protocols and strategies to help ensure every account is protected as much as possible from outside data breaches, insecure application programming interfaces (APIs), system vulnerabilities, and shared technology-related issues. These precautions tend to work after content has been stored online but often doesn't protect content as you upload or download it between the service and the equipment you're using.

Certifications from Recognized Organizations

Virtually all cloud computing platforms and services rely on the security guidelines and certifications overseen by independent, industry-accepted organizations, such as the International Organization of Standardization (ISO) and the Cloud Security Alliance (CSA). When you're researching a cloud-based service or platform's security, look for compliance with, or certifications related to, these two organizations.

There are also many organizations and government agencies that provide strict, industry-specific guidelines related to compliance and security issues when working with specific types of data or information. Companies working in the health, medical, finance, banking, and insurance sectors, for example, are required to adhere to strict information and data management protocols—including how content is stored and managed within a cloud-based computing platform—that are specific to those industries. For example, the Health Insurance Portability and Accountability Act (HIPAA) and the Health Information Technology for Economic and Clinical Health Act (HITECH) relate to how companies and organizations must handle health- and medical-related data and information related to individuals.

CAUTION

Adhere to Industry-Specific Compliance Regulations

Based on what industry you work in, before deploying or using any cloud-based computing service or platform, research which compliance regulations you must adhere to and determine whether the cloud service's internal security meets or exceeds what's required. Then figure out whether you need any additional security software or tools to further protect user accounts and related content.

Types of Security Threats

One of the most confusing and convoluted aspects of using cloud services or platforms is understanding what forms of cybersecurity are provided and whether they address the many types of threats that you might encounter.

The Cloud Security Alliance (CSA) has published a report, *The Treacherous 12: Cloud Computing Top Threats in 2016* (https://cloudsecurityalliance.org/download/the-treacherous-twelve-cloud-computing-top-threats-in-2016), that provides an overview of the most common threats, which were

- Data breaches
- Weak identity, credential, and access management
- Insecure APIs
- System and application vulnerabilities
- Account hijacking
- Malicious insiders
- Advanced persistent threats (APTs)
- Data loss

- Insufficient due diligence

- Abuse and nefarious use of cloud services

- Denial of service (DoS)

- Shared technology issues

Some of these threats are clearly beyond the scope of what individual users can do to protect their accounts and even what teams, companies, or organizations can do when managing the use of public cloud-based services that are operated outside of their own organizations.

The best strategy for protecting against some of these threats is to research a cloud service prior to deploying it and make sure that service adheres to the latest security guidelines, regulations, and certifications that have been established by recognized, independent organizations, such as the ISO and CSA.

In Practice

Check for Updates

Nefarious individuals are always working on developing new threats and attacks to our cyber-security. It's important to stay abreast of changes in security so that you keep your cloud-based content safe. Occasionally check the Cloud Security Alliance website and the threat report to find out whether an update to this report has been published.

Ways to Protect Yourself When Using the Cloud

It's important to understand that despite all of the security-related technologies and protocols that are in place by cloud services, a significant threat to the secure use of these services has to do with inadvertent user error and user misuse of these services. Fortunately, there are ways you can help to reduce or eliminate these problems.

CAUTION

Nothing Is 100% Secure in the Cloud

Despite all the research, technology, security-related compliance activities, and high-tech counter measures that cloud services employ to protect users and their online content, no cloud computing platform or service (public or private) is 100 percent secure. It's up to individual companies and users to determine what content should (and shouldn't) be stored, managed, or shared within a cloud-based environment and what added security-related precautions are necessary to protect accounts, data, files, documents, and content.

The following are some strategies that you can adopt when using any cloud-based computing platform or services.

- **Be aware of possible threats:** Understand what threats exist when using any cloud-based service or platform and learn how to detect and prevent these threats if they arise. In addition to individual user accounts, when a team or company deploys a cloud-based service, additional administrator tools or controls are often provided to allow one person within the team or organization to oversee the use of a cloud-based platform or service, implement optional security measures, and potentially detect user errors or suspicious activities that could result in security threats.

- **Understand compliance regulations for your industry:** Based on the industry you work in, determine what compliance regulations you must adhere to and ensure that all users are provided with the training and tools that will allow them to stay compliant.

    Unfortunately, in an effort to protect consumers and companies from any type of harm as a result of the poor management of sensitive information, various divisions of the U.S. government, as well as other governments and regulatory agencies around the world (including the ISO), have enacted what often turn out to be confusing laws and convoluted regulations relating to how specific types of information may be managed, handled, utilized, and stored. Because industry specific compliance laws and regulations are constantly changing, there are no shortcuts to take when it comes to researching what's required, based on the type of information you'll be working with.

In Practice

Seek Out the Guidance You Need

When it comes to adhering to compliance regulations, don't guess. Discuss your needs directly with representatives of the cloud service you're thinking about using. Also, do your own online research. From any search engine, try using a search phrase like [industry] compliance regulations. In addition, you can consult with a lawyer who specializes in industry-specific compliance regulations.

There are also independent consulting companies, like Rackspace (www.rackspace.com), that can help small to medium-sized companies choose and then migrate to platforms or services (such as Office 365) in the most secure and industry-compliant way possible.

FYI: Compliance Advice from Microsoft

Microsoft Corporation has published a document called *Think Cloud Compliance: An Introduction to Cloud Computing for Legal and Compliance Professionals* that offers advice to companies and individuals who need to follow compliance standards and regulations for managing data. You can read the document at http://download.microsoft.com/download/0/D/6/0D68AE95-6414-4074-B4B8-34039831E2BF/Introduction-to-Cloud-Computing-for-Legal-and-Compliance-Professionals.pdf.

- **Choose the most suitable platform or service:** Based on the needs of your team or organization, choose which platforms or services have the features, functionality, security tools, and security protocols that best fit your needs.

- **Use due diligence and common sense:** Make sure you and your associates use cloud-based services in a responsible manner. Content moved to and from the cloud should be transferred in the most secure way possible. When working with third-party software or mobile apps that store or retrieve data from the cloud, make sure that the APIs that are used by the software or mobile app(s) are secure and work flawlessly with the selected cloud service. This is particularly important if you're using third-party APIs that are related to software or service you're already using. Whenever possible, try to use APIs developed by the cloud service provider or the software developer that created the software you're using with the cloud-based service.

FYI: Advice from an Expert

According to Jon Ferrara, CEO and Founder of Nimble, Inc. (www.nimble.com), a social sales and marketing CRM platform that works in conjunction with Office 365 and Google G Suite, "A big part of working in the cloud is creating a login, and then accessing an app, such as one of the Office 365 apps on your computer or mobile device. Once you have done that, in order for it to be effective, you need to tie it into other apps. When you do that, you give that other app, and potentially its developer, access to your identity and the data.

"You really have to manage those integrations, because you may have given access to a third-party app two years ago that you have forgotten about, and the app's developer has since been sold, which means somebody else is now potentially accessing your data. Remember, some companies buy other companies just for their user base, and maybe even the access they might have to your data.

"On an ongoing basis, you need to manage your logins, and change your passwords, set up a two-step authorization, and manage the integrations and access that you provide. Make sure that passwords are changed periodically. The passwords should also be sophisticated. Too many people use their birthday, or something related to their names. If the tools you are using have the ability to check the IP address of the device that you are accessing them from, you might want to consider using these types of security precautions as well. Finally, VPNs are also powerful tools for controlling access to information by encrypting it."

- **Take advantage of security options:** Many services and platforms offer optional security tools that augment the basic security features you might get with a basic account. If the content you're working with needs to be as protected as possible, use tools like file and data encryption and two-factor authentication when users sign in to their accounts. When users are accessing a cloud-based service from an insecure Wi-Fi hotspot, consider having the users first establish a virtual private network (VPN) to use with their computers or mobile devices.

- **Identify and avoid common user errors:** Make sure all users are properly trained to use the tools at their disposal and that they adopt practices that will help to prevent the most common user errors that can result in serious security-related problems and issues.

User Mistakes That Often Lead to Security Problems

Security and compliance are important considerations that need to be taken seriously, not only by the people choosing which cloud computing service(s) to adopt but by everyone who will be using the cloud-based tools and services.

Several of the top cloud computing-related threats caused by user errors include

- Data breaches or theft as a result of a user accidently sharing his or her account password, account hijacking, or a user making account information easily accessible to unauthorized people.

- Not employing sufficient identity, credential, or access management for the service.

- Accessing a cloud-based service from an insecure, public Wi-Fi hotspot.

- Employees or users with authorized access to cloud-based accounts using their access for malicious purposes.

- Users sharing their devices without safeguarding their account information. In other words, someone lets the web browser automatically store the account username and password and then allows another person to use the equipment, which means the second user is to gain full access to the first user's accounts.

When organizations or companies experience data breaches, data loss, or other potentially serious problems, the cause often can be traced back to user error or the misuse of a service rather than to problems with the security and compliance features of the service. Mistakes are often caused when a user simply doesn't know how to use the tools. This is why user training is essential. Not only does good training boost individual productivity but it helps protect the security of content being accessed and shared on the service.

In Practice

Always Sign Out

For user convenience, many web browsers automatically remember all sign-in details for websites and then automatically sign in the user each time he or she returns to the website. Both Windows computers and Macs can be set up to sync a user's account usernames and passwords across all their computers and mobile devices, so the account credentials are available to all web browsers (see Figure 4.1).

For the most secure situation possible, refrain from allowing your web browser, computer, or mobile device to remember the usernames and passwords associated with any services you use. Also be sure to sign out from your account when you're done using it, as opposed to simply closing the web browser or mobile app you were using.

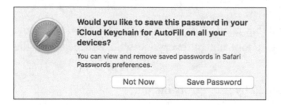

FIGURE 4.1   Do not allow the web browser you're using to automatically remember the account username or password that's associated with your account(s).

Strategies for Password Creation and Management

Just about every website you visit and interact with, including all of the cloud services and platforms, require users to set up a password for their account. As a result, most people wind up having to create and remember dozens of different usernames and passwords in their everyday lives.

To achieve the maximum levels of security these passwords can offer, use the following strategies for creating and managing passwords (not just the ones used to access cloud-based services):

- Do not use the same password for all of your accounts. If you have just one password and someone figures it out, you're basically giving them full access to everything you do online.

- Do not use a common or easy-to-figure-out password. Things like "password," "12345678," "87654321," your birthday, your spouse's name, your pet's name, your child's name, "football," "StarWars," and "login" are the most commonly used passwords. The password should also not relate to the application it's being used for, such as "OfficePassword."

- All passwords should be at least eight characters long, mix and match upper- and lowercase letters, and include one or more numbers.

- Get into the habit of changing each of your passwords, especially the ones that grant access to your most important accounts, on a weekly or biweekly basis. You can easily change an account-specific password in the Account Settings menu for each service you use (see Figure 4.2).

Change Password option

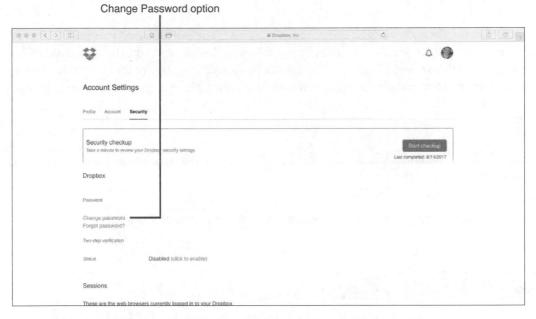

FIGURE 4.2   Manually change your account password on a regular basis to help protect your account. Shown here is the Account Settings Security menu for Dropbox.

- In addition to the password for the overall account, consider assigning different passwords for any files or folders that also have passwords. For example, if you're sharing a Word document via Dropbox and you have opted to set up a password for that document, make sure the document's password is not the same (or similar) to your account password.

- Do not write your passwords on a sheet of paper or sticky note that's kept anywhere near your computer or that you keep "hidden" in your office or wallet. One common mistake is writing passwords on a sticky note or piece of tape and attaching it under a computer keyboard. This is such a common activity that it's usually the first place someone looks if they're trying to break in to your computer or account(s).

- If you need someplace secure to store your passwords, use a specialized mobile app, such as Password Manager Vault, 1Password, or Keeper Password Manager. Dashlane (www.dashlane. com is both a mobile app and a secure, cloud-based service that protects your entire collection of usernames and passwords, plus syncs the database between all of your own computers and mobile devices for easy access. Type "password manager" in your mobile device's app store to find appropriate apps.

Two-Factor Authentication

One of the optional security features that most services offer is *two-factor authentication* (also known as *two-step verification*). To turn on or off this feature, log in to a service you're using and access the Account Settings menu. If you don't see an option for two-step authentication, check on the Account Security menu.

When you have two-factor authentication activated, you enter your username and password to sign in to the account, but the service also generates a special code and sends it to you via text message (see Figure 4.3) or email. You need to enter this code on the authentication page for the service (see Figure 4.4). A different, random code is generated and sent with each login attempt, and each code is valid only for a few minutes.

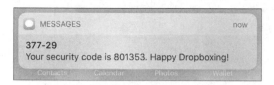

FIGURE 4.3   The service provides an authentication code for you to complete the sign-in process.

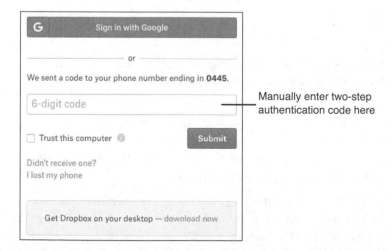

FIGURE 4.4   Enter the unique authentication code that you receive from the service.

Two-factor authentication makes it harder for someone to access your account. If someone has figured out your username and password, they will still need access to your smartphone to get the additional authentication code needed to sign in to and access your account. For this feature to work, when you activate it, you'll need to provide the service with your trusted smartphone phone number. In some cases, a special app will also need to be installed onto your smartphone, or you can set up the feature to send you an email that contains a unique sign-in code each time you need to access your account.

The benefit to using two-factor authentication is that it keeps your cloud-based account safer by making it much more difficult for someone to hack into. The drawback is that it takes you a little bit longer to sign in to your account because you need to receive and type in the verification code every time you want to sign in to it. This adds between 15 and 30 seconds to the sign in process, depending on how quickly you receive the code and then enter it.

In Practice

Two-Factor Authentication for Multiple Services

Google has implemented a two-factor authentication service that other cloud-based services (including Dropbox), software packages, and mobile apps have since adopted. After you've activated the Google two-factor authentication feature and sign in to a compatible account using your username and password, Google sends a code to you via text message, voice call, or its proprietary mobile app. (You must already have the app installed on your smartphone to be able to receive and display the necessary verification codes.)

For more information about Google Two-Step Verification, visit www.google.com/landing/2step.

Virtual Private Networks

When you log in to a cloud-based service using the Internet connection at your office, chances are that it's a secure connection. In other words, the connection between the computer (or mobile device) and the Internet router/modem is encrypted and secure.

However, if you connect to the Internet from someplace with a public Wi-Fi hotspot (airport, hotel, coffee shop, library), the wireless connection between your computer and the router/modem is not secure. This provides an opportunity for hackers and cyber criminals to access your information.

It's important to understand that the cloud-computing services all have secure servers, so once content is uploaded to a service and stored there it's automatically encrypted and well protected. The opportunity for a breach often comes from a user's own equipment and the way each user connects to the Internet.

To compensate for this potential problem, you can activate a virtual private network (VPN) from your computer or mobile device. The easiest option is to subscribe to a service that provides a proprietary mobile app or software that automatically establishes a VPN whenever you've established an insecure Internet connection.

Norton WiFi Privacy Service

Norton WiFi Privacy (https://us.norton.com/wifi-privacy) is one VPN service. It costs $4.99 per month, per user, and it allows each user to establish a VPN from one computer or mobile device. Once activated, the VPN encrypts all information being sent or received via the Internet from an insecure Wi-Fi hotspot. A second subscription plan ($7.99 per month, per user) makes it possible for each user to establish a VPN from up to five different devices (any combination of computers and mobile devices); a plan for $9.99 per month, allows ten different devices.

Signing up for Norton WiFi Privacy takes about three minutes, and requires a credit or debit card. After you've created your account, you download specialized software or a mobile app to each computer and mobile device that you'll be using with the service. The confirmation email you receive provides the link to the software for your Windows PC or Mac, or you can visit www.norton.com/setup. This email also contains a 25-character product key that you must enter the first time you attempt to install the software on a computer or mobile device. (Visit the app store for your mobile device to acquire the necessary Norton WiFi Privacy mobile app.)

Launch the software or app on your computer or device and then sign in to your Norton account. Each time you need to log in to a public Wi-Fi hotspot, first launch the Norton WiFi Privacy software (see Figure 4.5) or mobile app (shown in Figure 4.6), and then use your favorite web browser or applications to access the Internet, just as you normally would.

FIGURE 4.5   Norton WiFi Privacy is shown here running on a MacBook Air.

VPN icon

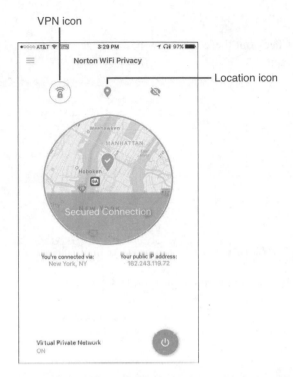

Location icon

FIGURE 4.6   The VPN icon in the top-left corner of the screen indicates that a VPN is active.

In Practice

Norton VPN Protects More Than Your Data

In addition to ensuring that all data that's sent or received from your computer or mobile device while you're connected to an insecure Wi-Fi hotspot is encrypted and secure, a Norton VPN creates a "virtual location" for your computer or mobile device, so a hacker can't determine where you're accessing the Internet from. Plus, this software allows you to turn on or off Ad Tracking, which means that as you're surfing the Web, advertisers can't track what sites you're accessing.

To adjust these privacy settings on your computer, launch the Norton WiFi Privacy software and then access the Account Setup menu by clicking the gear-shaped Settings icon (refer to Figure 4.5). From the mobile app, tap the Location icon (refer to Figure 4.6).

Additional VPN Service Options

Norton WiFi Privacy isn't the only VPN solution. Check out these other low-cost services that allow you to create a VPN from your computer or mobile app:

- **ExpressVPN** (www.expressvpn.com)

- **Hotspot Shield** (www.hsselite.com)

- **NordVPN** (www.nordvpn.com)

- **PrivateVPN** (www.privatevpn.com)

- **PureVPN** (www.purevpn.com)

FYI: Quickly Find Other VPN Service Providers

To find additional VPN service options, access any Internet search engine, and within the Search field, type "VPN Service Provider."

FYI: Resources for Security Information

To find out more about the security and compliance features and functions built in to the services covered in Chapters 5 through 16 of this book, use these links:

- **Box.com:** www.box.com/security
- **Cisco WebEx and Cisco Spark:** https://support.webex.com/LocalizedUpgrades/2014/bestpractices/best_practices_for_secure_meetings.pdf
- **DocuSign:** https://trust.docusign.com/en-us
- **Dropbox and Dropbox Paper:** www.dropbox.com/security
- **Evernote:** https://evernote.com/security
- **Google G Suite:** https://gsuite.google.com/learn-more/security-g-suite.html
- **Microsoft office 365 and Exchange Online:** https://products.office.com/en-us/business/most-secure-office
- **Salesforce:** https://trust.salesforce.com
- **Skype for Business:** https://support.skype.com/en/faq/FA34649/protecting-your-online-safety-security-and-privacy
- **Slack:** https://slack.com/security
- **Trello:** https://trello.com/security

Chapter | 5

Collaborating with Box

This chapter focuses on Box, a cloud-based file-storage and file-sharing tool that offers some additional functionality as well. This chapter introduces you to the following:

- The core features and functions offered by Box
- The ways Box integrates with popular software, mobile apps, and other cloud-based collaboration services
- How to collaborate using Box Notes

Box (www.box.com) is a cloud-based file-storage and file-sharing service that offers collaboration tools and can integrate with many popular software applications, mobile apps, and other cloud-based services. This makes it suitable for use by individuals or teams and organizations of almost any size.

Getting to Know Box

Since Box launched in 2005, it has helped individuals and businesses use cloud-based computing to meet their current and ever-evolving file-storage and file-sharing needs. Some the most appealing features of Box are that it works with virtually all computer and mobile device platforms, it provides the tools needed to securely handle several common cloud-computing tasks, and the service is easily scalable for the size of the group of people who will use it.

As of mid-2017, more than 41 million individual users and 59,000 businesses around the world, including 59 percent of Fortune 500 companies, use Box to help manage content in the cloud.

File Storage

The Box service offers online storage that is compatible with virtually all popular file types. Users can organize their files into custom folders and subfolders, which are securely stored online and are accessible from all of the user's computers and mobile devices that are signed in to the same Box account. In other words, a user can access their single Box account from any desktop, laptop computer, smartphone, or tablet from virtually anywhere.

As long as the computer or mobile device you're working with has Internet access, as you create or edit files, the latest version is uploaded to your Box account and is immediately accessible to all of your other computers and mobile devices. You can configure Box to automatically handle this file syncing.

When you use the Box website, you can preview almost any type of file that you've stored online without having to open another application and then import the file into it. The preview feature works with more than 120 different file types, including all file types associated with Microsoft Office, Office 365, Google G Suite, and digital image or video files.

CAUTION

Make Sure You Have Enough Online Storage

The biggest problem users run into when using a cloud-based service for storing data, documents, files, digital photos, video content, and other types of content, is that they quickly exceed the amount of online storage space that's allocated to their account. This is typically more of a problem for individual consumers. The business-oriented accounts offered by Box (and similar services) tend to provide much greater online storage allocations.

Box limits the amount of data you can upload per month based on the type of account you have. This could become a concern if you will be frequently uploading extremely large files to your Box account.

For example, a free Individual Box subscription plan offers 10GB of online storage but limits new file uploads to just 250MB per month. A Personal Pro, Business, Business Plus, or Enterprise plan increases this monthly new file upload limit to 5GB per month.

File Sharing

The file-sharing capabilities built into Box enable you to share any specific file(s) or folder(s) that are stored online within your account, with any other specific users, even if those other people don't use Box or are not employees within the same company.

When you share files that you have stored in Box, you manually select files or folders to determine exactly what content you are sharing, and you maintain control over the other user's privileges when it comes to accessing those files or folders. You can revoke the other user's access at any time. All other files and folders stored within the Box account are kept secure and private.

Based on how you set up the files or folders to be shared, the content can be encrypted and/or password protected. You can also set expiration dates for shared links, and you can share each file or folder with any number of separate people.

> ## CAUTION
>
> ## What Happens to Files After They've Been Shared
>
> After a file is accessed and downloaded by others, what those people can do with that file is no longer in your control. This is true when sharing files via any cloud-based service.

When you select one or more files to be shared with one or more other people, the Box service automatically emails an invitation to the intended recipients and provides a secure URL from which the files can be retrieved. One of the most popular uses of this feature is to allow users to easily and securely share or distribute extremely large files with others, which are too large to send as email attachments.

Alternatively, you can set up separate shared folders within your Box account and then allow specific people either full or limited access to those folders. This is particularly useful for online collaboration, where files continuously go back and forth between users as revisions are made or when a file is being used simultaneously by multiple people.

The benefit to using a shared folder that automatically syncs files is that all of the people working together can store related files that they're collaborating on in one secure online location. All team members or collaborators will always have access to the latest version of each file (along with past versions, if necessary).

One of the added features of Box is the extensive preview capability. Anyone using Box can preview more than 120 different file types without first needing to download the file.

In Practice

Take Advantage of the Version History Feature

Box (and many cloud-based file-sharing services like it) offers an automatic Version History feature to paid users, which means that each time a specific file is updated by a user, or online collaborators modify the file, a new version of it is created and saved. Older versions are still available to be accessed as needed. Box's various Business and Enterprise plans maintain between 25 and 100 versions of each file, as needed, which helps to ensure important content isn't accidently lost or permanently deleted. (The Personal Pro plan stores only up to 10 versions of a file, and this feature is not available with a free account.)

With services that don't have this versioning feature in place, once any change is made to a file that's stored in the cloud, the older version of the file is erased and replaced by the newest version. A cloud service that maintains copies of older versions of a file is extremely useful, especially when you're collaborating with others on shared files.

FYI: The People You Share with Don't Need Box

When you're using Box, you can share a file or folder with someone else who is not a Box user by using the Share tools. You use Box to send a link to another person, who then uses the link to access your shared file or folder, download the file(s) to their own computer or mobile device, and open and work with those files using whatever software or mobile app is required, such as Microsoft Word, PowerPoint, or Excel.

Integrated Collaboration Tools

Beyond just giving users the ability to share files and folders, Box has an ever-growing selection of real-time collaboration tools built into the service. Box also integrates with some of the most popular software packages, mobile apps, and other cloud-based services used in business, such as Microsoft Office and Office 365, Microsoft Outlook, most of the popular Google apps, Slack, DocuSign, Salesforce, and WebEx.

As a result, when you use any of these applications or services, you can set up the service so any content you create or edit with it is automatically stored within your Box account. There's no need to manually copy data, documents, or files to the cloud because the software or mobile app you're already using syncs the files you're working with.

For Box Business account users, the service always maintains an end-to-end audit trail of all files that are stored on the service, including Microsoft Office files. This allows team leaders or administrators to monitor who has accessed which files, see when those files were accessed, and determine what was done to a file by each user. Box is capable of tracking more than 70 user activities. The service automatically tracks and alerts team leaders or administrators of unusual uploads or downloads, which helps to prevent content and data theft or loss.

> ### FYI: Box Is Compliant with Security Standards
>
> Using granular permissions, data encryption, two-factor authentication, shared link password security, bulk managed user provisioning, admin role delegation, document watermarking, password policy enforcement, usage logs, file statistics, custom terms of service, and device trust, Box is fully compliant with global security standards. To learn more about Box's security features, visit www.box.com/security.

Understanding Box Subscription Plans and Pricing

Box offers a variety of user subscription plans to meet the needs of individuals, small teams, and large businesses. The following sections describe the various levels of subscription plans.

Individual Plans

Single users can start using Box for free. Simply visit www.box.com using any web browser and click the Sign Up button in the top-right corner of the screen. From a mobile device, you can download the free Box mobile app from the app store for your smartphone or tablet, locate the Box app using the app store's Search field, and then download and install the app. After you've installed the app, launch the app and tap the Sign Up option.

The Box Individual free plan includes 10GB of online storage, but new file uploads are limited to just 250MB per month. For about $10.00 per user, per month, the Personal Pro plan includes 100GB of online storage and bumps the new file uploads cap to 5GB per month.

Business Plans

The three Box plans for business users, include

- Starter ($5.00 per user, per month)
- Business ($15.00 per user, per month)
- Business Plus ($25.00 per user, per month)

The Starter plan offers a total of 100GB of online storage per user, but new file uploads are limited to 2GB per month. Under this plan, team leaders and administrators have limited control over Box users within an organization, and the integration features that work with other popular software, mobile apps, and cloud-based services is more limited in this plan than with some others. This plan includes fewer security and compliance features than what's offered by the Business, Business Pro, and Enterprise plans.

The Business plan includes unlimited online storage for each user and caps new file uploads at 5GB per month. Compared to Individual plans and the Starter plan, the Business plan offers more robust sharing tools, collaboration tools, security features, and more integration with popular software (including mobile apps and other cloud-based services). More advanced reporting and global compliance features are also included with this plan.

The Business Plus plan builds on the features and functions included with the Business Plan when it comes to file sharing and collaboration tools. It offers even better integration, security, data loss prevention, workflow automations, mobile device integration, and global compliance.

To download a free information sheet that highlights key features and functions offered by each Box business plan, visit https://cloud.app.box.com/v/BoxBusinessEditions.

FYI: More About Enterprise Solutions Using Box

Box also caters to the cloud-computing needs of large organizations. For more information about customizable Enterprise plans—which include a higher level of support, more security controls, unlimited app integrations, workflow automations, and other features—contact Box at 877-729-4269.

Using Box with PCs and Macs

When using Box with any Internet-connected Windows PC or Mac, you can securely access your account using any popular web browser. Simply visit www.box.com, click the Sign Up button to create an account, or click the Log In button to sign in to an existing account (see Figure 5.1). Within minutes after signing up for an account, you'll receive a confirmation email within your inbox. Click on the Verify Email button that's embedded within this email to begin using your new account immediately.

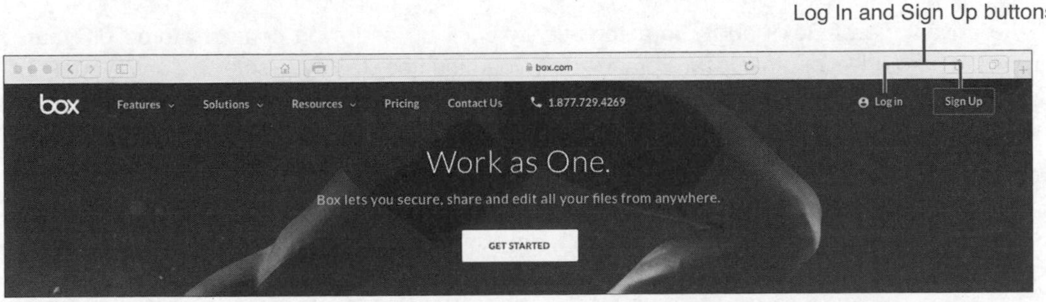

FIGURE 5.1   From the home page of Box.com, you can create a new account or log in to your existing account.

After you've signed in to your Box account, you have access to your online storage space, within which you can store your files and folders. Begin by creating custom folders and then uploading files into them. Alternatively, you can upload existing folders and their contents from your computer's hard drive (or other local storage).

Figure 5.2 shows the Box.com file management window, which is accessible after you sign in to your account. From here, you're able to upload, manage, view, edit, share, and collaborate.

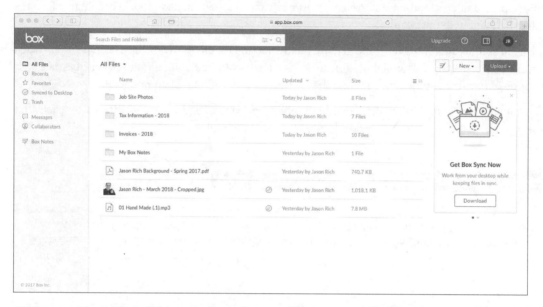

FIGURE 5.2   In this window you can view the files and folders stored online and directly access Box's file-management, collaboration, and sharing tools.

In Practice

Download the Box Sync Software

To take advantage of Box's ability to automatically back up and sync content stored on your computer's hard drive (or other local storage), download the free Box Sync software onto your PC or Mac. The link to this software is displayed when you access your Box account from your web browser.

If you don't use the Box Sync software, you have to manually upload files from your computer's local storage to your cloud-based account. Click the Upload button in the top-right corner of the Box browser window. Then select files or folders, drag and drop files or folders, or copy and paste files or folders into Box's Upload window.

The free Box Sync software enables your computer to automatically back up and sync files as you create and save them into a local folder. This software only needs to be set up once, but you can later add folders that you want to backup and sync automatically with your online-based Box account.

Another way to ensure that files and data automatically sync to your Box account when using specific applications, such as Microsoft Office or Office 365 applications, is to set up automated Box integration within each of these applications. You have to do this only once. After you've set up application-specific integration, your data, documents, files, or related content from that application automatically are synced and shared with your Box account. The same files can often be stored locally as well, based on which application you're using.

Anytime you're using Box directly from your favorite web browser, you also have access to the service's Messages and Collaboration tools, as well as Box Notes. These features are covered later in this chapter.

Customizing Your Box Profile and Account Settings

When you first start using Box, especially if you plan to share files or collaborate with others, be sure to customize your Box profile. Access your Box account using your favorite web browser and then click your initials in the round icon in the top-right corner of the browser window.

Next, click the View profile option and then click the Edit Information button. To add a profile photo, click the Profile Picture option (see Figure 5.3) and select the photo you want to use.

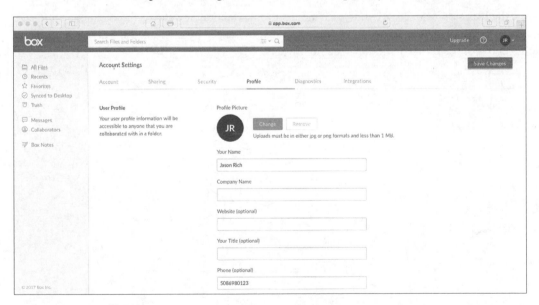

FIGURE 5.3 After creating your Box account, take a few moments to customize your profile and personalize your Account Settings.

Within each field, fill in the information that you want to make viewable to other people on your team, within your company, or with whom you'll be sharing files. These fields include Your Name, Company Name, Website (optional), Your Title (optional), and Phone (optional). Be sure to click the Save Changes button to update your profile.

You also can customize specific settings related to your Box account. Click the Account, Sharing, Security, Profile, Diagnostics, and Integration tabs to adjust whichever options you desire from the corresponding submenus.

For example, use the Account menu to associate additional email addresses with your account, change your account password, or activate the two-step verification process that helps protect your account against unauthorized logins.

The Sharing menu within Account Settings enables you to customize how content is shared with other people. From this tab, you can personalize when Box sends you notifications to alert you of specific events related to your account.

From the Security screen, you can view a detailed history of each login your account has made to the Box service. The Diagnostics tools are used by Box's tech support or your Box administrator to solve account-related problems, and the Integrations screen allows you to manage permissions for specific software applications, mobile apps, and other cloud-based services that you use.

Working with Box Messages

Anytime the Box service or one of your team members or collaborators needs your attention, a message is delivered to the Box Messages area. You access these messages by clicking the Messages button in the left sidebar of the browser window (see Figure 5.4).

FIGURE 5.4 Box Messages alerts you of files or tasks that need your attention from within your Box account.

On the Messages page, the list of messages related to collaboration invites, mentions in comments, tasks others have assigned to you, and file/collaborator expiration notices are displayed in reverse chronological order. After selecting and reading a message, you can take whatever additional actions are needed, typically by following links or menu options embedded within the message.

You can sort received messages based on a variety of criteria, such as Unread, Incomplete Tasks, Accepted Invites, Unread @Mentions, or pending Expirations.

FYI: @Mentions

The @Mentions feature allows users to address other users in a group by their username. This is useful when you're participating in a group conversation but when you need to bring something to a specific person's attention or need to mention a specific person in a comment.

Managing Files and Folders Within Your Box Account

You can manage the files or folders that you have created, copied, or synced to your Box account from the Box website. After signing in to Box, click the All Files, Recents, or Favorites option in the left sidebar of the window.

In Practice

Search for Any Stored Content

To quickly locate specific data, documents, files, photos, or other content in your Box account, type a keyword, filename, date, or search phrase in the Search field that's at the top of the Box browser window (see Figure 5.5) and then press Enter or Return. Search results are displayed below the search field, and an icon indicates the file type of each result. Click the file or folder that you want to view, manage, or access. In Figure 5.5, I used the keyword *Jason* to find any files stored within the Box account with filenames that contain that word.

When you're looking at the Box browser window and have clicked on the All Files option, for example, you see a complete listing of all folders and files stored within your Box account. Click the All Files pull-down menu option to sort your folders or files.

Create a new folder by clicking the New button, selecting the Folder option from the drop-down menu (see Figure 5.6), and then entering a custom name for the folder. From the All Files view within the Box browser window, all folders are displayed separately (by name), and all individual files (that aren't in folders) are also displayed.

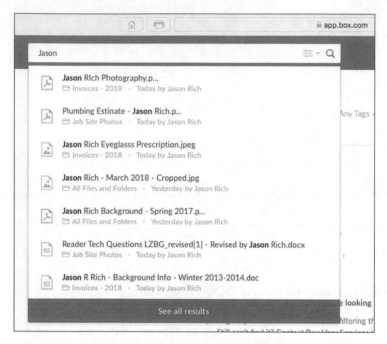

FIGURE 5.5   Use Box's Search tool to quickly find and access files or content that's stored within your account.

FIGURE 5.6   You can create folders to keep your files organized.

When you're using a Windows PC or Mac, you upload files simply by clicking the Upload option and then dragging and dropping or copying and pasting the files you're adding to Box.

Taking Advantage of Box's File Management and Collaboration Tools

After you have one or more files or folders in Box, you might want to initiate a new collaboration or share a file. View the files you've uploaded by clicking on the All Files, Recents, or Favorites option in the left sidebar of the Box browser window. In the list of files, you see a graphic icon that represents the file type, the filename, the date the file was last updated within the Box account, and the file size of the file. Hover your mouse over the file listing to reveal a More Options (…) button and a Share button (see Figure 5.7).

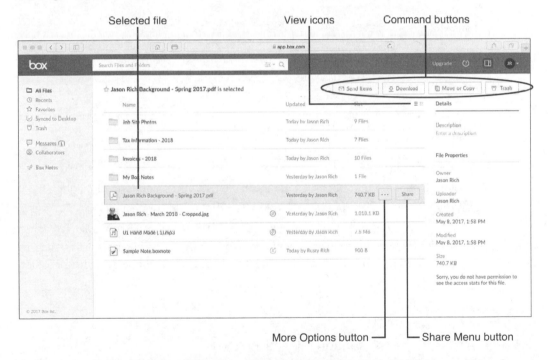

FIGURE 5.7 Once the listing for a file or folder is selected and highlighted, a variety of management, sharing, and collaboration items become active.

Click the List View or Grid View icon, displayed near the top-right corner of the file and folder listing, to switch viewing options. You can move one or more individual files into a different folder, or move folders into subfolders, by highlighting and selecting the desired files or folders and then dragging them to the desired location. Alternatively, use the options available from the More Options menu to manage the selected content.

You delete one or more files or folders by selecting the item and then dragging it directly over the Trash option in the left sidebar. You can also select an item and then click the Trash command button at the top of the window.

Click the More Options button associated with a file or folder listing to see commands to Share, Upload a New Version, Download, Favorite, Move or Copy, or Lock the file. You can also adjust the file or folder's Properties or Integrations (see Figure 5.8). (An integration allows a service like Box to integrate with or exchange information with other software applications and/or cloud-based services.)

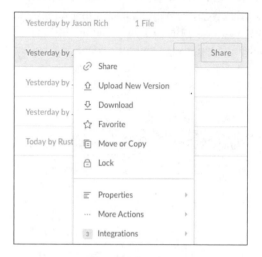

FIGURE 5.8   This More Options menu becomes accessible when you select and highlight a file or folder, and then click on the More Options (…) menu button.

Click on the More Actions submenu option to view additional options for handling tasks such as renaming a file or folder, deleting a file or folder, or adding text-based tags to the selected file or folder.

> ### In Practice
>
> ### Use Command Buttons to Manage Files or Folders
>
> When you've selected one or more specific files or folders, you not only see the More Options and Share buttons but you also see additional command buttons near the top-right corner of the browser window. These buttons include Send Items, Download, Move or Copy, and Trash. Click the appropriate button to quickly handle the desired task.

To share specific files or folders with other people, select the file or folder you want to share, and click the Share button that's associated with that file or folder. A Shared Link window opens (see Figure 5.9).

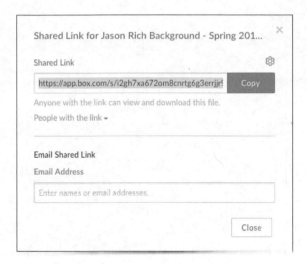

FIGURE 5.9 Share any file or folder in your Box account with other people, even if they're not Box users themselves.

Click the gear-shaped Shared Link Settings button to adjust the security settings you want to activate related to the shared file or folder. Figure 5.10 shows the Shared Link Settings menu. For example, you can add a password to the file or set an expiration to the Shared Link so it can only be accessed for a predetermined amount of time. The sender can also lock the option for the recipients to download the file, which means recipients are able only to open and view the file.

If you want to share the link via email, text message, or some other form of digital communication, click the Copy button that's located to the right of the Shared Link field. Anyone who has this unique link will be able to access the content you want to share.

Alternatively, you can invite specific people to access the file or folder you want to share. Enter each recipient's email address in the Email Shared Link field. Be sure you've used the gear icon to adjust the settings for the file or folder first.

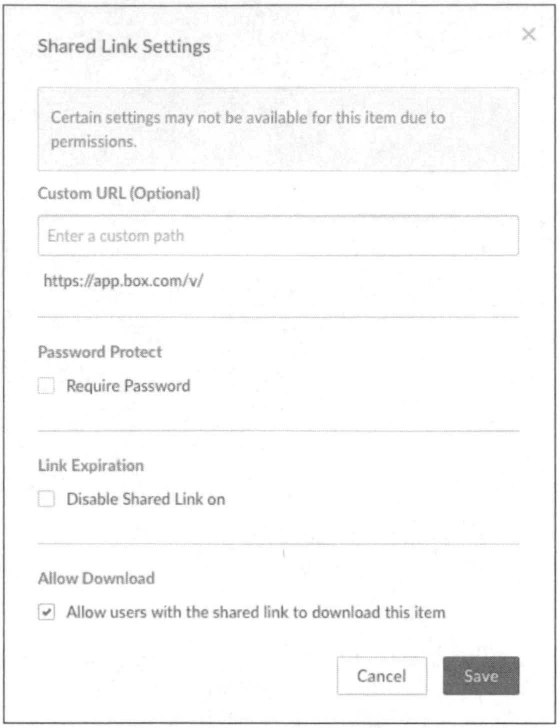

FIGURE 5.10   After clicking the Share button, click the gear-shaped Shared Link Settings icon to access this menu.

FYI: View Details About a File

As you're viewing the listing for a selected file within the Box browser window, the details about that file are displayed within the right sidebar of the window (refer to Figure 5.7). You can manually add a text-based description of the file and view the file's properties, which include the Owner, Uploader, Date Created, Modified date, and the File Size.

After you have one or more files or folders in Box, you might want to set up Box's collaboration tools. You can quickly access and manage each separate collaboration folder by clicking the Collaborators option in the left sidebar.

Using Box Notes

Box Notes is an interactive text editor that offers a handful of useful word processing and information gathering tools. With Box Notes, you can compose and format text-based documents, and you can embed photos into those documents (see Figure 5.11). The application offers a handy tool for note taking or for collaborating with others (with whom you're also sharing files and folders using Box).

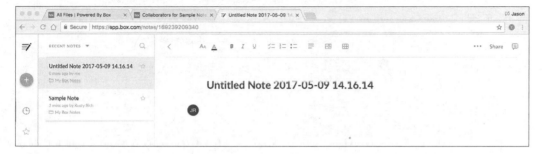

FIGURE 5.11 Box Notes is a text-editing, note-taking, and collaboration tool that's entirely online-based, and available to all Box users.

> **In Practice**
>
> ## Accessing Box Notes
>
> After logging in to Box in your web browser, click the Box Notes option in the sidebar to launch the application within a separate browser window. From the Box Notes browser window, you can compose, access, edit, share, and collaborate on individual note documents.

With Box Notes, you can create any number of separate notes (limited only by your account's online storage capacity) and then store each note in whichever folder the content applies to, including folders that are being shared with other people. Like all other files stored within Box, notes or note-related folders can be shared with others via the Box service. You can manually download notes to local storage on your computer or mobile device as needed.

Each separate note you create using Box Notes has its own filename and title. The application automatically records the time and date each note is created or modified and keeps track of the note's author and/or collaborators (including which aspects of a note were created or edited by other people).

Formatting tools allow you to adjust font size, font color, and typestyle, adjust paragraph formatting, and incorporate numbered lists, bulleted lists, or interactive check box lists into a document (see Figure 5.12). You can embed one or more photos into a document and create tables.

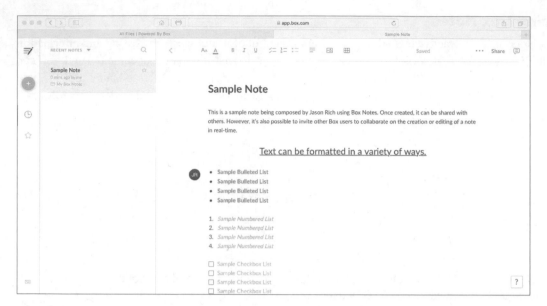

FIGURE 5.12   Use the built-in formatting tools to adjust the appearance of your Box Notes documents and custom format the text.

When using Box Notes as a collaboration tool, individual users have the ability to attach comments (by typing them in a dialog box) to a document. As you can see in Figure 5.13, comments within Notes can be addressed to all collaborators, or mention a specific collaborator by name using their unique username (using the *@username* format). Conversations between collaborators can be held in real-time. As one user makes a change to the note or posts a new comment, it automatically updates almost instantly on everyone's respective screen.

In Practice

Work in Real Time with Other Box Users

After you've shared a note with others, two or more people can work with that note simultaneously. With the Comments tool, the collaborators can hold a real-time, text-based conversation at the same time.

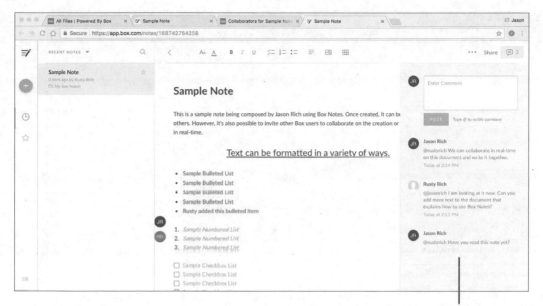

Interactive comments feature

FIGURE 5.13 Users can collaborate and share comments when working with individual notes.

Because every revision to every note is time and date stamped, and Box Notes keeps track of who created, edited, or added a comment to a note, it's possible to view the entire history of the note. You can also revert to older versions of a note by clicking the More Options (…) button and then selecting the Version History option. Remember that the number of versions of a file that can be stored and later retrieved varies based on your Box subscription plan.

Use the Search field to quickly locate content by searching for a keyword, search phrase, collaborator's username, or date that's associated with a note.

Using Box with a Smartphone or Tablet

One of the really useful features of Box is that you can access your account and manage or share files or folders stored within your account from virtually anywhere using the Box mobile application for your smartphone or tablet. The mobile apps provide almost all of the same functionality that's built into the Box.com website. Figure 5.14 shows the Box app running on an iPad.

FIGURE 5.14   Manage all aspects of your Box account and access any files stored within your account directly from the Box mobile app running on your Internet-connected smartphone or tablet.

In fact, using your Internet-connected mobile device, you can manage your entire Box account without ever needing to use a computer. This includes working with Box Notes in real time with other Box users (see Figure 5.15).

However, you can also use the Box mobile app to access files and documents that were created on your computer. This includes files or folders that were created by others and shared with you via Box.

Like the Box.com website, the Box mobile apps are regularly updated as new features, functions, and security tools are made available. Consequently, it's important that you make sure you're always using the latest version of the Box mobile app on your smartphone or tablet. You can download updates to the Box mobile app through your mobile device's app store.

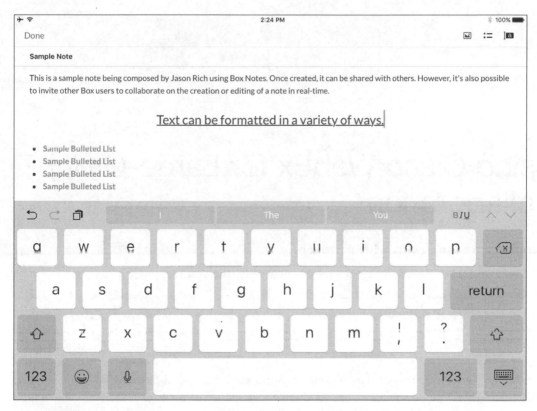

FIGURE 5.15 Box Notes and the real-time collaboration tools offered by Box are also accessible using the Box mobile app.

Getting Online Support

To get the most out of a service like Box, it's important that you and your team members or collaborators have a comprehensive understanding of what tools are available and how to use them. Free online help for Box is always available, regardless of whether you're using the website or a mobile app.

To access help through Box's website, sign in to your Box account, click on your profile photo or initials, and select the Help option from the menu. You will be granted access to a vast online community of Box users as well as how-to articles, help files, and a comprehensive *Get Started Guide for New Users* (https://community.box.com/t5/Box-Guides/ct-p/BoxHowtoGuidesEN).

Personalized tech support from Box (via phone or email) is also available, based on the type of paid subscription plan you have.

Chapter 6

Using Cisco WebEx for Large-Group Collaboration

This chapter covers the following:

- The web-based video-conferencing tools offered by the WebEx platform
- Uses for Cisco Spark with WebEx
- Features offered by WebEx that can help make a team more productive and cost effective

Cisco WebEx (www.webex.com) has become a world leader in cloud-based video conferencing, thanks to its WebEx platform and its toolset Cisco Spark, which is used for real-time collaboration in a virtual workspace. Although Cisco is known for addressing the cloud-based communication and virtual meeting needs of large corporations, the company also caters to small teams, along with organizations and companies of all sizes.

Cisco WebEx Overview

Cisco WebEx provides an ever-expanding toolset for virtually bringing people together from geographically disparate places. All conference or meeting participants are able to see and hear each other while they simultaneously share content from their own respective computers or mobile devices. The WebEx platform is primarily cloud-based, and it takes full advantage of the camera, microphone, and speakers built into most computers and mobile devices to transform that equipment into conferencing tools for voice or video conferences and virtual meetings.

It's important to understand that *only* the meeting or conference host needs a paid subscription to Cisco WebEx. The subscription plan determines the maximum number of individuals who can participate in each video conference or virtual meeting at a time. A paid account holder is able to host an unlimited number of meetings or video conferences per month.

Participants simply need to follow the invitation link that they receive via email. They don't need to be WebEx subscribers (or previous users) to participate from their Windows PC-, Mac-, or Linux-based computer, iOS mobile device, or Android-based smartphone or tablet. WebEx is compatible with all standards-based video conferencing systems, and offers its own collection of optional equipment, including the Cisco IP Phone, Cisco Spark Desk, Cisco Spark Room, and Cisco Spark Board, all of which offer seamless integration and additional functionality to the WebEx platform. These optional devices are specialized telephones, smart screens, and whiteboards that have web-conferencing functionality built in.

In Practice

Internet Is Required

Because WebEx is primarily cloud-based, everyone participating in a video conference or virtual meeting must be using equipment with a continuous Internet connection.

Each meeting or video conference can be set up so all participants can see each other on the screen in video windows. Alternatively, the service can be configured so that the meeting host is visible to the participants alongside whatever other things they're seeing on their computer screens. This second option makes WebEx a great solution for presenting content (such as a PowerPoint presentation or software demonstration) online, hosting webinars or training sessions, or handling remote support for customers and clients.

To facilitate higher quality audio during a voice conference or video conference, participants can simultaneously call into the service using their landlines or cellphones. Participants also can use their computer equipment to initiate a voice-over-IP (VoIP) connection for audio. Some WebEx plans include a Call Me feature that enables participants to join a particular meeting that they've been invited to simply by answering their phone or clicking a link that's embedded within their invitation email.

During a meeting, real-time group messaging allows individuals or groups to simultaneously communicate via text-based messaging. Participants can also take advantage of screen sharing, sharing a document or file, or marking up a virtual white board. Some of these additional tools require the use of Cisco Spark, a real-time collaboration service that fully integrates with WebEx (see the nearby FYI box). All meetings can be recorded and then later shared or archived, which enables people who weren't available for the meeting to later have access to it.

FYI: WebEx Is Scalable

In addition to traditional virtual video conferences and meetings attended by small groups of people, WebEx can be set up by a company to host training sessions or online events with hundreds or thousands of participants.

FYI: Overview of Cisco Spark

Cisco Spark (www.webex.com/products/cisco-spark.html) is included with all WebEx plans. This tool is designed to be used in conjunction with WebEx video conferences, but you can just as easily use it on its own to enable small to mid-size groups to conduct real-time group messaging, file sharing, and collaborating in a virtual, secure, cloud-based work space. Spark maintains its own user directory, so reconnecting with people is simple.

WebEx and Spark Service Plans

Cisco offers three paid subscription plans for meeting hosts that are ideal for small and medium-sized businesses and organizations. WebEx is also available in customizable and scalable Enterprise solutions. All three of the following plans allow the subscriber to host an unlimited number of meetings per month.

FYI: A Free WebEx Plan Is Available

In addition to the paid plans, one free plan is offered. A free account allows a maximum of three people to participate in video conferences or virtual meetings, provides Standard quality video for video conferences (rather than HD video), and offers just 250MB of online storage. To take advantage of this plan, visit https://signup.webex.com/webexmeetings/US/basic/meetings-plans-basic-free.html. If you start with a free plan, you can upgrade to a paid plan to unlock all of the features and functions built into the WebEx platform and Cisco Spark.

Premium 8 Plan

The Premium 8 Plan ($19.00 per month, per user, paid annually) allows the host to initiate HD video conferences and simultaneously use features like screen sharing. From a security standpoint, Cisco provides end-to-end encryption and lockable meeting spaces, which help to ensure that your data is protected while in the cloud and that unauthorized people can't access your virtual meetings. Meetings can be recorded, archived, or later shared with other people who couldn't attend. Real-time chat and collaboration tools are included with the plan via Cisco spark.

The biggest differentiator of this plan, compared to others offered by WebEx, is that each video conference can be attended by a maximum of eight people.

Premium 25 Plan

Priced at $29.00 per month, per user (paid annually), the Premium 25 Plan includes all of the features and functionality of the Premium 8 Plan but allows up to 25 people to participate in each video conference.

Premium 200 Plan

Priced at $39.00 per month, per user (paid annually), this WebEx plan also includes all of the features and functions offered by the Premium 8 and Premium 25 plans, but as many as 200 people can participate in each video conference.

In Practice

Only One Account per User Is Required

Each person within an organization who wants to host video conferences or virtual meetings with more than three people must have her own (paid) WebEx subscription and account. As previously mentioned, however, participants can attend meetings for free without being a paid WebEx subscriber.

Each participant in a meeting needs to sign in to the service using their email address and a password that they create. Only one account is needed per user, regardless of how many different computers and/or mobile devices they'll be accessing the WebEx platform from.

For added security, each user should turn on the two-step authentication feature, or one of the other account-specific security features to ensure unauthorized people can't gain access to their account. The platform's security features also protect any files, documents, and content that are stored within a company or user's cloud-based account.

As with any cloud-based service, for added account security, you should refrain from allowing a computer's web browser to automatically remember your username and password.

Cisco Mobile Apps

From any Internet-connected computer (Windows, Mac, or Linux), a paid WebEx subscriber can host a video conference or invite others to a virtual meeting using the Cisco WebEx or Spark tools. Participants can then join in using almost any web browser on their own Internet-connected computer; it's not necessary to download and install additional software. It is necessary, however, for Spark users to download and install the Spark desktop app or Spark mobile app onto the equipment they'll be using.

To host or participate in a video conference or virtual meetings from a smartphone or tablet, you must install one or more of Cisco's proprietary mobile apps on your device. Cisco supports Android-based smartphones and tablets, iOS-based mobile devices, as well as Blackberry and Windows Phone.

Available from a mobile device's respective app store, the Cisco WebEx Meetings mobile app allows paid users to host or attend meetings. Participants can use the apps to attend meetings, online events, or virtual training sessions. In either case, the mobile device has to have a continuous Internet connection.

From the App Store for the iPhone or iPad (shown in Figure 6.1), within the Search field, enter the keyword Cisco to locate the three mobile apps (WebEx Meetings, Spark, and Jabber) discussed in this section.

In Practice

Use Wi-Fi for the Best Results

Although the WebEx mobile app works with a cellular data Internet connection (via a cellular service provider's 3G or 4G cellular data network), you'll have the best experience (in terms of HD video quality clarity, for example) when you're connected to a Wi-Fi network. This is particularly important if your cellular data plan has a monthly usage allocation because participating in video conferences will quickly use up your allocation. As of mid-2017, Cisco had begun testing 5G cellular data connectivity with its platform.

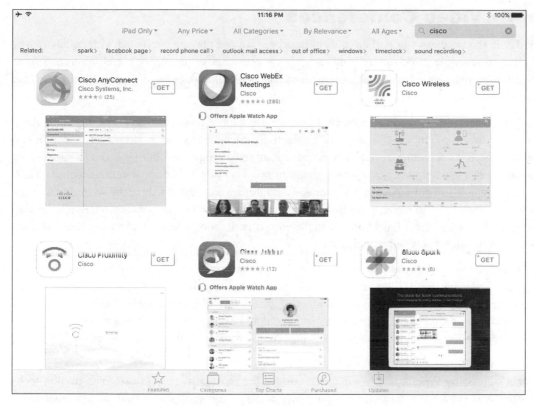

FIGURE 6.1   In the Apple App Store you'll find the three Cisco mobile apps: WebEx Meetings, Spark, and Jabber.

The Cisco Spark app allows mobile device users to participate in a virtual meeting and take full advantage of the majority of features and functions offered by the Spark collaboration and communications service. This mobile app allows users to participate in group text messaging, file sharing, and collaborate in real time. You can quickly switch between multiple virtual work spaces or conversations. Anything that transpires during a meeting in terms of file sharing or collaboration on documents or files is stored in the cloud and syncs with the user's computers and mobile devices.

A third mobile app offered by Cisco is Cisco Jabber. This is a group messaging app that also allows for voice and video messaging, desktop sharing, and conferencing. This app offers video calling or Internet-based voice-calling capabilities, as well as integration with Microsoft Office. This is an ideal solution for keeping in touch with team members and collaborators while individual participants are on the go.

This service is secure and similar in functionality to other popular one-to-one or group messaging apps and social media services, like Skype, iMessage, or Facebook Messenger, for example.

WebEx Video Conferences

Every day in the business world, thousands of hours are wasted playing phone tag with collaborators, attempting to schedule in-person meetings among a group of busy people, or travelling to and from in-person meetings. Some face-to-face interactions can't be replaced, but many types of meetings can be held virtually.

Not only can virtual meetings and video conferences save a lot of time and money but this technology can improve meeting outcomes in terms of productivity because anyone in almost any location can join a meeting from a mobile device. The collaboration technology used during a virtual meeting or video conference can help keep everyone's attention in a way that a traditional conference call can't, and people are able to communicate in a clear and straightforward way to reduce the wasted time often spent in meetings. Only in recent years has it become technologically viable and affordable to be able to host or participate in virtual meetings using the computer or mobile device technology that's already accessible to meeting hosts and participants.

As with any technology-based toolset, it's essential that everyone understands what's possible with a video-conferencing tool and learns how to use the features and functions that are at their disposal. Deploying a video conferencing or virtual meeting platform within an organization is an important first step, but then properly training all users is an equally important second step. Proper training will reduce miscommunications and user mistakes that could easily lead to data breaches or mismanaged data.

The tools offered by WebEx and Cisco Spark are, for the most part, easy to use, even by non-tech-savvy people. However, it remains the responsibility of the person assigned with admin responsibilities to ensure that these tools are being used correctly in accordance with company-created guidelines.

Cisco offers specialized in-person and online-based training for administrators (www.cisco.com/c/en/us/training-events.html). For individual users, a wide range of online tutorial videos (https://view.webex.com) and interactive Help tools (www.webex.com/support/getting-started.html) are available to provide all users with a working knowledge of how to use the WebEx platform in their work environments.

Getting Started with WebEx Tools

As a meeting or video-conference host, the first thing you need to do is set up a WebEx account. You set up the account from your favorite web browser by visiting www.webex.com and clicking the Try It Free or Buy a Plan button (see Figure 6.2).

FIGURE 6.2   Get started using WebEx for free by visiting www.webex.com and clicking the Try It Free button.

In Practice

Sign Up for a Free 30-Day Trial

The free trial period is 30 days, and it includes WebEx Premium 200 plan functionality, such as personalized video meeting rooms, Cisco Spark messaging and file sharing, and unlimited Cisco Spark video calling (with screen sharing).

After you complete the sign-up form (see Figure 6.3), you receive a verification email. Click the Get Started button in this email (see Figure 6.4).

Your web browser reopens, and you're directed to the WebEx sign-in page. Enter your email address and the password you created when you set up the account. Click the Sign In button to begin using the WebEx and Cisco Spark service on an unlimited basis during the trial period. No credit card is required, unless you opt to continue using the service beyond the trial period. During the trial period, virtually all WebEx and Spark features are unlocked so you can use them during meetings or conferences that include more than three participants; a free account limits the number of participants to three.

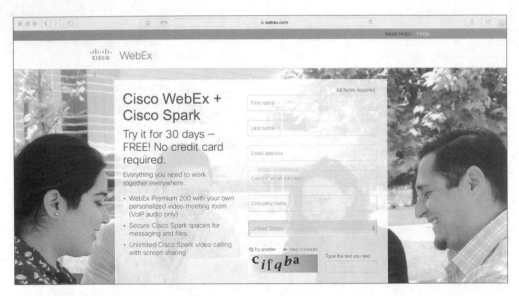

FIGURE 6.3   Create your WebEx account by completing the online form.

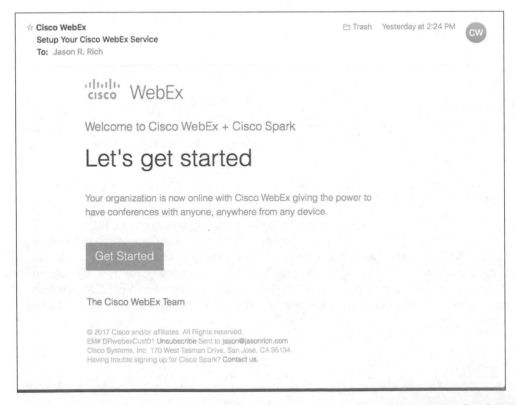

FIGURE 6.4   Respond to the confirmation email you receive by clicking on the Get Started button.

FYI: When You Already Have an Account

If you already have an account, from the WebEx home page, click the Host button to host a virtual meeting or video conference, or click the Join button to join a meeting. Jump ahead to the "Starting Your First Video Conference or Virtual Meeting" section later in this chapter for more information.

One of the first steps involved in creating a new WebEx account is establishing your team or organization's online presence. From the Let's Set Up Your Service window (see Figure 6.5), provide the name of your company, team, or organization. A unique virtual meeting center for your group is created, using the *[company name].my.webex.com* format. Note that the name you assign for this virtual meeting center must be unique.

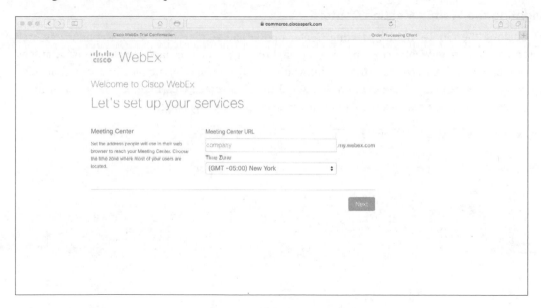

FIGURE 6.5   Establish your organization's presence on WebEx.

When you enter the name for your group, provide details about what time zone you're working in using the pull-down menu. This part of the account setup process only needs to be done once. Click the Next button to continue.

When you see the `Your services have been activated` message, click the Go To WebEx Meeting Center, Set Up Your Spark Team, or Administer Your Service link.

Regardless of which option you choose, the Terms of Service information is displayed the first time you sign in to your new WebEx account. Scroll to the bottom of this screen, and click the Accept button to continue.

> **CAUTION**
>
> ### Consider Compliance Regulations
>
> Depending on the industry you work in and the type of information you'll be sharing using this cloud-based service, be sure that WebEx and Spark meet the compliance regulations you must adhere to. Prior to placing any of your content online, consult directly with WebEx's security experts to determine whether using their platform will allow your specific team, group, or company to adhere to the necessary compliance regulations. Visit this link for additional information https://support.webex.com/MyAccountWeb/supporthome.do.

Navigating the WebEx Meeting Center

After clicking the Go To WebEx Meeting Center option and signing in to your account, your web browser loads the main WebEx Host Meeting screen. From here you can start a new meeting simply by clicking the Start Meeting button. At this point, you're ready to host or participate in a virtual meeting or video conference using WebEx. From this initial meeting screen (see Figure 6.6), you can invite participants, see who's already participating, and manage a virtual meeting.

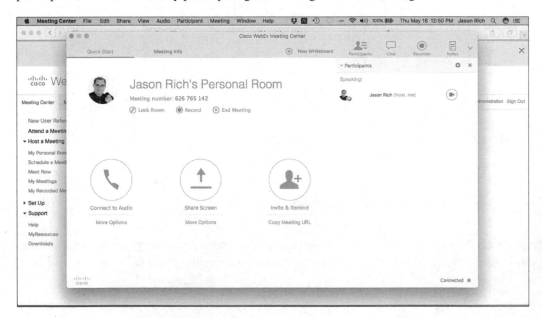

FIGURE 6.6 The WebEx Host Meeting screen.

Also, the first time you use WebEx, take the time to customize your Account Settings, and add your profile photo to your account. If all meeting participants add a profile picture, everyone can easily be identified (by their name and photo) during virtual meetings, video conferences, and collaboration sessions.

Setting Up Your Spark Team

The account administrator can set up a team or company's virtual workspace. Within this workspace, all users have access to Cisco Spark's group messaging, real-time collaboration tools, and Internet-based voice- or video-calling capabilities. The administrator needs to log in to his or her account and then click the Set Up Your Spark Team option.

In Practice

Download the Free Cisco Spark Desktop App

From any computer, Spark account administrators and users alike are encouraged to download the free Spark desktop app, which offers easy access to many of Spark's features and functions. However, the features can also be used directly from a user's web browser.

You can find links to each version of Cisco Spark's software and mobile apps at www.ciscospark.com/downloads.html.

Handling Administrative Tasks

When you (or the person assigned as the administrator) clicks the Administer Your Service option, your web browser goes to WebEx's Cloud Collaboration Management Overview screen (see Figure 6.7). From here, you can manage all aspects of your team, organization, or company's WebEx account and usage.

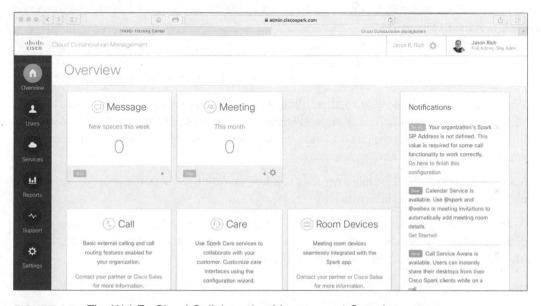

FIGURE 6.7 The WebEx Cloud Collaboration Management Overview screen.

Options displayed along the left margin of the browser window offer separate screens to handle the following:

- **Overview (Default):** Displays a dashboard and account overview screen, which provides details about WebEx usage.

- **Users:** Provides tools to manage users. From here you determine which WebEx and Cisco Spark features and functions each person can use by managing user-specific permissions.

- **Services:** Offers an overview of available WebEx services. Click the Setup button associated with Hybrid Calendar, Hybrid Call, and Hybrid Media to customize these options.

- **Reports:** Gives you a way to monitor account-wide WebEx and Cisco Spark usage. Click the Spark Rooms, Room Devices, or WebEx Reports tabs near the top-right corner of the browser window to view and work with specific types of customizable reports.

- **Support:** Provides access to WebEx customer support options.

- **Settings:** Enables you to manage account-specific settings, privacy options, and security settings. For example, from below the Authentication heading, the account administrator can turn on or off sign-on features for users. From below the Branding heading, video-conference rooms and virtual workspaces can be branded with a company logo.

Scheduling a Meeting

You can spontaneously host a meeting and invite participants (see the next section), but it's also possible to take advantage of WebEx's scheduling tools to preplan meetings and send out appropriate invitations. Use the following steps:

1. Log in to your WebEx account by visiting www.webex.com from any web browser.

2. Below the Host a Meeting heading, click the Schedule a Meeting option (see Figure 6.8).

3. Within the Schedule a Meeting window, fill in all of the necessary fields, which include Meeting Topic, Password, Date, Time, and Duration (see Figure 6.9). Within the Attendees field, one at a time, enter the email address for each person you want to invite. Separate each email address with a comma or semicolon.

4. Scroll down within the Schedule a Meeting window, and click the Start button to save the meeting details and send the invitations.

5. At the scheduled time for the meeting, return to the WebEx.com website, sign in to your account, and find the meeting you want to participate in or host (it'll be listed underneath the My Meetings heading). Click the Start button to proceed.

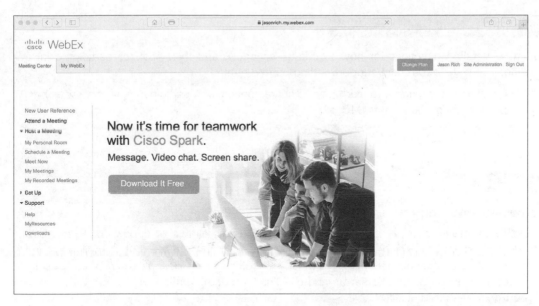

FIGURE 6.8   Pre-schedule a meeting or video conference and invite participants in advance.

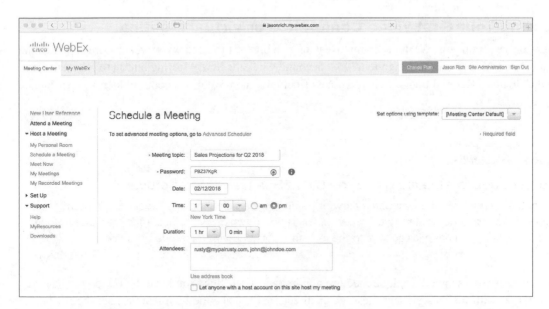

FIGURE 6.9   Complete this schedule meeting form, and WebEx sends out the necessary invitations.

FYI: More Detailed Instructions

For more detailed directions for how to create, schedule, and then host (or participate in) a meeting, visit www.webex.com/support/getting-started.html.

After a meeting is in progress, to learn how to share content with participants, visit www.webex.com/support/getting-started.html#MC-q2.

In Practice

Schedule a Meeting from Outlook

If your team, organization, or company uses Outlook, Lotus Notes, or another popular group scheduling and time management application, you can integrate WebEx with that application and then schedule and manage meetings from within Outlook or the application you're already using. For more information on how to set up and use this type of integration, visit www.webex.com/support/getting-started.html#MC-q4.

Starting Your First Video Conference or Virtual Meeting

After you've set up your WebEx account, use your web browser to go to www.webex.com and click the Host button. When prompted, sign in to your account. Click the Start Meeting button to proceed. Next, tap the Invite & Remind option to invite others (including non-WebEx account holders) to participate in your meeting.

In Practice

Host or Join a Meeting Using the Cisco Spark Desktop Software

Although much of WebEx's functionality for hosting or participating in a meeting can by handled directly from any computer's web browser, when you download and install the free Cisco Spark Desktop App, you have full access to the real-time collaboration tools offered by Spark.

Every meeting is assigned a unique meeting number and URL link. You have the option to share this information with invitees via text message or direct email. Once the recipients accept the invitation, your video conference/virtual meeting automatically gets underway.

From the Cisco WebEx Meeting Center screen within your web browser, click the video camera icon when a meeting is underway to activate your computer's camera so other participants can see you during the video conference (see Figure 6.10).

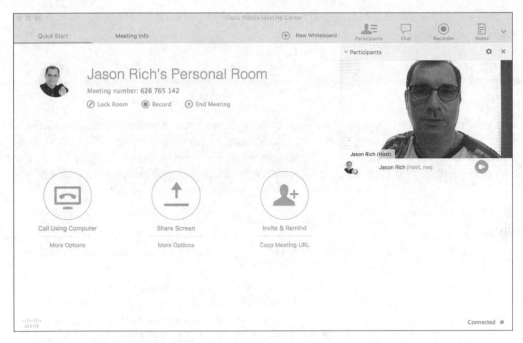

FIGURE 6.10   The Cisco WebEx Meeting Center screen.

Click the Connect to Audio option (see Figure 6.11) to determine how you will access the conference's audio. The default method is to use the established Internet connection and your computer's built-in microphone and speakers. If you need to mute your microphone during a meeting, click the microphone icon. You can still hear the conference, but the other participants won't be able to hear you.

During a video conference, video of the meeting host is displayed in the large portion of the video window; your own video feed is displayed in a smaller video window.

The Share Screen option is on the Quick Start tab; click it to begin sharing your computer screen with meeting participants. Click the Recorder option in the top toolbar to turn on or off the video-recording option. The Notes option gives you access to a virtual text editor; use it to compose notes for yourself during the video conference or meeting.

If you want to use an interactive whiteboard during a video conference or virtual meeting, click the + New Whiteboard option in the top toolbar.

You can conduct private conversations or group messages with specific meeting participants by using the Chat option. Click Chat in the top toolbar to start a conversation; the default setting for the Send To field is Everyone, which means that all participants will see the text message(s) you type and send. If you prefer to send a private message to a single meeting participant, click the Send To field and select that participant's name.

During a video conference, use WebEx's Polling feature to pose questions to participants and have them vote. This offers a way for meeting hosts to quickly gather information from participants while the meeting is in progress. When it's time to conclude the meeting, click the End Meeting option (refer to Figure 6.10).

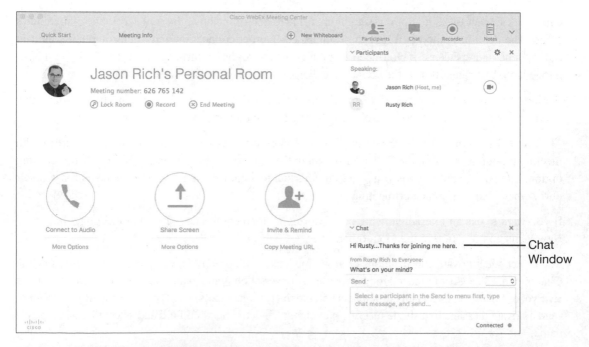

FIGURE 6.11 Send text messages to one meeting participant or group member, or address a text message to everyone.

Lock Your Meetings

Once a meeting is underway, the meeting host can click the Lock Room option to prevent additional people from joining the meeting without being granted access by the host. To unlock the room, simply click the Unlock Room option.

Collaboration in a Spark Virtual Workspace

The WebEx platform provides capability for video conferences or virtual meetings that include screen sharing, virtual white boards, and group messaging, but Cisco Spark (see Figure 6.12) includes a somewhat broader collection of real-time collaboration.

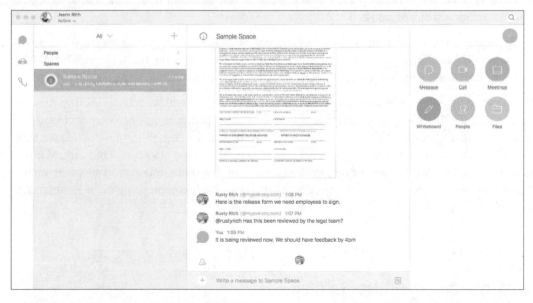

FIGURE 6.12 Download the Cisco Spark app to have access to real-time chat, voice calling, video calling, file sharing, and other real-time collaboration tools that work in conjunction with WebEx.

To use Spark, each user should download and install the free Cisco Spark desktop app or Cisco Spark mobile app, and then sign in to their WebEx account. Similar functionality can also be handled from any web browser.

The Spark software and mobile app (as well as the cloud-based Spark application) provide functionality for group text messaging, Internet-based voice or video calling, and the ability to collaborate in virtual work spaces. A user can create as many separate work Spaces as he needs to work with specific other people on various projects.

Likewise, Spark allows for any number of Teams to be created, which is a pre-defined group of people that can communicate and collaborate within a particular virtual Space. This feature is useful if you constantly work with the same group of people but you work with them on different projects or collaborative tasks. Each task can be assigned its own Space within Spark, which helps keep topic-specific content and discussions separate.

Each Space is given its own custom title, and any number of people (which is limited based on the type of paid account the host has) can be invited to collaborate simultaneously within that virtual work space.

Each virtual space is basically a separate group chat room, within which participants can send and receive text messages, share files, and share screens. As communication between team members occurs and as work is done within each Space, everything is tracked based on date, time, and user. All the meeting information is stored online.

Using the Search tool, you can quickly locate any content created, managed, or stored using Spark. When you're using the Spark Desktop app, you access the core functionality for the service by clicking on one of the command icons located in the right margin of the screen: Chat, Teams, and Calling.

Click Chat to initiate or engage in a text-based group conversation, which includes sharing files, for example. Click the Team option to create and interact with specific groups of people, or click the Phone icon to initiate a voice or video call. The official WebEx or Spark mobile apps provide the same functionality that's available via a computer, but the menu options, icon placement, and general layout of the screens are different because of the smaller screen size. For more information about the mobile apps and how to use them, visit www.webex.com/products/web-conferencing/mobile.html#cisco-webex.

In Practice

WebEx Can Be Used with Other Services

If your organization wants to rely on the proven video-conferencing capabilities of WebEx while users simultaneously use other collaboration tools—such as Dropbox Paper, Google G Suite, Evernote, Trello, or Slack—you can certainly do that. However, it's important that groups, teams, organizations, or companies choose just one conferencing/communications platform and one real-time collaboration platform to ensure everyone is using the same tools and that everyone can easily find related files and content on a single service.

The WebEx platform offers a superior video-conferencing platform. However, when it comes to real-time collaboration and file sharing, you might find that other services offer more robust tools that better cater to your needs.

Security Considerations

As you begin using the WebEx platform, you'll discover that Cisco has included all the security and data encryption features you'd expect. The platform has been certified by the SkyHigh CloudTrust Program, which is an independent agency that offers extensive and impartial evaluations related to cloud security. What's nice about this platform is that it's easily scalable. It can be used to conduct a virtual meeting with just a handful of people, or it can just as easily be used to host a virtual meeting attended by dozens of people.

Even with the most secure technology in place, it's up to a company's WebEx administrator to properly manage user accounts. It's also each user's responsibility to protect his or her account and use it according to company guidelines so as to not share confidential information with unauthorized people.

FYI: WebEx Offers Best Practices Guides

Any group or organization interested in using WebEx should carefully read the WebEx *Best Practices for Secure Meetings* document (https://support.webex.com/LocalizedUpgrades/2014/bestpractices/best_practices_for_secure_meetings.pdf) and adhere to the strategies outlined in it.

Account administrators and meeting hosts should familiarize themselves with the security strategies outlined within the document *Best Practices for Secure Meetings for Site Administrators and Hosts* (https://support.webex.com/LocalizedUpgrades/2014/bestpractices/best_practices_for_secure_meetings_admin.pdf).

Beyond utilizing account-specific security features offered by WebEx, be sure to review the security guidelines and strategies for individual cloud computing users that are outlined within Chapter 4, "Understanding Cloud-Based Security Concerns."

Chapter 7

Using DocuSign to Review, Edit, Sign, and Share Documents

This chapter covers the following:

- What sets DocuSign apart from other cloud-based document management and sharing services
- How DocuSign allows users to add legally binding signatures to documents, correspondence, and contracts
- Strategies for using DocuSign from a computer or mobile device
- An exclusive interview with Tom Gosner, founder and CEO of DocuSign

This chapter focuses on the core features and functions offered by DocuSign, explains how and why a small business should use this service, and provides tips on how to smoothly adopt this type of cloud-based service into your company's established workflow.

DocuSign Overview

Currently used by more than 200 million users in 188 countries, and by more than 300,000 companies worldwide (including 12 of the top 15 financial service companies, and 12 of the top 15 insurance carriers within the United States), DocuSign has become a world leader in *digital transaction management*.

> ### FYI: What Is Digital Transaction Management
>
> Digital Transaction Management (DTM) is the process of creating and sharing between two or more parties a contract or another type of correspondence that needs to be reviewed, possibly edited or annotated, and ultimately signed (via eSignatures) in a secure and legally binding way.
>
> A DTM service, like DocuSign, handles this process using cloud-based tools that can seamlessly integrate with more than 4,000 other software packages and mobile apps. Although DocuSign uses cutting-edge and complex technologies behind the scenes, the service offers a fast, secure, inexpensive, and extremely intuitive interface for managing workflows related to documents in an entirely digital way.

Although it's not a full-featured, cloud-based collaboration tool, DocuSign offers cutting-edge and highly secure tools for reviewing and signing legally binding documents and handling certain types of online payments that are directly tied to documents and contracts. For example, if someone needs to sign an agreement to rent a vacation condo, they can use DocuSign to sign the agreement and immediately make a deposit payment via check, debit card, or credit card. In other words, most companies use DocuSign as an add-on tool to other file-sharing and collaboration services.

Benefits of DocuSign

First and foremost, DocuSign is a low-cost and easy-to-use service that allows a document, such as a contract, to be sent to one or more recipients. That document can then be viewed, securely signed, and returned to the sender, 100 percent digitally (see Figure 7.1). This can be done from any Internet-connected computer or mobile device. As this service has evolved, functions have been added to allow for documents to be annotated or edited, for text-based discussions to be held about a document in a secure online environment, and for payments related to a document to be made.

Aside from the core functions related to signing, sending, and managing documents, DocuSign works with software and mobile app developers around the world and already offers more than 4,000 free connectors. These connectors allow DocuSign functionality to integrate seamlessly with popular applications, including Office 365, Salesforce, several of Google's G Suite applications, Evernote, Box, Dropbox, and many others.

After you set up a DocuSign account, you can import a document into DocuSign. The file can be on your computer or mobile device, or it could be stored in another cloud-based service (such as Box, Dropbox, Google Drive, or Microsoft OneDrive).

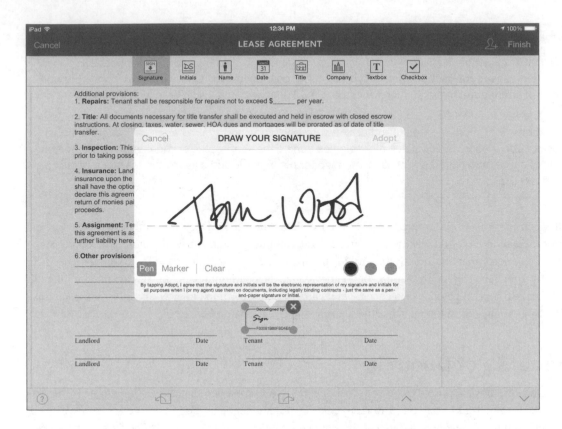

FIGURE 7.1   With DocuSign, a legally binding eSignature can be created and securely embedded into any type of document.

In Practice

DocuSign Supports Numerous File Formats

DocuSign accepts many popular file formats, including Microsoft Word (2003, 2007, 2010, 2013, and 2016), Microsoft Excel (2003, 2007, 2010, 2013, and 2016), Microsoft PowerPoint (2003, 2007, 2010, 2013, and 2016), Office365 documents and files, Text (.txt), Rich Text Format (.rtf), Image File Formats (.png, .jpg, .gif, and .tif), and Portable Document Format (.pdf).

After importing a document, you provide the recipient's name and email address, indicate the location in the document where fields need to be completed, and where full signatures, initials, and a date need to be provided (see Figure 7.2).

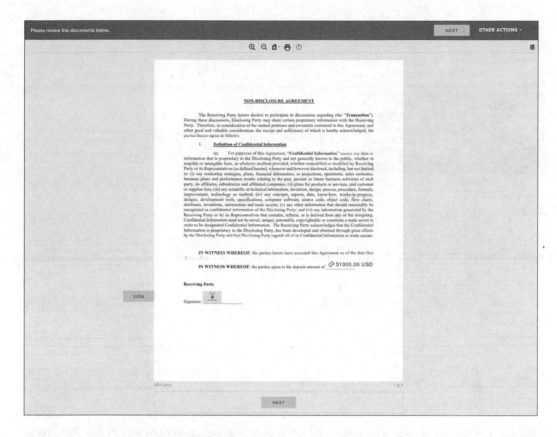

FIGURE 7.2   For the recipient (the signer), reviewing a document and knowing where to initial and/or sign is very straightforward. No special software is required.

With certain DocuSign subscription plans, you can make use of additional standard or custom fields for signers to fill in. Once the document is uploaded to and secured by DocuSign, the service emails a unique link to each recipient, which provides access to the document (see Figure 7.3).

The recipient has the ability to review and sign the document using any Internet-connected computer or mobile device. A paid DocuSign account is not required to review and sign documents. Tabs and simple instructions are provided for the recipient, which guides them, step by step, through reviewing and signing the document.

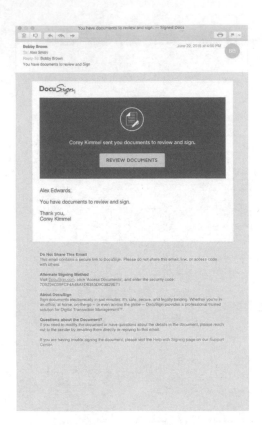

FIGURE 7.3   The recipient (signer) receives an email that provides a secure link to the document that needs to be reviewed and signed.

After a document has been signed by the recipient(s), you (the sender) can manage the document, which is securely stored within your DocuSign account. For example, you can check the status of the document at any time from the DocuSign dashboard. If necessary, you can have DocuSign generate automatic reminders and notifications to inform you when a document needs to be signed or when other parties have signed your documents. Both you and your recipients can access signed documents at any time so you can view, download, and print the documents as needed.

DocuSign is one of the few services of its kind that keeps documents secure and that enables signers to generate and apply a legally binding digital signature (an eSignature) to a document. DocuSign offers full compliance with security standards and document encryption. It also offers secure access to documents based on several different, user-selectable, authentication options.

> ## FYI: Security Is DocuSign's Highest Priority
>
> DocuSign meets and often exceeds most U.S. and global security standards. According to DocuSign, it's the only Digital Transaction Management (DTM) provider that's ISO 27001-certified and SSAE 16-certified (SOC 1 and SOC 2).

In comparison, other digital signature services allow someone's signature to be created and then pasted into a document in an unsecure way. DocuSign is one of the few services of its kind that verifies that documents have not been modified, and it incorporates a digital certificate that secures documents and signatures with what DocuSign refers to as "tamper-evident seals."

As a result, eSignatures added to documents via DocuSign are court-admissible and include a Certification of Completion, which contains a comprehensive audit trail that includes verifiable security information, including the signing parties' names, digital signatures, email addresses, public IP addresses, signing locations, timestamps, and a chain of custody related to the document.

DocuSign Subscription Plans

In addition to providing customized enterprise solutions, DocuSign offers three subscription plans that range in price from $10.00 to $40.00 per user, per month. The Personal Plan ($10.00 per user, per month) is designed for a single user who needs to send not more than five documents per month to be signed by other parties. This plan offers only basic fields within a document that can be filled in by the signing party.

The Standard plan ($25.00 per user, per month) allows for any number of documents to be sent out for signatures. It too allows only for basic fields to be filled in by the signing party. This plan also allows reminders and notifications to be generated, and the platform itself can be branded with a company's logo.

The Business Pro plan ($40.00 per user, per month) unlocks all of DocuSign's features. It allows a user to send any number of documents to be signed, and both basic fields and custom (advanced) fields can be embedded within a document for the signer to fill in. This plan also includes the ability to generate reminders and notifications, plus includes Signer Attachments with documents. The sender has access to a Bulk Send feature, so one document can easily be sent to multiple parties for a signature.

To learn more about Enterprise plans, which offer all of the functions of a Business Pro plan plus additional security features and account management tools, visit www.docusign.com/company/contact-us#sales.

Depending on the other software or cloud services your company already uses, you might be able to take advantage of other subscription plans that offer integration with third-party tools (www.docusign.com/products-and-pricing/api-plans). DocuSign also offers some subscription plans for companies working in specific industries, such as real estate (www.docusign.com/products-and-pricing/real-estate-editions).

The DocuSign Mobile App

In addition to using DocuSign via your computer's web browser, you can use the DocuSign mobile app that is available for both iOS and Android mobile devices.

Any user with a DocuSign account (including a free account) can import any incoming contract or document that needs to be signed and then use DocuSign's secure tools to review, sign, and return the document. The original document does not need to have been created by the sender using DocuSign.

The mobile app can convert forms within the document so they can be filled in and completed from within the mobile app. Figure 7.4 shows what a sample release form might look like when it's being reviewed with the DocuSign mobile app (shown running on an Android smartphone).

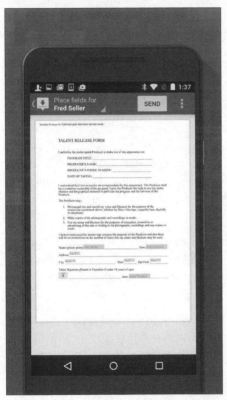

FIGURE 7.4   You can use the DocuSign mobile app to complete forms.

Copies of all documents imported into the mobile app are stored online within your DocuSign account (see Figure 7.5), so you can access them later using either the mobile app or the website.

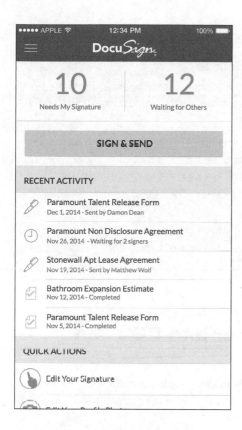

FIGURE 7.5 The DocuSign mobile app (iOS version shown here) keeps track of all documents imported and processed by the app.

FYI: Learn More About the DocuSign Mobile App

To see what's currently possible using the DocuSign mobile app, visit www.docusign.com/features-and-benefits/mobile. Check back often because the DocuSign mobile app is continuously being updated to include new features and functions.

iPhone or iPad should visit the App Store (https://itunes.apple.com/app/apple-store/id474990205) to download and install the free app. Android smartphone and tablet users can acquire the app from the Google Play Store (https://play.google.com/store/apps/details?id=com.docusign.ink).

In Practice

DocuSign Is More Widely Used Than People Realize

When a company chooses to begin using DocuSign to distribute correspondence, agreements, and/or contracts, one of their initial misconceptions is that, because it's so new, their customers or clients will be hesitant to use it.

In reality, this technology is not brand new, and most people working in today's business world have already been exposed to receiving and signing a document or contract digitally, so it's not typically something the recipient will be afraid of. Plus, the user interface offered by DocuSign has intentionally been created to be intuitive, even for people who typically shy away from using cutting-edge technologies.

One potential pitfall to avoid is trying to do too much with the service too quickly, before your organization's employees, customers, or clients have all become acclimated to the new, all-digital process of handling documents and contracts.

Interview with DocuSign Founder and CEO Tom Gosner

In this exclusive interview, DocuSign's Founder and CEO, Tom Gosner, shares additional information about the DocuSign service, plus offers useful strategies for effectively using the service to save time and streamline paperwork within any company or organization.

"I started the company in late 2002. At the time, I was involved with another company that was an early pioneer in online signatures and digital certificates. There are things that I refer to as inevitabilities. One of them back then was that in the near future, people were not going to be running around chasing paper-based contracts. I believed that eventually, this could all be done electronically," explained Gosner.

Using his professional experience and insight, Gosner began contemplating how to make what he knew was an inevitable future use of technology become a reality. "Anytime in my professional life when I have come across an inevitability with insight about it that other people don't have, it's hard for me to not try to make it happen. Back then, the way people were talking about handling electronic signatures was really broken and flawed. Not only was it inefficient and time consuming to use this technology, it was also way too complicated for most people."

Gosner believed that everything related to digitally signing documents could be done on the Web, and that encrypting files and emailing them back and forth was not a viable solution. His goal became, "to take a document, put it in the cloud, encrypt it, make it secure, and make it legally binding, in a way that the end user didn't need to see. The end user would only need to use a web browser to visit a document in order to authenticate, review, and sign it."

By focusing on the cloud-based aspect of digital transaction management, DocuSign was eventually able to make the process of digitally signing documents secure and easy, with the users knowing where each document is 100 percent of the time, so they have full audit control over the review and signature process.

"In the case of multiple signers, the document's sender can stipulate which order each person needs to sign in, and provide each signer with a different set of tasks they need to do within the document. Each signer can have a different set of form fields they need to complete, for example," explained Gosner. This is functionality that can't be done with standard PDF files, even today. "Our recipe for success was to create a method for digitally reviewing and signing documents that was fast, easy, and familiar. Achieving our goal is what has allowed DocuSign to take off."

Despite all of the advancements that have been made in recent years, many people still remain hesitant to use a digital tool for signing documents. "The biggest misconception people have about DocuSign is that it's risky, and that documents can be changed after they've been signed. This is not at all true, or possible, when DocuSign is used. There are also a lot of people who use freeware or other applications that can be used to digitally sign documents, but they're not aware that many of these alternate methods are not legally binding, or, in some cases, they're not even secure," stated Gosner. "DocuSign is not just about signing documents digitally. It's about taking entire business transactions and digitizing them to make them more secure and efficient."

In today's business world, there are now many different ways DocuSign gets used. Gosner added, "Every business runs on transactions. No matter what your business does, you can identify something in your business that would be a transaction, such as selling something or a consulting project, for example. Those transactions involve some sort of documentation, such as an agreement to move forward, a payment, or approvals. In many cases, those forms, payments, and approvals are manually done. This slows everything down. Any business that has any documents, no matter what they're about, can start using DocuSign to manage those documents and speed up the transaction rate dramatically. DocuSign fundamentally speeds up the transaction flow, which is probably the biggest benefit we offer to companies of any size, working in any industry."

Anything that needs to be signed, such as a sales agreement, letter of intent, or contract, can be handled using DocuSign. In some industries, like in real estate, documents need to be signed quickly, because it's a very competitive market, and in some cases, even FedEx is too slow. "People used to be forced to get in their car and drive across town to collect signatures. With DocuSign, a document can be prepared and sent, and then reviewed and signed, in a matter of minutes, and this can happen between two parties located anywhere in the world," added Gosner.

Because of the many security measures added to DocuSign, in many ways, signing a contract digitally using the service is more secure than signing a traditional paper-based document, sending documents via fax, or emailing documents back and forth, for example. "If a company processes all of its business communications through DocuSign, the user always knows where they are and has access to them. The service creates a comprehensive journal of everything that's ever been done using DocuSign and makes every document accessible. As a result, contract management and contract maintenance becomes really easy," said Gosner.

When asked about DocuSign's built-in document annotation tools, Gosner was quick to respond that this is a feature that exists, but that's rarely used. After all, once a document is ready for signatures, the sender does not necessarily want to make it possible for changes to be made to that document.

"Our customers don't want annotation tools to be readily available. In DocuSign, there is an ability, if a user wants to turn it on, to markup a document or line something out and write something else it, but this tool is not used too much," explained Gosner. "If the feature is turned on and a change is made, it requires both parties to review and initial the changes before it can be signed. Most users will compose a document using a word processor, such as Microsoft Word, and go back and forth on the creation of that document before it's ready to be signed. Then, when the document is ready for final signatures, it gets sent through DocuSign with the annotation and markup features turned off."

Within the United States, as well as in most other countries, a variety of criteria need to be met for a signature within a document, such as a contract, to be legally binding. In the United States, the E-Sign Act defines what needs to be true in order for a digitally signed contract to have legal effect. For example, once a contract is signed, its contents cannot be changed or altered.

Also, the identity of the person or people who signed the agreement are bound to the agreement. It must be provable that the person who digitally signed the document was the person identified within the document. This is not provable if a signature is simply cut and pasted into a Word document, for example.

In Practice

What You Should Know About the E-Sign Act

To learn more about the E-Sign Act and how it applies within the United States, visit any of these websites: www.gpo.gov/fdsys/pkg/PLAW-106publ229/html/PLAW-106publ229.htm, www.fdic.gov/regulations/compliance/manual/10/x-3.1.pdf, www.electronicsignatureact.net/index.html, or http://electronicsignature.com/esignact.

"How you bind the identity of the person who is signing the contract can be handled digitally in a handful of different ways," explained Gosner. "It's important to understand that not too many tools handle this very well, or in a legally binding way. In the case of DocuSign, we allow the person who is sending the document to choose how they want the person or people who are signing the document to authenticate their identity.

"This can be as simple as providing their email address, and by default their IP address, which is legally effective. However, authentication can also be done in any of several additional ways, such as providing a PIN that's been associated with the document. Phone authentication via SMS message using any smartphone is a popular security measure that DocuSign offers, as is knowledge-based authentication that requires the signer to answer security questions. Authentication technology is built into DocuSign and very simple to utilize. Senders can use as much or as little of this functionality as they'd like in order to be sure that the person signing a document is actually who they say they are."

Authentication tools are cryptographically sealed into the file. Thus, if someone were to tamper with a document later, DocuSign can identify the tampering and indicate exactly how the document was affected. This is all handled in a way that's recognized by the U.S. courts. DocuSign also adheres to laws in many other countries around the world when it comes to handling digital signatures.

"While a lot happens behind-the-scenes technologically to keep a document secure within DocuSign, all the user sees in their web browser, for example, is the document itself, along with clearly labeled fields that need to be filled in," stated Gosner. "The person who creates and sends a document within DocuSign determines what authentication tools will be used when the signer tries to sign the document online."

When asked if it's possible for someone to forge an eSignature when using DocuSign, Gosner responded, "Yes, it is possible, but it would take a Cray supercomputer a long time to hack into a document that utilizes the sophisticated encryption used by our service. So, in reality, it's next to impossible. The electronic record that's produced in conjunction with each document is more accurate and has much more evidence and traceability around it than a traditional paper-based record."

As a DocuSign user, the additional step you can take when sending a document to a signer includes manually turning on at least one or two separate authentication tools.

Gosner explained, "Regardless of which cloud-based service you use, Google Authenticator or a smart-phone two-factor authentication process where the signer needs to respond to an SMS message sent to their phone, both are very useful and secure tools. Taking these steps helps to avoid the chance that someone can hack into a cloud-based account using just someone's username and password."

According to Gosner, one reason for the global success of the DocuSign service is because it integrates so easily with so many other cloud-based services, as well as software packages and mobile apps that business people are already using. He added, "When we add a connector that provides integration with a third-party software package, mobile app, or cloud-based service, we work to ensure that the integration in no way compromises the security measures that DocuSign automatically puts into place for all of its users. These connectors are typically provided at no cost."

Another area that's new to DocuSign, but that's already having a huge impact, is online payment integration. This can be included within documents handled by DocuSign. "With DocuSign, it's now possible to take any document and easily transform it into an intuitive and secure payment surface area," said Gosner.

Additional functionality that's being incorporated into DocuSign in 2017 and beyond includes what Gosner refers to as "digital conversation" tools. This will allow someone receiving a document to pose a question about a page, paragraph, or specific wording within the document, and have the sender respond in context, using the conversation tools provided. The digital conversation tool will record everything that's discussed, so the negotiations or explanations can be referred back to later.

Another tool being implemented will be for sharing specific aspects of a document, with select other people, but only for a limited time. One use of this tool would be if the recipient of a contract, for example, has a question about a paragraph that he wants to forward to his lawyer prior to signing the contract. "This type of tool is part of the digital conversation which may need to happen around a document. At DocuSign, our ultimate goal is to be able to handle all aspects of a digital conversation pertaining to a document," said Gosner. "This includes offering a shared collaboration space when it's needed."

One step beyond the complete digital conversation that Gosner is excited about is what he refers to as the introduction of "smart contracts." Based on responses from people in a transaction, a smart contract will automatically be able to take alternative or additional actions, as needed. "Contracts will become little computer programs that execute based on input, which can make working with contracts much more efficient," said Gosner.

For a business that wants to incorporate DocuSign into their existing business practices and workflow, Gosner offered the following advice. "The first step is to set up a free DocuSign account, and then take some of your existing documents and pull them into the system. From there, you can naturally integrate the functionality that's offered with specific applications that are already being used, such as Office 365, Google Docs, or Salesforce.

"For individual users who want to become more productive using DocuSign, you'll save time using the free templates that we offer. This is a very powerful tool that's frequently overlooked. If you have a similar type of document that gets used over and over again, a DocuSign template will save you time. Templates can also cut down on user errors when creating documents or contracts, for example," he said.

In Practice

Learn How to Use DocuSign

The fastest and easiest way to learn how to use DocuSign is to take advantage of DocuSign University (www.docusign.com/support/docusign-university), which is a collection of interactive tutorials for individual, non-tech-savvy users, as well as administrators.

Chapter | **8**

Managing Collaboration with Dropbox

This chapter covers the following:

- Understanding the differences between Dropbox and Dropbox Business
- Using Dropbox for online file storage, file sharing, and data syncing
- Syncing content between popular applications, mobile apps, and Dropbox
- Getting to know the online collaboration tools offered by Dropbox Paper

This chapter focuses on Dropbox, a readily accessible, low-cost, and efficient cloud-based file-storage and file-sharing service that's compatible with all popular computer and mobile device platforms. Recently, Dropbox introduced Dropbox Paper, which provides users with a collection of online-based collaboration tools.

Dropbox Overview

Since being founded in 2007, Dropbox has been a pioneer in making cloud-based computing affordable and accessible to everyday people as well as to businesses of all sizes and in all industries. This service can be used with all of your company's existing equipment, and the Dropbox software and mobile apps integrate with the operating system of Windows, Mac, and Linux-based computers.

The initial goal of Dropbox was to provide an easy way for two or more people to share files (even really large ones) via the Internet, which would be a workaround to the file-size limitations imposed by email. This continues to be a popular use of the service. You can store any type of data, documents, files, photos, or videos within any Dropbox account. Dropbox even allows you to share your files with other people who are not Dropbox account owners.

Dropbox also makes it easy for individual users to use the cloud to automatically sync data, documents, files, photos, and content between all of their own computers and mobile devices.

In Practice

In Practice

Anywhere Access to Files

After you set up data syncing between Dropbox and your computer and mobile devices or manually copy or move data, documents, files, and photos to your cloud account, you can access that content anytime from whatever equipment you're currently working with.

You can also visit www.dropbox.com from any Internet-connected computer, log in to your secure Dropbox account, and work with your files using the web browser.

FYI: Who's Using Dropbox?

As of mid-2017, Dropbox boasts having more than 500 million registered users, as well as more than 200,000 businesses and organizations that use Dropbox Business. The service is used in more than 200 countries and territories, and it supports 20 languages. Every day, more than 1.2 billion files are saved to Dropbox.

Like everything else in the cloud, Dropbox has evolved a lot since its inception. Today, Dropbox offers a comprehensive set of powerful and secure data-syncing, file-storage, and file-sharing tools to its users.

Dropbox expanded its scope in 2013 and began providing enhanced tools for businesses of all sizes and in all industries under the name of Dropbox Business. In addition to the most powerful features of Dropbox, Dropbox Business has added security, team-oriented collaboration tools, admin controls, enhanced technical support, and useful deployment tools.

To keep up with the demands and needs of business users, the company continuously works with software and mobile app developers, which enables direct and seamless integration with popular applications used in business, including Microsoft Office 365.

FYI: Secure Dropbox Integration

Dropbox Business securely integrates with hundreds of other popular applications, tools, and mobile apps, including Salesforce, Slack, DocuSign, and Trello. Learn more by visiting www.dropbox.com/business/app-integrations.

In 2015, Dropbox expanded further with the introduction of Dropbox Enterprise), and in 2016 the company launched Dropbox Paper. Dropbox Enterprise is designed to be used by large companies. Each account includes the same features and functions as an Advanced account but also includes a series of Admin tools, plus added security features.

All Dropbox subscription plans include at least a 30-day version history and file recovery, which automatically protects files if someone accidently deletes them or a you want to restore a previous version of a file that has been overwritten with a revised version.

FYI: Dropbox Paper Is Included

All paid Dropbox subscription plans include Dropbox Paper, which is an entirely online-based collaboration toolset. The Dropbox Standard and Dropbox Advanced subscription plans include Dropbox Paper with added admin tools.

The next several sections focus a bit more on the core functions that Dropbox and Dropbox Business offer to individual users, teams, and organizations or businesses of any size.

File Storage in the Cloud

In its most basic form, Dropbox serves as cloud-based storage that functions with your Internet-connected computer or mobile device in much the same way as a local hard drive does. You can manually copy files to your Dropbox account. In your account, you can store files in the main Dropbox folder, or you can create custom-named folders and subfolders to help keep things organized.

Using copy-and-paste or drag-and-drop methods, you can copy files or entire folders to your Dropbox account; the content you copy or drag to Dropbox remains stored within your computer or mobile device's local storage. You can set up file syncing, though, so that when you make changes to a file on your computer or mobile device, the changes are updated in the version stored in Dropbox.

When you use the Move command, the content is transferred from one location (such as your local hard drive) to your Dropbox account. The original file doesn't remain in its original location on your computer or mobile device.

In Practice

Quickly Find Content Stored in Dropbox

To quickly find content stored within Dropbox, use the Search field in the top-right corner of the Finder (Mac) or Explorer (PC) window on your computer. You can also use the Search field in the top-right corner of the Dropbox.com browser window or in the top-center of the Dropbox mobile app (after tapping on the Recents or Files option).

Within the Search field, type a filename, date, keyword, or search phrase that will help you locate the content you're looking for. When the search results are displayed, click or tap the desired listing to access that file or content.

File-Sharing Functionality

After you've transferred files, folders, and/or subfolders to your Dropbox account, you can access that content from any Internet-connected computer or device. This feature makes Dropbox super convenient because you always have access to your content from anywhere you can access the Internet. For example, if you create a document on your computer at work, later—when you're on the road or at home—you can access that file remotely so that you can continue working on it without toting a flash drive or other storage device to and from the office.

You can also use the Share capabilities built into Dropbox to securely share specific content with one or more other people; everything else stored within your Dropbox account is private and not accessible to others. You determine whom you share content with and establish permissions (which determine what the other people can do with the shared content). How you establish the Folder Settings options when you share the content determines whether invitees may share the content with others. When looking at a listing of files and folders in Dropbox, hover your mouse over a listing, and a Share button will appear. Click it to access your sharing options.

The paid Dropbox accounts, which have more features than the basic account, expand how you can manage and share files—and they also incorporate additional security and compliance tools. Read more about the different account types in the "Dropbox Subscription Plans" section later in this chapter.

In Practice

File Listings Show When They're Being Shared

Regardless of how you're accessing your Dropbox account, as you view a listing for a file or folder, you can see whether that content is currently being shared, and, if it is, how many people it's shared with. If you're using Dropbox.com, for example, hover the mouse over the # Members option in a file or folder's listing to see the names of the people that particular content is being shared with (see Figure 8.1).

When you hover the mouse over one file or folder listing or select multiple files or folders, click the Share button to manage permissions for the shared file or folder or to invite additional people to share the content. If you want to revoke someone's access to the shared content, click Share and in the dialog box click Remove (see Figure 8.2).

The highlighted folder is being shared with four people.

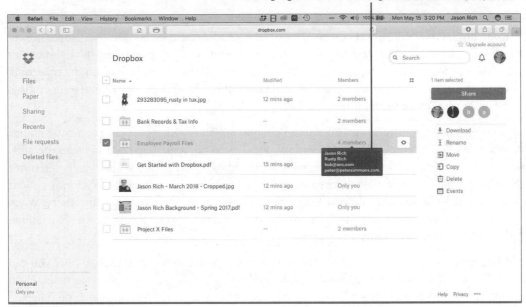

FIGURE 8.1   Quickly determine whether a file or folder is being shared, and with whom.

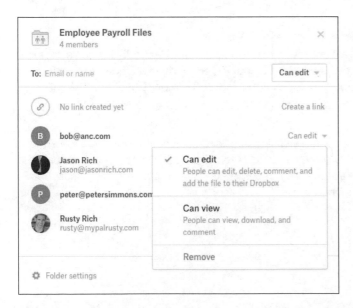

FIGURE 8.2   The person sharing a file or folder, or the administrator, can edit permissions at anytime, or invite additional people to share the selected content.

Data Syncing

With the free Dropbox software, mobile app, or applications that include Dropbox integration, you can set up your account so your important documents, files, or data automatically sync between all of your computers and mobile devices. For example, if you compose a Microsoft Word document on your desktop computer at work, when you have the syncing settings enabled, that document automatically is saved to your Dropbox account, which means you can download it from Dropbox to another device that has Microsoft Word installed so that you can work on it there. This capability ensures you're always working with the most current version of your work, regardless of what equipment you're using or where you're using it from, as long as Internet access is available.

To learn how to set up and use the Dropbox syncing feature using the Dropbox software, visit www.dropbox.com/help/syncing-uploads/syncing-overview.

In Practice

Internet Is Required

As with any cloud-based service, a continuous Internet connection is required on all of your computers and mobile devices in order to keep your content synced in real time. If a device lacks Internet access for a while, as soon as an Internet connection is re-established, Dropbox can sync whatever content has changed.

Likewise, if you take photos with your smartphone that get stored within the internal storage of your mobile device, you can set up the Dropbox mobile app to automatically back up and sync your photos with your Dropbox account as they're taken or edited. This automatically creates a remote backup.

In Practice

Take Advantage of Smart Sync

Dropbox's Smart Sync feature is designed to make finding your important content faster. One of the biggest problems computer users have these days is remembering where their content is stored—locally, in a variety of cloud-based services, or within which folder. It's a good idea to set up project- or topic-specific folders within your Dropbox account and then sync related content to the appropriate folder. This method helps you and your team to always know where relevant files are located and have easy access to the most current versions of files or content.

When you access content stored on your computer, right-click the file or folder and select the Move to Dropbox option. Going forward, that file or folder will automatically sync with your Dropbox account anytime you alter it. To learn more about this feature, visit www.dropbox.com/business/smartsync.

> **FYI: Real-Time Collaboration Tools**
>
> If you need to compose, review, or edit a document in real time with one or more collaborators, or gather information and brainstorm ideas with a group, you can use the functionality in Dropbox Paper, which is covered in more detail later in this chapter in the "Dropbox Paper" section.

Dropbox Subscription Plans

Depending on the needs and size of your team, organization, or business, Dropbox offers several different subscription plans that cater to different types of users.

Each Dropbox user must have an individual email address to establish an account and sign in to the Dropbox service. However, only one Dropbox account is required per user, regardless of how many computers or mobile devices that user will use Dropbox with.

> **FYI: Basic Dropbox Functionality Is Free**
>
> The Dropbox Basic account is free, but it offers just 2 gigabytes (GB) of online storage space. From a security standpoint, AES-256 bit encryption is used on all files stored using this plan, and optional two-step verification can be turned on to further secure a user's account.
>
> To get started, simply download and install the free Dropbox software or mobile app, or create and manage your account using any web browser by visiting www.dropbox.com and signing in to your account. Bear in mind that the web browser doesn't allow for automatic application-specific file and data syncing. You can do that only if you're using the Dropbox software or mobile app or you're using software that has built-in Dropbox integration.
>
> Note that many features and functions offered by paid Dropbox plans are limited or inaccessible to a free account. However, as your file storage, file sharing, data syncing, and real-time collaboration needs change, you can instantly upgrade your free Dropbox account to a paid account.

The Dropbox Plus Plan

The Dropbox Plus plan ($8.25 per month, per user, paid yearly) is ideal for individual users or small teams. It includes Dropbox's file-sharing and data-syncing features, along with 1 terabyte (TB) of online storage space per account. Some of the additional features this type of account offers include

- 30-day file recovery

- 256-bit AES and SSL/TLS encryption

- Dropbox Paper integration

- Office 365 integration

- Enhanced sharing and permissions features

- Remote device wipe

- The optional ability to activate two-factor authentication to further protect an account

This type of account is ideal for someone who wants to easily back up and sync content across all of their computers and mobile devices, occasionally share individual files or folders with others, or who need to collaborate with just a few team members who each have their own Dropbox Plus, Dropbox Standard, or Dropbox Advanced account. Priority email support is available from Dropbox. This plan lacks certain features, like a Team Folder and Admin console, that make using Dropbox with larger groups much easier.

The Dropbox Standard Plan

The Dropbox Standard plan is suitable for small groups, teams, organizations, or companies. The cost is $12.50 per month, paid yearly, which includes three user accounts. Additional accounts cost $12.50 per month, per user. This plan includes 2TB of shared online storage space, as well as all of the features included with a Plus plan. However, the Standard plan extends the file recovery and version history feature to 120 days.

This plan also offers admin tools and a detailed audit log for files stored online, more advanced security features, the ability to create user and company-managed groups (for file sharing), and custom branding. Live chat or email support is available from Dropbox.

The Dropbox Advanced Plan

Organizations, teams, or companies of almost any size can make use of the Dropbox Advanced plan. This plan, which costs $20.00 per month, paid yearly, includes three user accounts. Additional accounts cost $20.00 per month, per user. Each user has access to unlimited online storage space as well as all of the functionality provided by the Standard plan. The plan also provides more sophisticated admin, audit, and integration tools than the other plans.

For example, you can establish tiered admin roles (see the nearby In Practice sidebar for more information), and everything stored within Dropbox includes file event tracking. The administrator also has access to additional security features and audit controls, as well as invite enforcement, domain verification, and device approvals. Email, live chat, and phone support is provided by Dropbox.

In Practice

Why Tiered Admin Roles Are Useful

When using any cloud-based service as a company, one person is typically assigned the role of administrator. This is the person who can oversee and manage all user accounts and who is able to customize the security and compliance features the service offers.

Tiered admin roles allow administrators with different levels of clearance and authority to manage an organization's Dropbox usage, allowing for certain types of content to only be accessible to certain Administrators. For example, you might not want one administrator to have access to all content because only top-level executives should be privy to that information; this person would not be granted the top tier of administrator access.

For Dropbox Business plans that support this feature, three levels of admin roles are available: Team Admin, User Management Admin, and Support Admin. Only a Team Admin can sign in to any user's account, reset admin passwords, create or assign admin roles, and view the company-wide Dropbox activity feed.

A team admin can set team-wide security and sharing permissions, manage team members, manage team folders, and adjust the permissions of team members. They can also add, remove, or suspend other admins related to a team. A user management admin can remove team members, manage groups, and generate per-user activity logs, while a support admin can manage team member passwords, manage team member account security, and is the person who can contact Dropbox when support is required.

You can find more information about this functionality and how an organization should use it at www.dropbox.com/help/business/tiered-admins-overview.

FYI: Dropbox Enterprise Plans

For large organizations, Dropbox offers customized Enterprise plans. For more information, visit www.dropbox.com/enterprise.

Dropbox Software

To get the most out of Dropbox from your computer, you definitely want to download and install the free Dropbox software. This software adds integration between Dropbox and your computer's operating system, which means you can access Dropbox content directly from an Explorer window (PC), Mac Finder window, or when using a Linux-based computer.

To acquire the free Dropbox software, visit www.dropbox.com and click the Install option near the very bottom of the welcome screen. Next, click the Download Dropbox button and then follow the onscreen prompts to install the application onto your computer using the Dropbox Installer (see Figure 8.3).

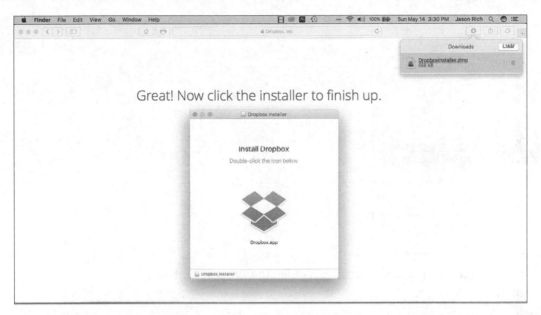

FIGURE 8.3   Follow the on-screen prompts to install Dropbox once the software is downloaded to your Windows PC or Mac.

After you've installed the software, you need to sign in to your Dropbox account using your email address and password. If you don't yet have a Dropbox account, click the Sign Up option (see Figure 8.4).

If you've already used Dropbox via other means (through the web browser or on mobile devices), you have to determine whether you want to sync everything stored within your Dropbox account to the computer where you just installed the software; another alternative is to choose specific folders to sync.

At this point, close the web browser window that was used to acquire the software and visit the Dropbox website. What you'll discover is that Dropbox now appears as a folder on your computer, and it works just like your Documents or Pictures folder that was already automatically set up by your computer's operating system (see Figure 8.5).

Within this main Dropbox folder, you can create custom-named subfolders in exactly the same way as you create new folders locally on your computer.

FIGURE 8.4   Sign in to your Dropbox account from the Dropbox software.

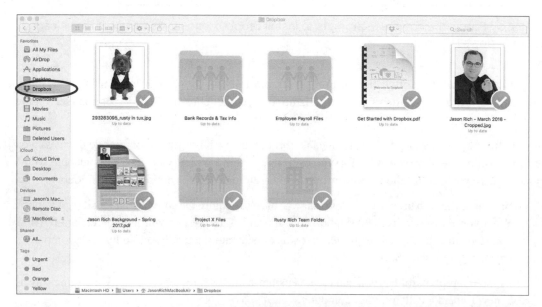

FIGURE 8.5   You can treat the newly created Dropbox folder just as you would any other main folder on your computer's hard drive.

The difference between the other folders on your computer and the Dropbox folder is that when you copy or move any files (data, documents, photos, and so on) to the Dropbox folder, that content automatically is backed up and stored online within your Dropbox account.

To adjust account or software-specific settings, click the Dropbox icon, which is at the top of the screen in the menu bar on your Mac (see Figure 8.6) or in the Taskbar at the bottom right on your Windows 10 PC.

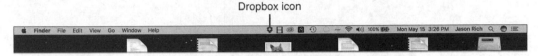

FIGURE 8.6 Click the Dropbox icon (shown here on a Mac) to manage your Dropbox account.

After clicking on this icon, click the gear-shaped Settings icon, followed by the Preferences option, to adjust account- and software-specific settings. (See Figure 8.7.)

FIGURE 8.7 Click the General, Account, Import, and Network tabs to adjust various Dropbox settings.

The Dropbox window opens; click the folder icon to access the main Dropbox folder on your computer. (Alternatively, click the Web icon to access your online Dropbox account and its contents.) Right-click any file or folder to access a menu (shown in Figure 8.8) from which you can share the file with others, view the file's version history, open the file within its associated app, or handle certain other file-management tasks.

FIGURE 8.8 You can use any of Dropbox's file management or sharing features directly from the Dropbox folder on your computer.

In Practice

Tips for Sharing a File or Folder

To share content, select one or more files, folders, or subfolders and click or tap the Share option. In the Share window, enter the email address for each person you want to share the selected content with. Remember, the invitees will be able to access only the content you're choosing to share; everything else that's stored within your Dropbox account remains private and inaccessible to those other people (unless they have certain Dropbox Admin privileges).

Next, adjust the permissions being granted for the content you're sharing by clicking or tapping the menu to the right of the To field. For most types of files that can be edited or altered, your options include Can View or Can Edit. Can View means the people you're sharing the content with are able only to view the file—not alter it. Can Edit means the invitee can view and edit the content being shared.

Type an optional message that will be sent to your invitees. Click or tap the Folder Settings button to determine who will be able to invite additional people to the folder that's being shared. When you're ready to share the selected content, click or tap the Share button.

The people you've invited to share content with receive an email from you (see Figure 8.9) that contains a secure and unique link that will grant them access to the selected content. If the people you've invited are Dropbox users, the files and folders will be added to their respective Dropbox accounts. Otherwise, invitees who are not current Dropbox users are able to access the file from the computer or mobile device they're using via their web browser.

FIGURE 8.9   People invited to share content receive an email message like this one.

CAUTION

Carefully Choose Whom You Share With

After you've shared a file or folder with other people, you can add other invitees or revoke access to specific people. However, if an invitee already has accessed the content and has downloaded it to a computer or mobile device, they will be able to do with it as they please. By revoking access to the file or folder, you simply prevent them from re-acquiring the content or being able to access updated versions of the content.

The Dropbox Mobile App

The Dropbox mobile app, which is available from the App Store for iOS devices or from the Google Play Store for Android devices, integrates directly with your mobile device's operating system as well as compatible third-party apps you have installed on your devices. Through the app you have full access to all of your files, folders, and content in your Dropbox account. You are able to manage and share content from your account (see Figure 8.10).

For example, tap the Recents option to select and view your files and folders stored online within your Dropbox account that you've worked with recently, and then use any of the Share tools to share the file (or folder) with other people. Choose the Files option to view all content stored within your account.

On an iOS mobile device, the Recents, Files, + (Add), Photos, and Offline command icons are displayed along the bottom of the app screen. On an Android device, tap the Menu icon (in the top-left corner of the screen) to access the Recents, Files, Photos, Offline, and Notifications options. You add a file or folder by tapping the + icon.

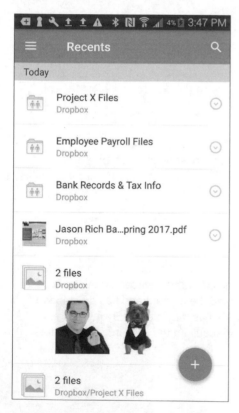

FIGURE 8.10   Manage your Dropbox content from your mobile device.

> ### FYI: Dropbox Paper Has Its Own App
>
> To take advantage of the Dropbox Paper real-time collaboration tools from your smartphone or tablet, you have to have the separate Dropbox Paper app.

Another feature of the Dropbox mobile app is the Dropbox Document Scanner. This feature allows you to use the rear-facing camera on your mobile device to photograph (scan) paper-based documents; you can store, manage, and share those documents from within your Dropbox account. The Document Scanner enables you to reduce paper-based clutter in your life while enabling you to access your scanned documents from all of your computers and mobile devices. You can also use it to scan a conference room's whiteboard during a meeting, which saves you from taking notes.

You access the Document Scanner feature of the Dropbox app by clicking the + icon (refer to Figure 8.10). When the device's camera activates, center the blue frame around a page or document and press the Shutter (scan) button (see Figure 8.11).

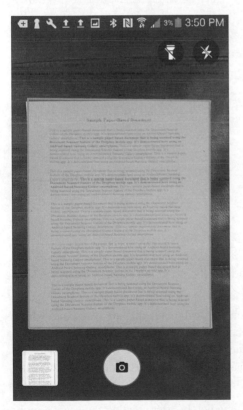

FIGURE 8.11   Center the blue frame around the paper-based document you want to scan.

To achieve the best scanning results, position the paper on a flat surface in a well-lit area and hold the camera steady directly over the paper. After you tap the Shutter button, you see a preview of the scanned page (see Figure 8.12).

Tap the Add Page icon to scan additional pages; the pages will be saved as a single document. Tap the Rotate icon to rotate the document 90 degrees with each tap. Tap the Adjust icon to adjust the Contrast (using a slider), or select a filter to enhance the readability of the scanned document.

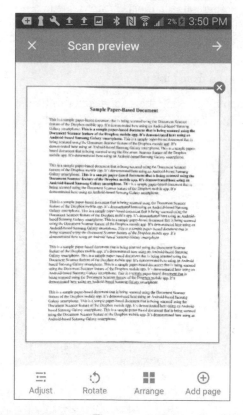

FIGURE 8.12   Tap one of the command icons to edit or adjust the scanned page.

After tapping the Adjust icon, select the default B&W option for documents that are black and white. Select Whiteboard if you've scanned the contents of a whiteboard. Select Original if you want to adjust or crop the edges around the scanned document. Tap the Done option (which is the check mark icon on an Android device) when you're finished making changes and then tap the Next option (which is the check mark icon on an Android device).

If you don't need to adjust the document, you can save it immediately after creating the scan; simply tap the Next option (which is the right-pointing arrow icon on an Android device) in the top-right corner of the screen. The Saved Settings screen opens. From there you can customize the document's filename, choose between saving the document as a PDF or PNG file, and then select the Dropbox folder in which you want the document stored.

> **FYI: PDF Documents Can Be Edited Later**
>
> By storing a document that you've scanned as a PDF file, you have the ability to edit the text using a PDF editor (such as Adobe Acrobat or PDF Expert) on your computer or mobile device. If you have scanned and saved the document as a PNG file, it is saved as a graphic image that you can later annotate but not fully edit.

The Dropbox.com Website

When you sign in to your account at www.dropbox.com, the Files option is selected by default, and the main area of the Dropbox browser window displays all your folders and files that are stored within your main Dropbox folder (see Figure 8.13).

FIGURE 8.13 Manage all aspects of your Dropbox account, as well as access all files and folders stored within your account using any computer's web browser.

Use the commands in the menu in the left margin of the Dropbox browser window to access additional Dropbox features. Your options include the following:

- **Files**—Access all files and folders stored online within your Dropbox account. Click a folder to open that folder and view its contents. Click a file or folder to select it, and then click on the More icon (…) to access a menu of commands you can use to manage that content (see Figure 8.14). After selecting a listing or hovering your mouse over it, click on its Share button to share the selected content with others.

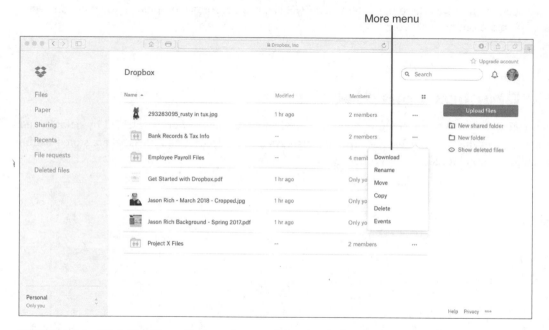

FIGURE 8.14   Click the More Options icon to Download, Rename, Move, Copy, or Delete the selected content. Click Events to view the file's history.

- **Paper**—Use the online collaboration tools offered by Dropbox Paper.

- **Sharing**—View and work with only files and folders that are being shared with others or that are being shared with you via your Dropbox account.

- **Recents**—View a listing of files and folders within Dropbox that you've recently worked with.

- **File Requests**—Invite others (team members, collaborators, and so on) to upload content to a specific folder within your Dropbox account.

- **Deleted Files**—Access files that have been deleted from your Dropbox account. How long these files are accessible depends on the type of account you have.

Use the Search field near the top-right corner of the Dropbox browser window to find any content that's stored within your Dropbox account, or use any of the command icons or options displayed along the right margin of the browser window to manage your account. For example, click the Upload Files option to manually upload files to your account. Click the New Shared Folder option to create a new folder within your account and grant access to it by select other people. Click the New Folder option to create a new (private) folder within your account.

To turn on and manage global Dropbox notifications, click the bell-shaped Notifications icon at the top-right corner of the browser window. To manage your Dropbox account, click your account profile photo or username, which is near the top-right corner of the browser window.

> ### CAUTION
>
> ### Always Sign Out When Done
>
> If other people will have access to your computer, or you're using someone else's computer to access your Dropbox account via www.dropbox.com, when you're done working with Dropbox, be sure to sign out from your account—don't just close the browser window when you're done. Click your account profile photo or username near the top-right corner of the browser window, and select the Sign Out option.
>
> Also, when signing in to your Dropbox account from a new computer (or someone else's computer), don't allow the computer's web browser to remember your Dropbox account email address or password. To add an extra level of protection to your account in order to prevent unauthorized people from accessing it, consider turning on the two-step authentication feature. You do this from the Account Settings menu, which is on the Security tab (located near the top-left corner of the browser window). The feature needs to be turned on only once per account.

Dropbox Paper

Dropbox Paper offers a flexible document-creation (and text-editing) tool that can be viewed and worked with simultaneously by two or more people. (An individual user can use Paper as an information-gathering and note-taking tool, but the application was designed to make it easy for two or more people to collaborate or brainstorm in real time.) The collaborators see changes or edits as they're being made, and all work is automatically saved online in Dropbox. While collaborating, the users can add comments to the document. Comments can be addressed to all collaborators or individuals (using the @username format). These comments use a group messaging format similar to a text conversation.

The first time you access Dropbox Paper, you're prompted to create a username. A special Dropbox Team folder is automatically created within your Dropbox account to give you a workspace in which to save your Dropbox Paper documents.

When you opt to create a new Paper document, you see several template options (see Figure 8.15)—Brainstorm, Project Overview, Meeting Notes, and Create New Doc.

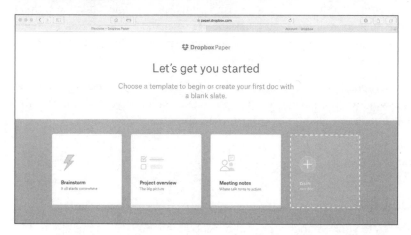

FIGURE 8.15 Take advantage of Paper's built-in templates to help you gather, format, and organize information as you're collaborating.

Click the Create New Doc option to create a free-form document from scratch, or use one of the templates to start with some extra formatting. If you choose a template, fill in the fields to help you gather and present the necessary information that will bring your collaborations together and focus everyone's attention on the task at hand.

The first step in the collaborative process is to give each new document a name (title). As with any document stored within your Dropbox account, it remains private until you opt to share it with one or more people by clicking the Share button in the top-right corner of the browser window (see Figure 8.16). From there you share the document the same way you'd share any file or folder using Dropbox.

After you've shared the document, you and your collaborators can begin typing content into the document or import content from other sources. Click on the + icon to import content; create a table, bulleted list, numbered list, or checkbox list; or add a page divider or code (see Figure 8.17) to the document. As text is being added by individual collaborators, Paper displays who has added content and tracks when each addition or edit is made. All work, as well as a detailed audit trail and version history, is automatically saved to your Dropbox account.

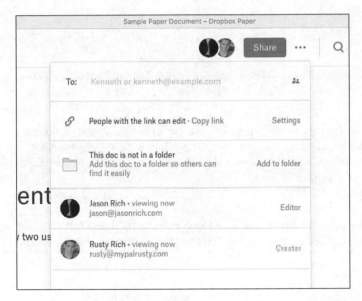

FIGURE 8.16. Dropbox Paper's Share tools are virtually identical to the Share tools offered by Dropbox.

+ icon

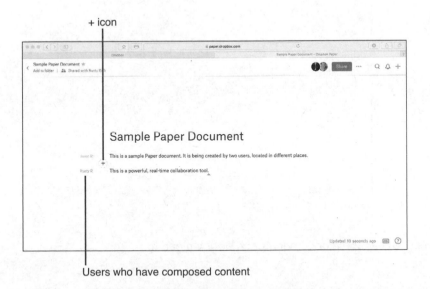

Users who have composed content

FIGURE 8.17   As you're typing content into a Paper document, click the + icon to gather and import content or format the text you're working with.

In Practice

Format As You Type

When you're working in Paper, select text to access the text formatting options, which include Bold, Strikethrough, Large Header, Medium Header, Bulleted List, Numbered List, Checkbox List, Create Link, and Add Comment.

The comments are like sticky notes that are displayed in the margin of a document. You can address a comment to one collaborator or to all collaborators. The content within comments is displayed in the right margin of a Paper document, but it isn't actually embedded with the text and imported content into the main body of a document.

As you're working with a document, click on the More icon (...) to access a menu that offers tools for managing, printing, or downloading the document. You can also view its word count or version history (see Figure 8.18).

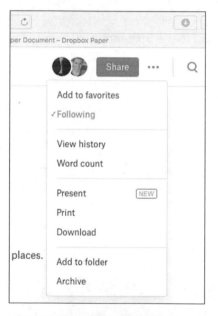

FIGURE 8.18   Use this menu to manage a document, print, or download it.

In Practice

Take Advantage of the Shortcuts Menu

In the lower-right corner of the Paper window is the Shortcuts menu icon (which looks like a keyboard). Click this icon to reveal the Shortcuts menu (see Figure 8.19), from which you can quickly format text, insert content, or manage the document you're working with.

places

FIGURE 8.19   Dropbox Paper's Shortcuts menu. Scroll down to see all of your options.

FYI: Dropbox Paper to Go

To use Paper from your smartphone or tablet, be sure to download and install the separate Dropbox Paper mobile app.

FYI: Get Instant Help Using Paper

Learn about the latest features added to Paper or obtain detailed directions for using each of Paper's tools by clicking the Help icon (the question mark) in the lower-right corner of the Paper browser window. You can then enter what you're looking for within the Search field or access a list of Featured articles.

FYI: Content Organization

After you opt to adopt Dropbox—whether it's for your own use or use within a team, organization, or business—get into the habit of storing all content within your Dropbox account. Making it a practice to store everything in Dropbox ensures you know where everything is stored and makes it possible for you to find what you're looking for using the Search tool.

CAUTION

Avoid Common Mistakes

Perhaps the biggest security-related mistake a person can make using Dropbox is accidently storing confidential files within a folder that's being shared with other people. It's up to every user to make sure only appropriate information is placed within folders that are being shared and to use common sense and due diligence when it comes to deciding with whom to share specific files and folders.

It's best to activate the necessary account-specific security features, and make sure you fully understand how to use the Share tools to set permissions for shared files and folders. Make sure you pay attention to what information is stored within each folder and keep an eye on who you're sharing those folders with.

As with any other online accounts, be sure to use strong passwords and, as suggested earlier in this chapter, enable two-step verification. To get more detailed information about how to use each of Dropbox's security and compliance features, visit www.dropbox.com/help/security.

Chapter 9

Taking Notes and Staying Organized with Evernote

This chapter covers the following:

- An overview of the writing, note-taking, and information-gathering tools that Evernote offers
- How the different versions of Evernote vary
- Ways to share files and handle real-time collaboration using Evernote

This chapter focuses on the core features and functions of Evernote, explains how and why Evernote may be more useful to you than a traditional word processor when it comes to note taking and information gathering, and provides tips on how to use Evernote's file-sharing and online collaboration tools.

Evernote Overview

Although Evernote is not designed to be a full-featured word processor, like Microsoft Word, Google Docs, or Apple's Pages, it does provide an ever-growing selection of text formatting tools, along with functionality that enables you to easily collect information from a wide range of sources and then import that information directly into notes in Evernote. After you have created notes, you can organize them within custom-labeled virtual notebooks.

Some versions of Evernote offer additional tools that enable you to share notes or notebooks with specific other people. You can also collaborate in real time with other Evernote users who are using a paid Evernote account.

In addition to the 200+ million individual Evernote users around the world, more than 20,000 companies utilize Evernote Business, which offers premium tools that focus on security, data syncing, file sharing, online collaboration, user management, and administration. Evernote Business is designed for organizations with more than 25 users.

Many individuals and organizations use Evernote in an effort to attain a paperless work environment. They rely on Evernote to compose documents, take notes, collect and organize information or research (including text, PDF files, photos, drawings, audio files, and other types of content), and to manage lists.

FYI: How Evernote Utilizes the Cloud

You can use any web browser to work with the cloud-based edition of Evernote to create, organize, and share content in the form of notes and virtual notebooks. In this case, the Evernote application, and all content that's created, is stored online. Each user must have his or her own Evernote account, but no special software is required. Alternatively, you can download and install the official Evernote software onto your computer or install the Evernote mobile app on your smartphone or tablet to access greater functionality when working with Evernote and your own content.

When you use the Evernote software on a PC or Mac or use the Evernote mobile app, the content and information that you gather and place into notes and virtual notebooks is stored online in your Evernote account. You also can store content locally (on the computer or mobile device you're using) if you have a paid Evernote account. The content automatically syncs between all devices and versions of Evernote that you work with.

To take advantage of Evernote's file-sharing and online collaboration tools, you (and the people you're sharing with) have to have your own paid Evernote account.

Evernote is different from some other cloud-based collaboration tools because you can download and install the Evernote software on your computer. You can also download and install the Evernote mobile app on your smartphone or tablet. See the "Setup of Evernote" section later in this chapter for information about how to download the software or app for your device.

CAUTION

All Versions of Evernote Are Compatible, But Not Identical

The Windows PC, Mac, iOS, Android, and online-based version of Evernote are pretty compatible with each other. However, each version has its own set of note-taking, editing, information-gathering, file-management, file-sharing, and online collaboration tools, many of which overlap, but some are unique to specific versions..

Evernote is an ever-changing platform. Throughout the year, Evernote updates the various versions of its software and mobile apps to introduce new features and functions as well as provide better integration with other software, mobile apps, and cloud-based services. Recent updates have focused on security, collaboration, and file sharing, as well as providing new ways for users to collect and organize a broad range of content types within notes and notebooks. Check for updates frequently to make sure you're using the most current version of the software or app.

In Practice

Many Add-Ons Are Available for Evernote

Regardless of which version of Evernote you're using, many add-ons are available to provide additional information-gathering tools. To learn more about add-ons offered by Evernote, which include Skitch (a drawing tool), Scannable (a paper scanning tool), Evernote Web Clipper (used for collecting content directly from web pages), and Penultimate (a drawing and text annotation tool for the iPad), visit https://evernote.com/products.

For information about third-party software and mobile apps that work with Evernote, visit https://appcenter.evernote.com. For example, there are apps that allow content from other applications to be imported directly into Evernote as separate notes, and other apps that enhance the way Evernote handles to-do lists.

Evernote Pricing

For individual users and small groups, Evernote Basic is free. However, this type of account has limits to Evernote's functionality and the amount of online storage that's available. For example, a Basic account includes just 60MB of online storage space per month for new uploads, and Evernote data can be synced between only two of a user's own computers and/or mobile devices.

The Evernote Plus plan, which is priced at $34.99 per user, per year, allows each user to upload up to 1GB of new content per month and sync their files across all of their computers and mobile devices. This plan also allows users to store Evernote content locally for offline access, and it provides additional security tools for encrypting notes and notebooks.

The Evernote Premium plan, which is priced at $69.99 per user, per year, offers the same features as the Evernote Plus Plan and also allows each user to upload up to 10GB of new content per month to their online-based account and to sync their files across all of their computers and mobile devices. This plan also offers tools that can search text within PDF files and Microsoft Office files. Users with this plan are able to annotate PDF files within Evernote. You can scan, organize, and store business cards, and there's a version-history feature that enables you to recover and view previous versions of notes.

For organizations with more than 25 users, Evernote Business is priced at $12.00 per user, per month ($144.00 per user, per year). Evernote Business includes all the functionality of the Evernote Premium plan, and it has better tools for real-time collaboration, security, user management, and administration.

Setup of Evernote

The Evernote software and mobile apps are all free, regardless of which subscription plan you use (which determines your storage space and available features). Use the following directions for the type of computer or mobile device you use:

■ Visit https://evernote.com/download to download and install the free Windows PC or Mac version of Evernote onto your computer (desktop or laptop). The website automatically determines which operating system your computer is using and downloads the appropriate version of the Evernote software. After the software has downloaded, double-click the file and follow the on-screen installation directions. When prompted, sign in to your Evernote account by providing your email address and account password, or create a new account from scratch.

■ Download and install the free iOS edition of Evernote by visiting https://evernote.com/ and clicking the Download button on the App Store icon. You can also visit https://itunes.apple.com/us/app/evernote-stay-organized/id281796108.

■ Download and install the free Android-based mobile device edition of Evernote by visiting https://evernote.com/download and clicking the Get It on Google Play icon. You can also visit https://play.google.com/store/apps/details?id=com.evernote.

To use Evernote through a web browser, visit www.evernote.com. Sign in with your username (email address) and password (see Figure 9.1).

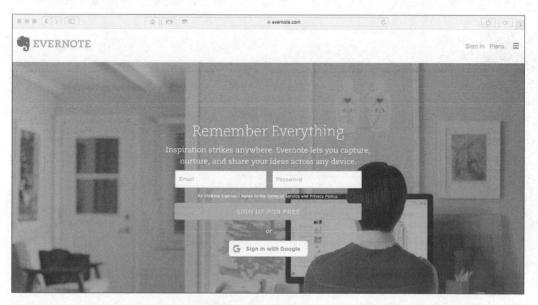

FIGURE 9.1 From any computer's web browser, securely sign in to the Evernote website (www.evernote.com) to access the online edition of Evernote.

> ## FYI: Only One Evernote Account Per User Is Required
>
> The first time you use any version of Evernote, you're prompted to either create a free Evernote account or sign in using your existing Evernote account. Regardless of how many different devices you plan to use with Evernote—on your work computer, laptop computer, home computer, smartphone, and/or tablet—you need only a single (paid) Evernote account. Each version of Evernote should then be linked with the same account so you can have access to all of your notes and notebooks. If you use a free account, only two computers and/or mobile devices can be synced to an account at one time.

Note-Taking in Evernote

Evernote is designed to be a note-taking and information-gathering tool. Regardless of which version of Evernote you're using, you can compose or collect content within individual notes (see Figure 9.2). You create a note by clicking or tapping the Create Note option. Give the new note a custom title, which also serves as its filename. Click or tap within the main body of the note area and start typing. You can also use one of the information-gathering tools to cut and paste, drag-and-drop, or import content into the note. The time and date when the note was composed and last edited is automatically recorded and saved.

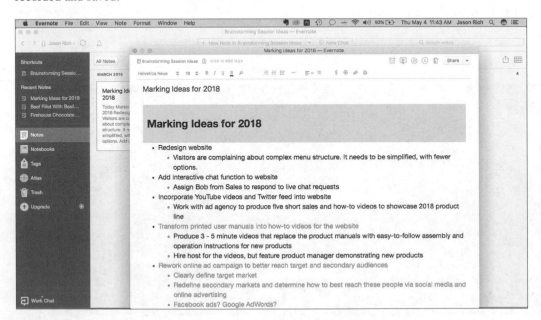

FIGURE 9.2 A sample note created using the Mac version of Evernote.

A note starts off as a blank document, but you can add as much content and information as is needed to the note (you just keep scrolling down). In other words, a single note is not limited to a single 8.5" × 11" page of content, for example.

Although Evernote is not designed to be a full-featured word processor, most versions of Evernote include features that enable you to select a font, font size, typestyle, and font color for your text. You can also alter the alignment of the text. You can change this text formatting as often as needed as you create a single note.

Because it's meant to be an information-organizing and -gathering tool, Evernote includes tools to create and manage bulleted lists, numbered lists, and interactive to-do lists that display check boxes for each item in the list (so that you can tick off tasks as you complete them; see Figure 9.3).

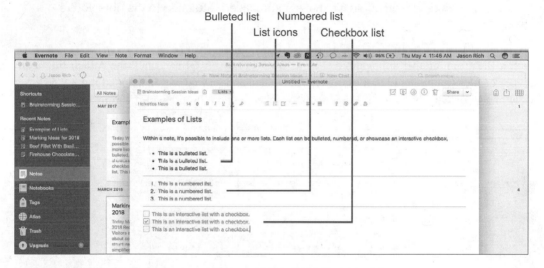

FIGURE 9.3   You can create several types of lists in Evernote.

To help organize how information is displayed within a note, most versions of Evernote allow you to create and edit tables. You can also import content from other files into a note, including photos, audio files, video clips, or content from another compatible application. Some types of Evernote subscriptions enable you to import and embed a PDF file into a note, which you can then annotate by using Evernotes markup tools. (Other subscriptions enable you to import PDFs, but you can only view them. Check the features of your subscription for more details.)

The Evernote software for the PC and Mac includes an audio-recording tool (see Figure 9.4), which enables you to use the microphone that's built into your computer to record meetings or dictation. The audio file is stored within the note you're currently working with.

Recording icon   Recording status bar

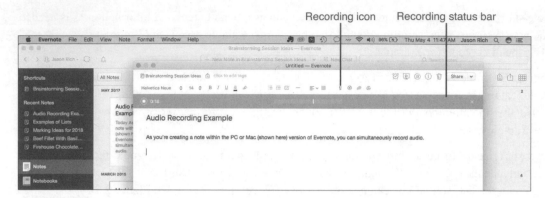

FIGURE 9.4   You can record an audio file that's automatically attached to the note you're working with.

To attach a file from another application, such as from Microsoft Office, click the Attach File icon. Some types of files (including PDF files) can be embedded and viewed within a note. Figure 9.5 shows a preview of a PDF. Click the Import Photo icon to embed a photo or video clip within a note.

File Attachment icon

Embedded PDF file

FIGURE 9.5   Embed or attach a file from another application, such as a PDF file or Office file, directly into the note you're working with.

Another handy feature of Evernote enables you to add a reminder to the note. You can set a specific date and time that you want an alarm to remind you of time-sensitive information you need to access or address, such as an item on a to-do list.

You can group individual notes in notebooks. You can create as many separate notes and notebooks as you need. Notes within notebooks are sorted alphabetically based on their titles, but you can choose to have them sorted based on other criteria, such as the time and date each was created. Some versions of Evernote enable you to color-code notebooks and give them custom names. Integrated search tools allow you to quickly locate and access text and/or content stored within notes or notebooks, although only certain paid Evernote plans allow for the contents of attached files to be searched from within Evernote.

You're able to create as many notebooks as you need to properly store and organize notes. You can create separate notebooks to store and organize notes related to meetings, specific projects, research, or clients, for example. All of your content is automatically saved within your cloud-based account. (Local storage of content on your computer or mobile device is only available with certain paid plans.)

In Practice

Use Tags and Geo-Tags to Organize Information

Within each note, you're able to link an unlimited number of tags. A tag is a searchable and sortable keyword you want to associate with a note. You're able to add to a note as many separate tags as you desire. A centralized list of the tags you use within Evernote is maintained for you. For example, if a note is a summary of a meeting, sample tags might be "meeting," "sales meeting," "meeting agenda," "meeting outcome," "meeting synopsis," or "meeting handouts."

It's also possible to associate a location with each note (which is also referred to as a geo-tag). After a location has been added, you're able to sort and search through notes or notebooks based on location. You do this using Evernote's Atlas feature, which you can learn more about by visiting https://help.evernote.com/hc/en-us/articles/209005037.

Evernote's Data-Syncing and File-Sharing Tools

Be default, as you compose and edit content within Evernote, all your notes and notebook content are saved automatically within your online Evernote account. That content can automatically sync between two or more of your own computers and mobile devices that are linked to the same Evernote account (the number of devices depends on the type of account you have).

To ensure that the automatic data-syncing feature works properly, you must sign in to the Evernote software or mobile app on each device that you want to have syncing with the cloud. For your notes and notebooks to sync across all of your computers and mobile devices, you need to sign in with each computer or device using the same Evernote account information.

If you're using a version of Evernote that enables you to share with others, you can share a specific note or an entire notebook with specific other people. Simply click the Share option or icon to access the Share menu (see Figure 9.6).

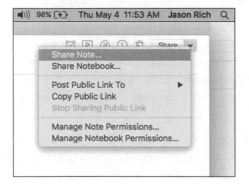

FIGURE 9.6   Use the Share menu (shown on a Mac) to share a specific note or entire notebook.

When you share a note or notebook, you can indicate whether the recipient will be able to read the note; read and edit the note; or read, edit, and share the note with others (see Figure 9.7).

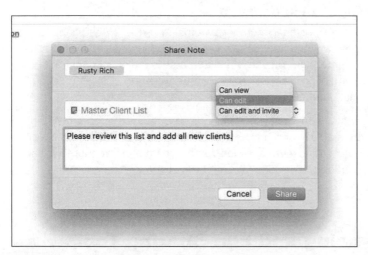

FIGURE 9.7   As the sender of a note or notebook, you decide what permissions to grant to the recipient(s).

Depending on the Share tool that you use, the recipients either receive an email inviting them to access the note or notebook using a secure webpage URL, or they receive an invitation in Evernote to access shared content (see Figure 9.8). When you prepare the invitation to share, you can personalize the message of the invitation.

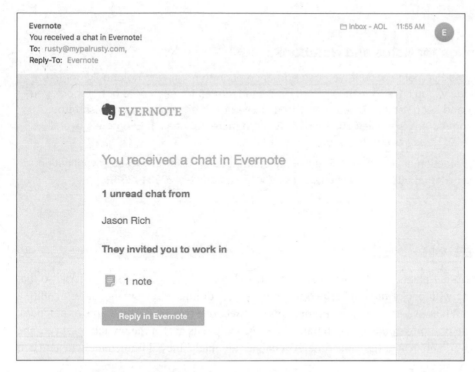

FIGURE 9.8 Recipients receive a notification when a note or notebook from another user is shared with them.

Once the recipient of a shared note or notebook accepts the invitation, the content is accessible to them via their own version of Evernote. If you later change your mind about sharing access to the note or notebook, you can revoke access. You can also use the Share menu to adjust the access permissions.

In Practice

Content Can Be Shared Publically

If you want to share content from a note or notebook in an unsecured and public way—such as through a social media post, blog post, mass email, website, or another form of digital communication—you can use Evernote's Post Public Link To or Copy Public Link commands. Just remember that when you share a note or notebook with someone else, and you give that person permission to edit and share the content, or when you share the content, you lose the ability to control what happens to that content in the future.

CAUTION

Data Encryption for Notes and Notebooks

When using a paid Evernote account, you can add encryption to notes and notebooks for extra security and privacy. You have to manually turn on these features for each note or notebook you want to protect and keep secure. To learn how to use Evernote's encryption tools, visit https://help.evernote.com/hc/en-us/articles/209005547. To learn more about all of Evernote's overall online security, visit https://evernote.com/security.

For additional protection of your overall Evernote account, you can set up two-step verification. Use the steps outlined at https://help.evernote.com/hc/en-us/articles/208314238.

Collaboration

With some subscription plans, you're able to activate the online, real-time collaboration tools so that you can collaborate with one or more other people on creating, editing, or reviewing content within a specific notebook. When Evernote's collaboration tools are used, one person creates a note or notebook and then invites one or more people to collaborate. After the recipients accept the invitations, everyone is able to view and edit content at the same time. As changes are made, they'll immediately be updated on all collaborators' screens.

Collaborators can easily refer to older versions of a note and take advantage of Evernote's live presentation tools, which allow one user to use screen-sharing features to highlight or bring attention to specific content as other users watch their respective screens.

The benefit to Evernote's collaboration tools is that everyone's work related to a note or notebook is stored in and accessible from one location. This includes file attachments as well as content that is embedded into notes. Evernote's messaging functionality enables collaborators to chat in real time using text-based messages (see Figure 9.9).

When collaboration tools are in use, the person who initiated the collaboration can add or revoke permissions for the other users. If Evernote Business accounts are being used for collaboration, the administrator also has the ability to handle permissions and access to specific content that's stored within notes and notebooks.

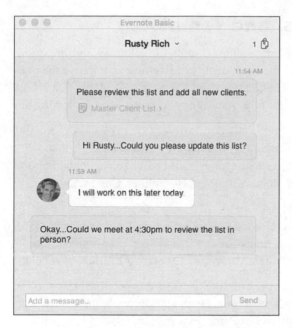

FIGURE 0.0 From within Evernote, two or more users can use a real-time chat feature to correspond via text messaging.

In Practice

Offline Editing Is Permissible

When collaborators with a Plus, Premium, or Business account take advantage of Evernote's offline options, a user can work with a note or notebook while not connected to the Internet, and as soon as that user's computer or mobile device reestablishes its Internet connection, all changes to the content sync with the cloud. All collaborators with access to that note or notebook receive the latest version of the content after it syncs.

Changes or edits made by specific users are identified, so all collaborators can see what was changed, who made the changes, and when the changes were made.

FYI: True Collaboration Requires a Paid Subscription

Although you can use the free version of Evernote, to truly benefit from the real-time collaboration and communication tools offered, it's necessary to have a paid Evernote account. Before making this investment, look carefully at what's offered by other online collaboration tools for content creation, including Google G Suite (which is covered in Chapter 10, "Working in Google's G Suite") and Office 365 (covered more in Chapter 11, "Using Microsoft Office 365 for Collaboration and File Sharing"), to determine which service provides the tools you need at the most affordable price per user.

Add-Ons, Third-Party Apps, and Templates

Many add-ons from Evernote and third parties provide additional tools for gathering and importing content into notes. These add-ons and apps enhance the functionality of Evernote or improve the integration of Evernote with other tools. To discover what add-ons and software is available that works directly with Evernote, visit the Evernote App Center (https://appcenter.evernote.com). Following are just a tiny handful of the add-ons that are available:

- Evernote's Web Clipper (https://evernote.com/products) is a free web browser add-on that makes it easy to grab the contents of an entire webpage (or even just part of a page) and import it directly into an Evernote note. Web Clipper works with Internet Explorer, Chrome, Firefox, and Safari web browsers.

- The Scannable mobile app (https://evernote.com/products/scannable/), which works with iOS devices, uses the built-in camera as a portable scanner for digitizing paper-based content. The photographed ("scanned") pages are imported directly into a user-specified Evernote notebook.

- Evernote Business for Salesforce (https://appcenter.evernote.com/app/evernote-business-for-salesforce/web-apps) integrates Evernote Business accounts with many types of paid Salesforce accounts, so content and information can easily be imported, exported, and shared between these two cloud-based services.

- If you have a newer tablet that allows users to write or draw on the tablet's screen with a stylus (such as the iPad Pro with Apple Pencil), you can use Evernote's Penultimate (https://evernote.com/products/penultimate/) to create handwritten or hand-drawn notes that are transferred directly into an Evernote note. This app enables you to handwrite content, rather than typing it, to embed it into your notes.

In Practice

Office 365 Offers Its Own Note-Taking and Collaboration Tools

Evernote differentiates itself by offering powerful note taking and information gathering tools, which can be used by individual users or teams collaborating together in the cloud. Although Microsoft Office files and documents can be imported into or attached to Evernote notes, it's important to understand that Microsoft Office 365 applications all have file-sharing and collaboration tools of their own built in.

Office 365 (which is covered within Chapter 11) includes Microsoft OneNote, which is a note-taking and information-gathering application that's similar in functionality to Evernote. If you're already using Office, it might make more sense to use OneNote, as well as the file-sharing and collaboration tools built into the various other Office applications, rather than adopting a separate application, such as Evernote.

One way for beginners to get up and running using Evernote for collecting and organizing specific types of information, particularly in a collaborative situation, is to use optional Evernote templates. Templates can help you set up some common types of notes with appropriate formatting, so that you don't have to start from scratch. Some of the Evernote templates available include Company Directory, Employee Handbook, Customer/Client Consulting Session Details, Customer/Client Relationship Management, Incident Response, Expense Tracker, Marketing Calendar, Conference Session Notes, Meeting Agenda, Phone Log, Project Plan, and Applicant Tracker.

You can find information about how to use templates, as well as links to specific templates, at https://help.evernote.com/hc/en-us/articles/209006007-Tools-Templates or https://help.evernote.com/hc/en-us/articles/210176028-How-to-Save-time-with-templates.

Ten additional templates, including Meeting Notes, Employee Goals, Project Budget, Work Order, and Business Trip Checklist, are available at https://blog.evernote.com/blog/2017/02/14/solve-small-business-secret-problem-take-evernote-work-free-business-templates.

Chapter 10

Working in Google's G Suite

This chapter covers the following:

- What's included with G Suite and how the suite's tools work seamlessly together
- Ways to use email, shared calendars, online chats, video conferencing, shared files, and real-time collaboration tools to make working with others more productive
- How to implement G Suite's security and compliance features to protect your data, files, and privacy

Google (www.google.com) is much more than the world's most popular Internet search engine. The company also offers more than a dozen popular online applications that are used by millions of people worldwide. G Suite offers a low-cost and comprehensive collection of Google's online applications that are designed to provide business professionals with a complete cloud-computing solution.

Google G Suite Overview

Throughout this book, you've read about separate solutions that handle video conferencing, group messaging, file storage, file sharing, and real-time collaboration for working with data, documents, and files. The goal of G Suite is to offer a complete cloud-based solution to handle all of these tasks, and more, for a low monthly subscription fee per user. Unlike the free versions of Google apps, G Suite provides an entirely ad-free environment, as well as added security and account management tools.

FYI: G Suite Has Plenty of Users

G Suite, which was formerly known as Google Apps for Work, launched in August in 2006 and was renamed in September 2016. It has evolved into a comprehensive cloud-based toolset. As of January 2017, G Suite was used by more than three million paying businesses.

The focus of G Suite is enhancing and streamlining communication, real-time collaboration, file sharing, and file storage while providing security and administration tools that can be managed by an in-house administrator. In its current iteration, G Suite comprises the following online applications:

- **Admin:** A comprehensive toolset for managing teams, groups, or employees using G Suite. The assigned administrator for an organization can quickly add users, manage devices, configure and manage organization-wide security settings, and monitor user activity.

- **G Suite Training:** An online collection of tutorials, how-to articles and videos, as well as an interactive Help feature that assists G Suite users in becoming more proficient using each of the suite's tools.

- **Google Calendar:** An individual and group scheduling and time-management application that can sync data with Microsoft Outlook and other tools.

- **Google Cloud Search:** A comprehensive search tool that allows users to quickly search through content created or managed by any G Suite application and that's stored within the cloud.

- **Google Docs:** A full-featured word processor, similar to Microsoft Word, that offers built-in file-sharing and collaboration tools.

- **Google Drive:** A cloud-based file-storage and file-sharing solution that can be used on its own or in conjunction with other Google apps for automatic file, data, document, and content storage. On its own, Drive works very much like Box, Dropbox, or OneDrive.

- **Google Forms:** A tool for creating, distributing, and analyzing the response from digital forms, surveys, and other interactive documents.

- **Google Hangout Meet:** A secure video-conferencing and virtual meeting tool designed for business.

- **Google Mail (Gmail):** Full email account management services that meet all current security and compliance regulations (particularly when used in conjunction with Google Vault). Provides a customized email address that features the *name@username*.com format, as opposed to a *name@*gmail.com format.

- **Google Sheets:** A spreadsheet tool, similar to Microsoft Excel, that offers built-in file-sharing and collaboration tools.

- **Google Sites**: A website creation and management tool.

- **Google Slides**: A digital slide presentation tool, similar to PowerPoint.

- **Google Vault:** An archiving tool that can be used to store emails, chat transcripts, and other important information in a way that makes it easy to create audit reports, search for content, and adhere to compliance regulations.

- **Google+:** A social media-like service for sharing topic-specific ideas and information.

Unlike other business application suites, all of the G Suite applications are based entirely online. As a result, all users are always working with the most up-to-date version of the application. There's no need to worry about manually installing software updates or security patches.

In Practice

Google Applications Can Import and Export Content

Docs, Sheets, and Slides are all compatible with popular file formats used by competing applications. As a result, a Microsoft Word document, for example, can be opened and worked with using Docs (and vice versa), and an Excel file is mostly compatible with Sheets (and vice versa). The same is true when working with Slides and PowerPoint. In general, this document or file cross-compatibility makes it possible for G Suite users to easily exchange files with Microsoft Office or Office 365 users, but there can be some incompatibility.

For example, when transferring any documents or files between applications, such as Word and Docs, formatting and fonts may not be fully compatible. For example, if a Word document is created and formatted using specific fonts and typestyles that are not built into or accessible using Docs, the Docs application substitutes what it perceives to be a similar font. This has the potential to negatively impact the appearance of a formatted document.

CAUTION

Internet Connectivity Is a Must-Have

The drawback to G Suite applications is that for users to have full access to all content stored in the cloud, they need a continuous (high-speed) Internet connection. Functionality and access to data is hindered, or in some cases not possible, if a user is working from a computer that's not connected to the Internet or is connected to a slow Internet connection from a remote location.

Although you can use each of the G Suite applications on its own, most are designed to fully integrate with one another to create a seamless, cloud-based work environment. For example, virtual meetings and conference calls can be scheduled through Calendar. Data, documents, and files that are created, viewed, or edited using Docs, Forms, Sheets, or Slides are automatically stored online within the user's Google Drive account. Forms or questionnaires created using Forms can be distributed via Gmail, and the results can be analyzed and viewed within Sheets.

A single Google account grants users access to all of the different Google tools and applications. The applications are accessible from any Internet-connected computer.

> ### In Practice
>
> ### Real-Time Collaboration Works with Most Google Apps
>
> Docs, Sheets, and Slides all include similar real-time collaboration tools that allow two or more people to securely work on the same document or file at the same time but from different locations, regardless of what type of equipment they're using. This ensures file compatibility and that everyone is always able to access and work with the latest version of a file.

G Suite Plans and Pricing

G Suite offers easy-to-understand pricing for individual and business plans. Individuals can use most of the separate applications offered by G Suite for free and link them with the same Google account. For teams, groups, or businesses, two different G Suite plans are offered. With either of these two plans, users can be added or deleted at any time.

G Suite Basic

Priced at $5.00 per user, per month, the G Suite Basic plan includes

- 30GB of online storage space

- A business email account (via Gmail)

- Smart shared calendars

- Access to Google's video-conferencing tools

- Full access to Docs, Sheets, and Slides

- Basic security and administration controls

- 24/7 access to tech support via phone, email, or online

A user's business-related Gmail email account is personalized using their name and company name (*name*@*company*.com). You can also have free alias accounts, such as sales@*company*.com, press@*company*.com, marketing@*company*.com, or support@*company*.com, and they don't count as separate users.

G Suite Business

Priced at $10.00 per user, per month, the G Suite Business plan includes unlimited storage per user for their data, documents, files, and content, as well as whatever additional file storage is needed for archiving purposes, such as storing emails and chat transcripts for compliance regulations. (For organizations with fewer than five users, each user's online storage is capped at 1TB.)

In addition to the functionality offered by the Basic plan, Business plan subscribers get automatic archiving of email and chats. The Business plan also includes standardized retention policies for all users within an organization, which means that backups of important data, documents, and files are automatically created and stored in the cloud.

eDiscovery, which allows administrators to track user activities and generate audit reports, is provided for emails, chats, and files. It's also possible to access the detailed history or activities related to specific files or documents. Additional security functionality, including data loss prevention for Gmail and Drive and the ability to integrate Gmail with compliant third-party tools, is provided.

FYI: G Suite Caters to Many Industry-Specific Needs

G Suite caters to the needs of many specific industries, including retail, manufacturing, professional services, technology, government, small business, new businesses, enterprise, and healthcare. It's especially robust in areas that address security compliance issues.

Getting Started with G Suite

Adopting an entirely new cloud-computing platform, even one that the majority of your employees might already be familiar with, can be a daunting task. To reduce the possibility of user error, and to take an organized approach to adopting G Suite within any organization, Google offers a handful of tools to make the migration of users and data as straightforward and secure as possible.

According to Google, the following are the core steps in this process:

1. **Set up G Suite:** Set up your organization's domain using the Setup Wizard (see Figure 10.1) to create an administrator account, and then add up to 10 initial users for a pilot program. You can manually add more users after you've completed the Setup Wizard. This initial setup also involves redirecting company and individual employee email accounts to the newly established Gmail accounts.

2. **Run a pilot:** Set up a five-step test program among a small team or group of employees. With any cloud service, it's a good idea to have a small team begin using the tools before you have your entire organization adopt something entirely new. The pilot program will help you determine whether G Suite meets the needs of the team and the organization as a whole. For more information about the pilot program, visit https://gsuite.google.com/setup/resources/pilot/.

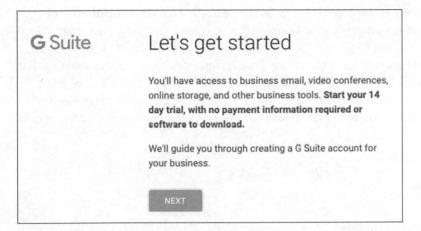

FIGURE 10.1   The G Suite Setup Wizard helps you set up and customize user accounts and transfer relevant email, contacts, data, documents, and files to each new account.

FYI: Free Trial

Google offers a 14-day free trial for any G Suite plan and includes support. To sign up for the free trial, visit https://gsuite.google.com.

3. **Add remaining users:** If the pilot is successful, create accounts for the other users in the organization and then have them sync their existing email, files, and data with the G Suite applications as needed.

4. **Prepare your communications:** Use the series of resources that Google has prepared to inform your employees of the transition to G Suite. The resources include a series of templates that can be used to compose emails and announcements. You can preview these tools at https://gsuite.google.com/setup/resources/templates.

5. **Migrate email, calendar, contacts, and files:** Use Google's free migration tools to import email accounts, calendar data, and contacts into G Suite. You can import data from Microsoft Exchange, IBM Notes, or another IMAP server. To learn about the available data-migration tools, visit https://support.google.com/a/answer/6250450.

6. **Set up mobile devices:** Set up additional security features for users who will be using a smartphone or tablet to work with G Suite applications. Each user will need to install mobile apps on the devices that are to be used. A summary of how to prepare mobile devices to use G Suite and the Google apps that are required is at https://support.google.com/a/answer/1734200.

7. **Train all team members on how to use the G Suite applications, communications tools, and collaboration tools:** Visit the G Suite Learning Center (https://gsuite.google.com/learning-center) to find a series of quick-start user guides, how-to articles, and video tutorials. You can find additional training resources at https://gsuite.google.com/setup/resources/user-training. For organizations transitioning from a different cloud-based service, Google offers special guides and tutorials to make the transition go smoothly. Visit https://gsuite.google.com/training/ to access the tutorials. If an organization has more than 200 users, Google recommends deploying its G Suite Enterprise solutions.

In Practice

Choose and Train Your Administrator

Especially if you plan to integrate G Suite into a mid-to-large size organization, it's essential that the person you assign to be the G Suite administrator understands your business, knows how to work with your business's technology, has a thorough understanding of G Suite, and understands how to manage its users. It will be this person who controls and sets the security and compliance tools built into G Suite and who oversees each employee's account.

After you decide to adopt G Suite, consider having the person who will be the administrator participate in the Administrator Fundamentals Course (https://gsuite.google.com/setup/resources/admin-training/) provided by Google. You might even want the person to earn the Google Certified Associate – G Suite Administrator designation (https://cloud.google.com/certification/gsuite-administrator). Not only will a Certified Administrator help your organization be able to migrate to G Suite more smoothly, this person will be able to help protect your organization's data, documents, files, and content during the migration process and beyond.

FYI: An Expert Offers Reasons to Test Drive Any Cloud Service

According to Ross Smith, Chief Architect at PITSS (www.pitss.com), "Any tool you want to try should only be adopted after a reasonable pilot by a limited test audience. Many cloud platforms structure their user agreements to facilitate this. In fact, many offer small-team licenses for free. You don't know how well a cloud solution will behave until you've learned to live with it a little while and have observed where the problems crop up."

Assuming serious problems don't arise, Smith suggests that you determine in advance, whether "the subscription costs are reasonable, and if the service will scale with your growth, but still remain an affordable solution. Also, determine if it's trainable and teachable with a little hands-on guidance, and if the service provider is a stable company with a good support line."

He added, "The important thing is not that you have the perfect tools, but that they serve a more perfect process, which has much more to do with your habits than their features. If you aren't working in a vacuum, you'll have to deal with someone else's file share and chat system eventually. That team will certainly use tools other than yours. As long as human beings keep making software, working across alternate tools will simply be our reality. The best thing you can do is admit that the one true platform is a myth."

Collaborating Using Docs

G Suite users can plan virtual meetings and collaboration sessions via Calendar or Gmail, for example, and then participants can use one of Google's online applications to work on the same file or document. For example, to handle word processing tasks to compose, review, or edit a document, G Suite users rely on Google Docs (see Figure 10.2).

FYI: Docs, Sheets, and Slides All Share Similar Collaboration Tools

Docs, Sheets, Slides, and several other G Suite applications have similar collaboration and file-sharing tools and similar user interfaces.

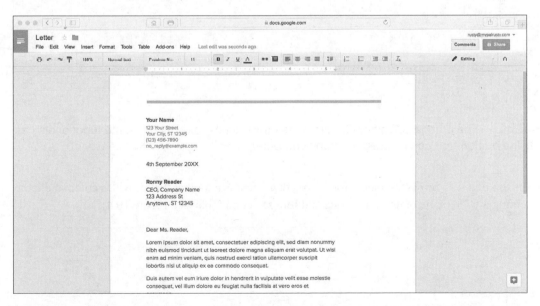

FIGURE 10.2 Google Docs is an entirely online-based word processor that offers built in collaboration and file-sharing functionality.

Docs is a full-featured word processor, but it works entirely from your web browser rather than from software running on your computer. There's no separate software to download and install. As one or more people are working with a document, Docs automatically saves the work to a designated Drive folder. Smartphone and tablet users need to download the free Google Docs mobile app, which grants them access to word-processing tools that they can use online or offline. Figure 10.3 shows Google Docs running on an iPhone.

FIGURE 10.3   The iPhone edition of Google Docs offers almost exactly the same functionality as the online edition that can be used from any computer.

Near the top of a web browser window for a Docs document is a toolbar that provides command icons representing a wide range of text formatting and font selection tools (see Figure 10.4).

Toolbar

FIGURE 10.4   On-screen icons can be used to handle many text formatting tasks as you're working within Docs.

Pull-down menus—such as File (see Figure 10.5), Edit, View, Insert, Format, Tools, Table, Add-ons, and Help—also grant users access to the majority of word-processing features and functions offered by Docs.

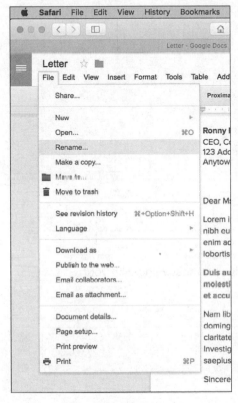

FIGURE 10.5 Additional document management and formatting functionality is available from the Docs pull-down menus.

When working with two or more people, users can hold real-time discussions using the app's built-in Chat feature (see Figure 10.6), or users can include comments within a document and address them to an individual person or to all collaborators (see Figure 10.7).

Chat window

FIGURE 10.6   Use the Docs Chat tool to communicate via text messaging with your collaborators as you work on a document.

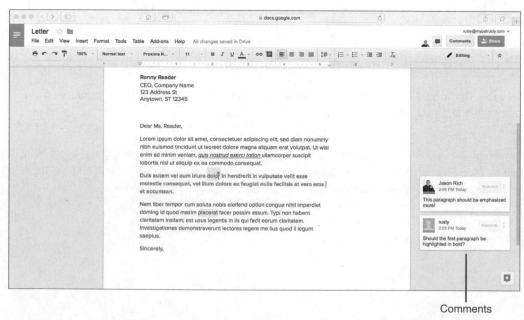

Comments

FIGURE 10.7   Use a virtual sticky note to pose questions or share thoughts about a document without actually embedding them within the document.

Changes or additions made to a document are reflected immediately on each user's screen. Docs also maintains a complete revision history for each document and allows users to refer to older versions of the document or undo any changes, deletions, or edits that were made accidently. Docs allows you to import Microsoft Word and PDF files, and you can use it to export work in the .docx, .pdf, .odt, .rtf, .txt, and .html file formats.

FYI: Work History Does Not Count Against Someone's Online Storage Allocation

Even if someone is using a G Suite account with an online storage limit, as documents are edited or revised, Docs maintains a complete revision history indefinitely, and the storage space needed for unlimited revisions is provided by Google.

It's important to remember that Docs is primarily an online application, which means Internet access is required to use the app and to collaborate with other users. Docs mobile app users can work offline and then sync their work with their Drive accounts when an Internet connection is reestablished. When using Docs on a computer via the Google Chrome web browser, you can do some offline work on Docs documents.

When using Docs' built-in real-time collaboration or file-sharing tools, the user who initially shares the file can determine exactly who has access to it. Either this person or the G Suite administrator can also determine if collaborators or people the document gets shared with are able to edit, view, or add comments to each document.

Many third-party add-ons are available to enhance the file-sharing and collaboration functionality of Docs. Add-ons can provide other types of capabilities, such as additional formatting, word look up, and mail merge functionality.

In Practice

Where to Find Google Docs Add-Ons

The G Suite Marketplace (https://gsuite.google.com/marketplace) is the place to find add-ons for Google applications, including Docs, Sheets, and Slides. You can also use the Google search engine (www.google.com) to search the phrase *Google Docs Add-Ons* to find add-ons that might not be in the G Suite Marketplace. You'll also find many articles in publications like *InfoWorld, TechWorld,* and *BetterCloud.com* that rank and describe top Google Docs add-ons.

Use these steps to begin a real-time collaboration session using Docs:

1. Load a document or begin composing a document from scratch.

2. Click the Share button in the top-right corner of the browser window to open the Share with Others window (see Figure 10.8).

3. Enter the email addresses for the people you want to collaborate with.

4. Click the Permissions button (which looks like a pencil) to determine what the collaborators will be allowed to do. Options include Can Edit, Can Comment, Can View.

5. Optionally adjust other options offered by the Sharing Settings menu to prevent others from changing access to the file and adding new people or to prevent others from downloading, printing, or copying the document.

FIGURE 10.8   You can invite one or more additional people to collaborate on a document in real time, even if they're not G Suite subscribers.

Switch Between Editing Modes

While working with collaborators on a document, you can select one of three editing modes. Editing mode allows all collaborators to make additions, changes, or deletions to the document in real time. In Suggesting mode, others can make suggested edits, additions, or deletions, but their actions aren't applied to the document until the document owner has approved them. Viewing mode allows collaborators to simply read and print the document but not alter it.

People invited to collaborate on a document receive an email containing a secure link to that document (see Figure 10.9). As soon as the recipient clicks the link, a version of Docs opens on their screen, and the shared document is accessible to them. Documents can also be shared via Google+, Facebook, or Twitter, or you can make the document public by copying the URL and pasting it into other applications.

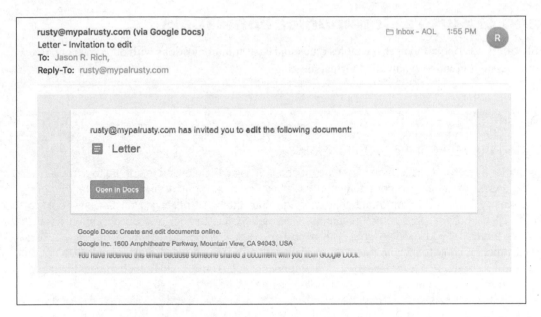

FIGURE 10.9   People invited to collaborate on a Docs document will receive an invitation email like this one.

Based on the permissions set by the sender, the collaborator can view, edit, and/or add comments. The Chat tool serves as an in-app conversation tool where text messages can be sent in real time between collaborators as they're working on a document.

The Comment tool allows individual collaborators to attach a text-based comment (which is like a virtual sticky note) to a document. These comments are displayed in the right margin. Other users can respond to a Comment or click the Resolve (hide) button when the issue the comment pertains to has been resolved. Resolved comments aren't deleted, however. Users can refer to comments at anytime, add a response, or re-open a resolved comment.

The name and profile photo of the user who posts the comment is displayed in the Comment box. The date and time each comment was created or modified, as well as the name and profile photo of anyone who responds to a comment, are also displayed (refer to Figure 10.7).

Any changes or edits made to the document by any of the collaborators are displayed in real time on all collaborators' screens. For a short time, an icon with the user's initials is displayed near the change within the document.

Because Docs is based entirely within a browser window, a user can work with multiple documents simultaneously by opening two or more browser windows on their screen.

Using G Suite's Communications Tools

G Suite offers a variety of tools that enables quick and easy communications with others via email, text (group) messaging, video calling, and virtual meetings.

In Practice

Making the Most of the G Suite Tools

In order for a team or organization to get the most out of using G Suite and to adhere to compliance regulations while keeping all communications and work stored together and accessible from one cloud-based location, it's important that users get into the habit of relying on G Suite tools to handle all of their relevant communications, file-sharing, file-storage, and collaboration needs. In other words, if you need to chat with a co-worker or collaborator about a document, use the communications tools built into G Suite rather than leaving a voice mail message, faxing a document, or sending a text message using another service. The G Suite apps can only track and store communications and work that is handled using G Suite.

Hangouts Meet

Hangouts Meet offers an easy way to set up and host secure virtual meetings and group video conferencing. It provides the same core benefits as meeting face-to-face, but it doesn't require everyone to actually gather in one place. This saves on travel time, and often makes scheduling easier because participants can join a meeting from their Internet-connected computers, smartphones, or tablets from virtually anywhere.

One of the benefits of G Suite is that Calendar can be used to share meeting invitations, coordinate schedules, and send email invites in a manner that's highly automated. Meetings held using Hangout Meets can be attended by anyone, even those who aren't G Suite users.

Google+

Google+ is a social media tool that allows groups of people to share topic-specific information and ideas in a less formal way—not necessarily in real time. You can adjust the security settings so that interactions can be kept between just a restricted group within the company or be opened up to approved vendors—or even the general public.

Gmail

Gmail on its own is a free email service available to anyone who wants to utilize a *username*@gmail. com email account. When used as part of a G Suite account, a user's Gmail email address can be customized to a company's domain name (*user*@*company*.com), and all work-related email can be managed through a user's Gmail account.

Gmail works seamlessly with Google Calendar, Microsoft Outlook, Apple Mail, and other popular email clients, and it keeps track of someone's contacts, so managing and organizing incoming and outgoing emails becomes an easier task. G Suite also archives all emails for compliance purposes, and allows other Google functionality, like Google Translate (a language translator), to be used from within Gmail.

In Practice

Start a Video Chat from Your Inbox

As a G Suite user, you're able to add anyone you exchange emails with to your Hangouts Chat list with just a few mouse clicks. After you've done this, you can be reviewing an incoming email and launch a video call with that person. A basic Google account allows for up to nine participants in a Google Hangout video call. This limit is higher for Business users.

Unlike a free Gmail account, G Suite-related email accounts are ad-free and include 24/7 support, as well as additional security-related features and functions.

Chapter 11

Using Microsoft Office 365 for Collaboration and File Sharing

This chapter covers the following:

- How Office 365 differs from other editions of Microsoft Office
- How to choose an Office 365 subscription plan that's best suited to you and your company
- What file-sharing and collaboration tools are built into Office 365 applications
- How Office 365 integrates with many other popular cloud-based services

Microsoft Office 365 is a subscription-based version of Microsoft Office that gives individual users access to the latest editions of popular Office applications from all of their computers and mobile devices. Built-in file-syncing, file-sharing, and collaboration tools that work with Microsoft OneDrive and other cloud-based services make it easy to sync, manage, and share all Office-related documents, files, and data.

Office 365 Overview

Even with plenty of competition from Apple's iWork apps, Google G Suite, and other companies' productivity suites, Microsoft's Word, Excel, PowerPoint, Outlook, and OneNote continue to be the most popular, powerful, and feature-packed options when it comes to handling everyday tasks like word processing, spreadsheet management, digital slides presentations, email management, scheduling, and note taking. In addition to working on their own and providing built-in file-sharing and collaboration tools, Office 365 applications integrate with several of Microsoft's other services, including OneDrive, SharePoint, Skype for Business, and Exchange. (Read Chapter 12, "Handling Large-Group Collaboration with Microsoft Exchange Online" for more information about Exchange.) Plus, the majority of the other cloud-based services that are used in business also somehow integrate with Office 365.

FYI: How Many People Use Microsoft Office 365?

Office 365 now has more than 100 million monthly, active commercial users worldwide. Outlook and Exchange email and calendar tools, for example, are used by 04 percent of Fortuno 100 companies.

Between early 2016 and mid-2017, the use of Office 365's collaborative applications and tools has more than doubled, and at any given time, OneDrive for Business now stores more than 60 petabytes of data.

In the past, individual users could purchase each Microsoft Office application separately or pay a flat fee to acquire the entire Office suite. A separate version of the applications needed to be purchased for each computer they'd be used on. Then, every year or two, a user needed to purchase a software upgrade, to be able to continue using the latest versions of these applications. More recently, Microsoft has made some changes to keep up with competition and demand from consumers by introducing Office 365 and a subscription-based price model. Now, users can pay a flat monthly fee for unlimited access to all of the popular Office applications. As long as a subscription is active, it includes unlimited updates.

Office can be installed on 1, 5, or 10 of a user's computers and/or mobile devices. (The number of devices is determined by the type of subscription plan.) This model is particularly useful because all the Office 365 applications are fully integrated with Microsoft OneDrive and can be set up to automatically and securely back up and sync all data, documents, files, and content via the cloud.

The goal of Office 365 is not only to give users access to Microsoft's entire suite of popular applications but also to allow a user to use the cloud for backing up and syncing files among all computers and mobile devices she uses. For example, a user can begin working on a Word document on her Windows PC and then continue working with that same document on a MacBook Air notebook computer— or a smartphone, or tablet—from anywhere she happens to be, as long as an Internet connection is available. As the user creates or modifies work, the latest revision of the file is immediately uploaded to the cloud, from where it can be synced with all of the user's other devices.

In addition, Office applications are typically cross-compatible with competing applications, so a document composed using Word can be opened and edited using Apple Pages, Google Docs, or another popular word processor (and vice versa). Likewise, a spreadsheet created using Excel can be opened and used with Apple Numbers or Google Sheets, or another popular spreadsheet management application. Meanwhile, it does not matter whether the Windows, Mac, online, or mobile device version of an Office application is used, as Office files and documents are cross-platform compatible.

Each Office 365 application also has built-in file-sharing and collaboration tools, which make it easier than ever to use the cloud so that two or more people in different locations can collaborate when working on the same Office-related documents or files. An Office 365 subscriber can share Office files or documents with non-subscribers. The collaboration tools integrate seamlessly with other Office applications, like SharePoint, Exchange, Skype for Business, Microsoft Teams, and Yammer, for example, making it easier for people to communicate, interact, and share content.

FYI: Full Versions for Mobile Devices

In addition to file compatibility across the Windows PC and Mac platforms, Microsoft offers full versions of its popular Office applications for iOS and Android smartphones and tablets, which also fully integrate with Microsoft OneDrive. As a result, all of a user's Office-related content is always accessible to them and can easily be accessed and shared with others from virtually anywhere.

There are also entirely cloud-based versions of some Office applications, including Word, Excel, PowerPoint, Outlook, and OneNote, that can be used from any web browser. A paid Office 365 subscription includes unlimited access to the available online versions of Office apps, although in most cases, users rely on the Office software that's installed on their computers because these versions are more robust and feature-packed than the online versions.

In Practice

Office Applications Get Downloaded and Installed

After any Office 365 subscription is paid for and a Microsoft account is active, each user needs to download and install the Microsoft Office applications onto each of their computers or mobile devices. The number of computers or mobile devices that a user can install the applications onto varies based on the subscription plan. The less feature-packed online editions of the Office apps can be used from any computer's web browser after a user signs in to the Microsoft website using her Microsoft account.

Windows PC and Mac users should visit https://stores.office.com/myaccount/home.aspx to manage their Microsoft accounts, download all included Office applications at once, and then activate each application by signing in to it using their Microsoft account.

To download and install the separate Office mobile apps onto your smartphone or tablet, visit the app store for your mobile device. Find, select, download, and install Word, Excel, PowerPoint, Outlook, OneNote, and/or OneDrive. When you launch each app for the first time, sign in to your Microsoft account to activate it and unlock all of each app's functionality.

One of the biggest benefits to Office 365 subscribers is the ability to work with the latest version of each application. As Microsoft releases updates, users can automatically download and install them. Keep in mind that only one active Microsoft account is required per user. A single Microsoft account can be used to activate or sign in to Microsoft Office applications running on any of a user's computers and/or mobile devices, as well as the online editions of the Office apps, as long as the paid subscription plan supports more than one computer or mobile device.

FYI: Managing Accounts

To create or manage an individual user's Microsoft account to update billing information, create a user profile, and/or change an account password, visit https://account.microsoft.com/account. The person assigned to be a company or team's Office 365 administrator can manage all user accounts from a single website. To learn more about managing an administrator account, visit https://support.office.com/en-us and click the Admin tab.

Office 365 Subscription Plans and Pricing

All of the Microsoft Office 365 subscription plans include Word, Excel, PowerPoint, Outlook, and OneNote. Some plans also include Publisher and Access, as well as access to other Microsoft applications and online services, including Skype (or Skype for Business). All subscription plans include a cloud-based OneDrive account for each user. There are several different tiers of Office 365 Home, Office 365 Small Business, and Office 365 Enterprise plans, as well as separate plans that bundle Office 365 with other Microsoft services, such as Microsoft Exchange, so it's sometimes not clear what's included with each plan.

Microsoft Office 365 Home Subscription Plans

The two main Office 365 subscription plans, which are ideal for individual users, are Office 365 Personal ($69.99 per user, per year) and Office 365 Home ($99.99 per user, per year).

The Office 365 Personal plan includes Word, Excel, PowerPoint, Outlook, OneNote, Publisher (PC only) and Access (PC only), along with OneDrive and Skype. These applications can be installed on only one computer or mobile device. The provided OneDrive account includes 1TB of online storage.

The Office 365 Home plan includes all of the same applications as the Personal plan, but the applications can be installed and used, on an unlimited basis, by any combination of five computers or mobile devices that are linked to the same Microsoft account. Alternatively, up to five family members can install and use the Office applications on their computers or mobile devices, and each family member is provided with 1TB of OneDrive cloud storage space.

Microsoft Office 365 Small Business Subscription Plans

The two main Office 365 Small Business plans are Office 365 Business ($8.25 per user, per month) and Office 365 Business Premium ($12.50 per user, per month). These prices are based on an annual commitment. Both include the ability to install Word, Excel, PowerPoint, OneNote, and Outlook on any combination of up to five computers and mobile devices per user. The Business plan also includes OneDrive for Business, 1TB OneDrive online storage per user, and full access to the online versions of Word, Excel, PowerPoint, and Outlook.

The Business plan does not include hosted email or access to other Office applications and Microsoft services. This plan is available to companies with up to 300 users.

The Business Premium Plan also includes Microsoft Exchange Online hosted email with a custom email domain address (*username@yourcompany*.com) and the ability to use a cloud-based version of SharePoint to communicate and collaborate with others. This plan includes Skype for Business, one-to-one and group chats using Microsoft Teams, team planning using Microsoft Planner, and the ability to collaborate and communicate with team members using Microsoft Yammer and Skype for Business. This plan is also available to companies with up to 300 users.

In Practice

Admin Responsibilities for Office 365 Management

After a company signs up for Office 365 Business for its employees, one person is assigned the role of Global Administrator. This is the person who is given control over all accounts and who has the ability to add or delete individual user accounts.

Microsoft has established several different administrator roles, which can be handled by one person or separate people. The Global Administrator has full access to all administrative features built into Office 365 applications and services. The person who initially establishes the Microsoft account for a business is by default assigned this role.

Other admin roles that can be assigned to different people include Billing Administrator, Exchange Administrator, SharePoint Administrator, Password Administrator, Skype for Business Administrator, Compliance Administrator, Service Administrator, and User Management Administrator.

All of the online-based tools available to the Global Administrator (and other administrators) are online. Visit https://support.office.com/en-us and click the Admin tab.

If your company lacks its own IT department or doesn't have the resources to manage the use of Office 365 applications by all of its employees, one solution is to hire an independent, third-party Microsoft Hosting Provider. Hiring this type of company can eliminate the need for an in-house, tech-savvy Microsoft Office 365 Global Administrator. Working with a Microsoft Hosting Provider offers a company more personalized technical support options and additional tools related to data security, email storage and retention, user training, and adherence to industry-specific compliance regulations.

> **FYI: More Information About Microsoft Hosting Providers**
>
> For more information, see the "Working with an Independent Microsoft Hosting Provider" section in Chapter 12.

Microsoft Office 365 Enterprise Subscription Plans

If your organization has more than 300 users, you can choose from several different Microsoft Office 365 Enterprise subscription plans, which range in price from $8.00 per month, per user, to $35.00 per month, per user. You can find more information about these plans at https://products.office.com/en-us/business/compare-more-office-365-for-business-plans.

> **FYI: Office 365 Meets Most Compliance Requirements**
>
> If your company must adhere to strict compliance regulations when managing data, files, and communications, Office 365 can be configured to adhere to these regulations, although in some cases additional software and/or services may be required. To learn more about achieving organizational compliance, and how to manage and protect data with Office 365, visit https://products.office.com/en-us/business/compliance-tools-ediscovery.
>
> Alternative subscription plans, such as Office 365 Enterprise E1, Office 365 ProPlus, Office 365 Enterprise E3, and Office 365 Enterprise E5, which are priced between $8.00 and $35.00 per month, per user, include Microsoft's eDiscovery tools, along with advanced data governance, auditing, data loss prevention, and security features. You can find additional information about these Office 365 subscription plans at https://products.office.com/en-us/business/compare-more-office-365-for-business-plans.

File-Sharing and Collaboration Tools

This section explains how to easily share Office-specific documents and files directly from an online-based OneDrive account or from within the individual Office applications.

File Sharing Directly from OneDrive

OneDrive comes preinstalled on Windows 10 PCs but can be integrated with most recent versions of the Windows operating system. It's a cloud-based file-storage, data-syncing, and file-sharing service that also integrates directly with Office 365 applications, as well as many other software packages and mobile apps. By downloading and installing the Microsoft OneDrive software onto a computer or a smartphone or tablet, you gain the ability to access and manage all your content that's stored within your cloud-based OneDrive account.

> **In Practice**
>
> ## OneDrive Services
>
> Whether you use OneDrive or OneDrive for Business, after the account is set up to work with the operating system for your computer or mobile device and also set up to work with Office applications, the OneDrive service stores, syncs, and makes your data, documents, files, and content available to share with others. However, you can also set up OneDrive to store your Office-related data, documents, and files locally so content is always available regardless of whether you have an Internet connection. Of course, after you re-establish an Internet connection, everything syncs with the OneDrive account. This happens automatically and in the background. At the time of writing, OneDrive doesn't store older versions of a file and make them available. When a file is updated or changed, the older version is overwritten and replaced. This will likely change in the future, however.
>
> You can also configure Office 365 to work with other cloud-based file-storage and file-sharing services, such as Dropbox or Box.com. That said, Office 365 users are encouraged, but not required, to use OneDrive or OneDrive for Business.

Any type of file can manually be copied or moved into your OneDrive account and stored online. You can manually create folders and subfolders within your OneDrive account to organize and manage their content. However, you can set up each of the Microsoft Office applications to automatically back up and sync all Office-related documents, data, and files with your OneDrive account, so that you can access content anytime, either from within a compatible Office application or by accessing the OneDrive account directly.

When it comes to file sharing, you can securely share with others files and folders that you have manually saved to your OneDrive account or that have been automatically synced or saved within the OneDrive account by an Office application. You do this using any web browser by visiting https:// onedrive.live.com or by using the OneDrive mobile app to access and select specific files or folders to share. You select one or more files or folders and then click the Share option (see Figure 11.1).

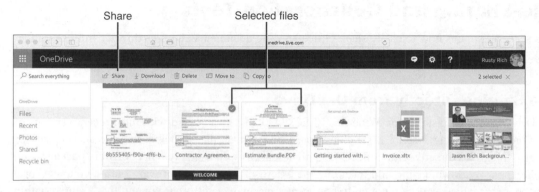

FIGURE 11.1   Manage and share content stored online, within a OneDrive account, by accessing the OneDrive website and signing in to your account.

The person sharing the content can then choose whether the recipient(s) of the content will be able to edit it or only view it (see Figure 11.2). To allow editing, add a check mark to the Allow Editing check box. To add an expiration date to the shared file, add a check mark to the Set Expiration Date option within the Share window and then adjust the expiration date.

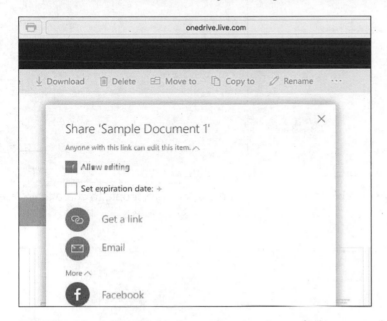

FIGURE 11.2   A file or folder's owner can set permissions associated with the content they're sharing.

You can share a file or folder privately via email, or you can copy the special link created by OneDrive and then share it by embedding it within a document or text message. You can even copy the link into a social media post, such as on Facebook, Twitter, or LinkedIn.

When you choose the Share via Email option, you're prompted to provide the email address for each person you want to share the selected file or folder with. You can also personalize a message that will be sent with the invitation (see Figure 11.3). When you click the Share button, each invitee receives an email that contains a secure URL to use to access the shared content (see Figure 11.4).

FIGURE 11.3   A file or folder owner is able to invite one or more additional people to share their content with.

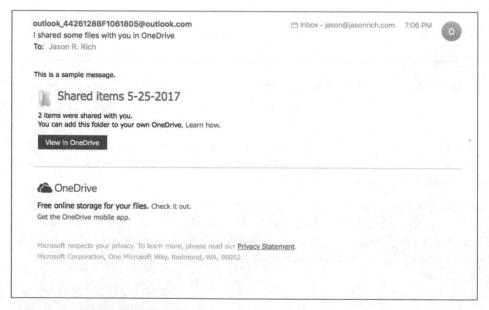

FIGURE 11.4   When someone is invited to access a file or document, he receives an email that contains a secure link to that content.

> **In Practice**
>
> ### Keep Track of Shared Files
>
> After you sign in to the OneDrive website, you can see all the different files and folders that are being shared, edit permissions, and see who specific files or folders are being shared with by clicking the Shared option along the left margin of the browser window. A similar Shared option is also available within the OneDrive mobile app.

Collaboration Tools Within Office Applications

Most Office 365 applications offer several built-in tools for sharing files and collaborating. After you've shared a file with someone else or with multiple people, the recipients take possession of the file and can work with it independently. Following are some of the things you can do with a shared document or file within an Office application (such as Word):

- The recipient can acquire a shared document and then view, edit, print, and share it with others, assuming the original document owner has not locked down the document in any way. If the owner has used the Protect Document feature (see Figure 11.5) that's built into many Office apps, he or she can add password protection and permissions to each document.

FIGURE 11.5 Word, Excel, and PowerPoint offer a Protect Document (or Protect File) feature that can be customized by the owner of the content.

In Practice

Using the Send As Attachment Feature

From within Word and most other Office applications, a document owner can opt to simply share it with others by attaching it to an outgoing email. When this feature is used, the recipients receive a copy of the document or file to work with it as they please. How the content owner configures the document (by turning on/off the Protect Document and Track Changes features) determines what recipients can actually do with the document.

To share a document or file via email, open it within the appropriate Office application, click the Share option, and then select the Send as Attachment option at the bottom of the Share pane (see Figure 11.6). Next, choose between keeping the file in its original file format or converting it to a PDF file before sharing it.

You can then compose a new outgoing email message, which already has the selected file attached to it. Fill in the To and Subject fields, and add text to the body of the email as needed. You can also modify the Cc:, Bcc:, and From fields, if necessary. Click the Send button to send the email to the desired recipient.

Recipients can locally store the attachment and then open and use it in any way they desire (based on how you set the Protect Document feature). As changes are made to the document, they are not automatically synced and shared among collaborators. The Send Attachment option is used to share a document or file from within an Office application that is not meant for collaboration.

- The owner or recipient can turn on the Track Changes feature so that every change made by each user within the document is recorded and displayed in a different color. Within the document's margins, each change is identified and logged by date and time, and the name of the person who made each edit is displayed (see Figure 11.7). The document owner can later accept or reject changes, and anyone can turn on or off the View Track Changes feature. When turned off, Word (or the Office application being used) continues to track all user changes in the background, but the document is displayed in one color, without any tracked changes indicated on the screen. This makes the document easier to read.

FIGURE 11.6 To email someone a file or folder from within an Office application, click the Share option and then choose Send as Attachment (shown here on a Windows PC).

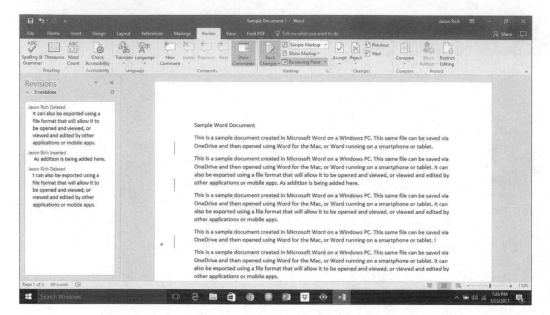

FIGURE 11.7   The Track Changes tools (shown here in Word) make it easier for people to collaborate and keep track of modifications made to a document.

■ People who access a document or file also have the ability to add comments to it. A Comment appears like a virtual sticky note within the document or file (see Figure 11.8) without altering the original content. Comments are color-coded by user. After someone composes and attaches a comment to a document or file, everyone who accesses or works with it is able to view and respond to the comment. It's a bit like having a text-message conversation directly within a document.

In Practice

Composing a Comment

To compose and add a comment (Word is used as the example here), position the cursor within the document at the location that relates to the comment to be added. Next, choose Insert and then Comment. Type the comment within the comment text box in the margin. Anyone can reply to a comment by clicking the Reply icon in the comment's window.

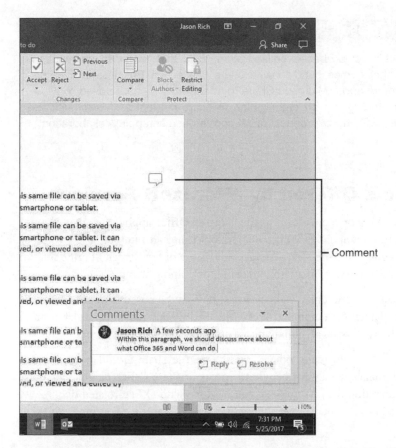

FIGURE 11.8   Comments can be added to a document. Other collaborators can read and respond to comments or add their own.

- Each user that makes changes to a document can use the Save As command to rename the document and then share the new version of the document with others. By renaming the document, a new version is created. Thus, all old versions of the document remain available for review. The drawback is that everyone needs to pay attention to file names, as well as the date and time information associated with a file, to ensure they're working with the latest or correct version.

- Multiple people can coauthor (collaborate on) a document or file using an Office application. This eliminates the need for the document to be manually sent back and forth between collaborators, because one file that's stored in the cloud becomes accessible to everyone, and as changes are made, they're immediately reflected on everyone's screen, or when all collaborators view the document or file. To do this, click the Share option and then click the Invite People option (rather than the Send Attachment option).

> **FYI: Learn More About Microsoft SharePoint**
>
> Microsoft SharePoint is a set of cloud-based collaboration tools that works in conjunction with Office applications and that comes bundled with some Office 365 Business and Enterprise subscriptions. To learn more about Microsoft SharePoint and how it can be used to allow co-workers or team members throughout an organization to share content and communicate using intranet sites and portals, visit https://products.office.com/en-us/sharepoint/collaboration.

Collaboration Tools Offered by Microsoft Services

While two or more people are working on a document or file using an Office application, they can use Skype (or Skype for Business) to communicate with collaborators using an Internet-based voice or video call or group instant messaging. One user can also take advantage of the Screen Sharing feature in Skype to showcase Office content to others in a virtual meeting or training session.

Depending on which Office 365 subscription plan each user has, it might be possible to use Microsoft Teams, SharePoint, Yammer, or Planner for communication, file sharing, and real-time collaboration. For it to be possible to work with these tools, all collaborators need to have access to them.

Office 365 integration has been built into many other cloud-based file sharing, collaboration, and communications services, which makes it easy for people to access or share Office documents, data, and files. In some cases, this integration focuses on what can be done with Office-related documents and files after they've been saved to the cloud rather than while someone is still working with them using an Office application.

> **CAUTION**
>
> **Collaboration of Office Content Requires Office 365**
>
> Collaboration functionality works best when all users are fellow Office 365 subscribers with their own paid accounts, and they're using a full working version of a specific Office application, such as Word, Excel, or PowerPoint.
>
> When an Office 365 user shares an Office document or file with someone who's not an Office 365 user, that content can be opened, viewed, and worked with using any compatible application. For example, a Word document can be opened using Apple's Pages, Google's Docs, or most other popular word processors.

Decision Time: Avoiding Office 365 Confusion

When two or more people within an organization will be using Office 365, they'll get the most out of this suite of applications if all users have the same subscription plan and ultimately have access to exactly the same collection of Microsoft software and services. The trick is figuring out which Office 365 subscription plan is best for all users. Instead of trying to figure out the convoluted and often overlapping Office 365 subscription plans yourself, consult with Microsoft directly by visiting https://resources.office.com/en-us-landing-o365-contactus.html or seek advice from an authorized Microsoft Hosting Provider who will help analyze and address the specific needs of your organization.

What you may discover is that Office 365 is ideal for managing your team or organization's word processing and related file-sharing needs, but for group messaging, video conferencing, or hosting virtual meetings and collaboration sessions you might need other cloud-based platforms that work with Office 365. Just because Office 365 offers a vast selection of applications and services doesn't mean you, or your entire organization, need to use all of them. What's more important is that everyone within your team or organization ultimately works with the same collection of software and cloud-based tools, has access to the content they need, and each person understands how to use the tools available to them.

Chapter 12

Handling Large-Group Collaboration with Microsoft Exchange Online

This chapter covers the following:

- An overview of Microsoft Exchange Online and the email solutions it offers
- A discussion of how Microsoft Exchange Online differs from Microsoft Exchange, which is a cloud-computing solution for large companies
- Guidelines for determining whether Microsoft Exchange Online can provide the most suitable cloud-computing tools to your company or organization
- An explanation of why it might make sense to take advantage of a Microsoft Hosted Exchange partner to manage your Microsoft Exchange email and Office 365 services

Microsoft Exchange Online, which is designed for small to mid-sized businesses, offers tools and functionality beyond what's provided by just Office 365. It's a more accessible and affordable solution than self-hosted Microsoft Exchange and Microsoft SharePoint solutions (which are designed to provide comprehensive cloud-computing solutions for large companies).

> **FYI: More About Microsoft SharePoint**
>
> Microsoft SharePoint includes a collection of cloud-based tools, mainly for enterprises, that allow two or more people to simultaneously collaborate and share files when working with data, documents, and content, including work being done using Microsoft Office applications. SharePoint's document management features enable multiple people to work on the same document or file simultaneously and have access to the latest version of the file that includes changes that were made by other users. A cloud-based (remotely hosted) version of SharePoint is offered with some Office 365 Business subscriptions.

Microsoft Exchange Online Overview

Just about everyone is familiar with Microsoft Office, which includes Word, Excel, PowerPoint, OneNote, Outlook, and other popular applications that provide companies of all sizes, in all industries, with a comprehensive collection of software, mobile app, and online-based tools designed to handle a wide range of common, work-related computing tasks. Microsoft Office 365 (which is covered in Chapter 11, "Using Microsoft Office 365 for Collaboration and File Sharing") includes applications that provide tools for handling many common tasks, like word processing, spreadsheet management, digital slide presentations, note taking, contact management, scheduling, online communications (including email, group messaging, voice calling, and video calling), and database management, but there are other cloud-computing tasks that Office 365 can't handle alone. To cater to the more expansive and growing needs of small to mid-sized companies, Microsoft Exchange Online can combine Office 365 with a complete (and scalable) hosted email solution for business, as well as other cloud-based tools designed to improve communication, online collaboration, and information management.

By itself, Microsoft Exchange Online is a hosted, entirely cloud-based email solution. This means that Microsoft uses its network of servers to securely host and manage the customized email accounts and email management tools used by a subscribing company's employees.

Employees and departments at a company that use Microsoft Exchange Online can have fully customized email addresses (featuring a custom domain), using the *username@companyname.com* or *departmentname@companyname.com* format.

These email accounts contain zero advertising, and Microsoft does not track any user content or activity for the purpose of sharing it with its advertisers. Individual users within an organization can take advantage of the online edition of Microsoft Outlook to manage their email accounts.

Because Microsoft Exchange Online operates from Microsoft's servers and is entirely cloud-based, companies don't need to invest in any specialized equipment to have a secure, scalable, customizable, and feature-packed email management system. Accounts can be managed from Windows PCs, Macs, and any Internet-connected mobile devices.

FYI: Email Security Is Included

Email accounts hosted and managed by Microsoft Exchange Online include enterprise-level security, including a multifactor authentication option. Even though Microsoft's servers are used to host a subscribing company's email using an entirely cloud-based solution, each subscribing company maintains full control over its own data and is given administrator controls to manage individual users and accounts. In addition to providing a 99.9 percent uptime guarantee, Microsoft provides tools to ensure remote access to email is as secure as using a computer from your office. Plus, antivirus and antispam tools are fully integrated.

According to Microsoft, Exchange Online and Office 365 also adhere to 10 privacy compliance standards that meet or exceed the requirements imposed on companies working in many industries, including medical, education, banking, government, and homeland security.

> **In Practice**
>
> ### Effortless Updates
>
> One of the biggest benefits of using Exchange Online is that companies don't need to purchase or manage their own servers, and all necessary updates are automatically installed and implemented by Microsoft. This means that in addition to cutting IT costs, all users are always working with the very latest email management tools.

If your company already has its own email domain, management system, and hosting service set up and operational in a way that works and meets your needs, then the time, effort, and expense of migrating to Microsoft Exchange Online may not be worthwhile. However, if you're establishing email for your company for the first time, Microsoft Exchange Online, combined with Office 365, offers a comprehensive solution. Microsoft utilizes software and mobile apps that you install directly on your equipment and also cloud services for online file storage, file sharing, data syncing, email hosting, and collaboration. The result is a comprehensive toolset that enables you to handle many tasks associated with the operation of your business.

Google offers similar functionality via G Suite; the main difference is that G Suite is entirely online. Also, G Suite offers a free trial, which isn't available for Microsoft Exchange Online. (Read more about G Suite in Chapter 10, "Working in Google's G Suite.")

> **In Practice**
>
> ### Microsoft Exchange Online Is Scalable
>
> As your company's size changes, Microsoft Exchange Online can scale up or down to meet your company's needs as you grow or shrink. The assigned administrator can easily create or delete individual email accounts for users. At all times, the company maintains full control over its user accounts and all of its data.

Microsoft Exchange Online Plans and Pricing

Pricing for Microsoft Exchange Online can get a bit confusing because it integrates fully with Office 365 (as well as other software applications, mobile apps, and cloud-based services offered by Microsoft and also third-party software publishers), so depending on a company's needs, pricing plans for per-user subscriptions get a bit convoluted. This section gives basic pricing information, but you need to investigate pricing for the specific solution that best fits your needs.

The Exchange Online Plan 1 is priced at $4.00 per user, per month and requires an annual commitment. When used on its own, this plan offers business-class email with 50GB of online storage per user (used to manage an email account's mailbox folders and content). Individual users within a company can send messages as large as 150MB and take advantage of Microsoft Exchange Online or Outlook Online. Each Microsoft Exchange Online email account automatically includes anti-malware and antispam protection, shared contact and calendar management, and the ability to archive all email-related data, files, and activities, which is a compliance requirement for most industries.

The Exchange Online Plan 2 option is priced at $8.00 per user, per month and also requires an annual commitment. This plan includes all tools and features offered by Exchange Online Plan 1, along with unlimited online storage for each user account (including 100GB of mailbox storage and unlimited archive storage), hosted voicemail, and data loss protection.

FYI: Data Loss Prevent Explained

The Data Loss Prevent (DLP) feature of Microsoft Online Exchange allows companies to adhere to many email-related, industry-specific compliance regulations by providing added controls for managing, tracking, monitoring, and archiving sensitive data that's sent and received via email.

Beyond these two subscription plans, Office 365 Business plans include all features and tools included with the Exchange Online Plan 1, plus full access and integration with select Office 365 applications, 1TB of online file storage space, file-sharing capabilities, and video-conferencing functionality. Users can also take advantage of the Outlook mobile app (in addition to the cloud- or software-based versions of Outlook) to manage their email account, calendar, and contacts, for example.

With the Business plans, each user can install and use Office 365 applications on up to five computers and mobile devices. This Office 365 plan includes unlimited use of the software and mobile app editions of Word, Excel, PowerPoint, Outlook, Publisher, and OneNote, as well as the online-based editions of Word, Excel, Outlook, and PowerPoint.

Using cloud-based communications tools, users can host or participate in virtual meetings, video conferences, voice calls, and group or direct text messaging/instant messaging conversations, plus take advantage of a corporate social network that's designed to help employees from different departments or different locations easily collaborate using virtual workspaces.

The Office 365 Business Premium plan, for example, is priced at $12.50 per user, per month and requires an annual commitment, but there are other Office 365 subscription plans for individuals, business users, and companies that are priced between $5.00 and $12.50 per month, per user. (Read Chapter 11 for more information.)

> **FYI: Get the Scoop on the Latest Subscription Plans from Microsoft**
>
> To learn more about the current subscription plans related to Microsoft Exchange Online, visit https://products.office.com/en-us/exchange/compare-microsoft-exchange-online-plans. To compare all of the current Microsoft 365 Business plans, visit https://products.office.com/en-us/compare-all-microsoft-office-products?tab=2.
>
> For details about current enterprise solutions that encompass Office 365, Microsoft Exchange, and Microsoft SharePoint, visit https://products.office.com/en-us/business/compare-more-office-365-for-business-plans. These plans range in price from $8.00 per user, per month to $35.00 per user, per month. All require an annual commitment.

Depending on the Microsoft Exchange Online or Office 365 Business plan a company adopts, different levels of technical support from Microsoft are available and included with the plan. This includes self-help community support, assisted support via web or email, and several levels of phone tech support (available during specific hours, or 24/7, depending on the plan).

> **FYI: Microsoft Exchange and SharePoint Require Your Own Server(s)**
>
> When you adopt Microsoft Exchange Online you can rely on Microsoft's remote servers and equipment to securely host your company's email service and all customized email accounts via the cloud. If your company already manages its own servers, it can use Microsoft Exchange and SharePoint to host and manage your email service, using software and applications created by Microsoft.

> **FYI: Using Skype with Microsoft Exchange Online**
>
> Be sure to refer to Chapter 14, "Communicating via Skype," for additional information about how this Microsoft service provides capabilities for Internet-based voice calling, video calling, video conferencing, virtual meetings, group messaging, and other forms of online collaboration that can be used in conjunction with Microsoft Exchange Online and Microsoft Office 365 applications.

Setup Options

When it comes to a small to medium-sized business getting started with Microsoft Exchange Online, you have two main options.

Interacting Directly with Microsoft

A company representative can contact Microsoft directly to discuss company needs, and then choose a subscription plan for the desired services. From there, the company assigned administrator can easily set up and manage the company's account and service via Microsoft's website (https://products.office.com/en-us/business/get-the-most-secure-office-with-exchange-online).

For someone who is somewhat tech-savvy, this is the fastest, easiest, and most cost-effective solution. To learn more about the responsibilities and capabilities of an administrator for Microsoft Exchange Online or Microsoft Office 365 Business, visit https://support.office.com and click on the Business Admins option.

Working with an Independent Microsoft Hosting Provider

A potentially more expensive option—but one that requires virtually no technical expertise whatsoever—is to hire an independent Microsoft Hosting Provider to handle all of the management and tech support activities associated with migrating to Microsoft Hosted Exchange and/or Office 365 A Microsoft Hosting Provider is authorized to sell Microsoft cloud services and license Microsoft software, in addition to their own value-added services related to tech support, user training, cybersecurity, and hosting. Pricing for these services vary because all solutions are customized for each individual company.

When you work with a Microsoft Hosted Exchange service, that third-party hosting company owns and manages the remote servers on which your organization's Microsoft Exchange and Office 365 accounts are hosted. In other words, that company serves as your virtual (off-site) IT department. Instead of using your own servers or Microsoft's servers, you use a third-party's servers in conjunction with Microsoft's tools.

When you choose a third-party Microsoft Hosting Provider, make sure the organization has earned the necessary certifications from Microsoft and is licensed to offer Exchange email services and Office 365 software and tools. Next, make sure the company is well established and reliable. The company should understand the needs of your business and have experience working with other businesses within your industry.

After your cloud-based services are set up and operational, your daily interaction with the third-party provider will likely be minimal. However, the company you work with should provide regular performance reports and detailed billing. The service should also regularly evaluate your company's needs to make sure that you have the proper cloud-based solutions and security measures in place based on your organization's current email, online storage, file-sharing, communications, and collaboration requirements.

In terms of the value-added services the Microsoft Hosting Provider offers, these should all be tools and resources your company actually needs and uses, such as individualized user training, on-call tech support, automated cloud-based data backup and archiving services, and/or added cybersecurity. Ideally, you want to create and maintain a positive, long-term relationship with a Microsoft Hosting Provider, which evolves as your company's needs change or expand over time.

FYI: How to Locate a Microsoft Hosting Provider

To find a Microsoft Hosting Provider and discuss your company's needs, visit www.microsoft. com/en-us/CloudandHosting/Find_a_Hosting_Provider.aspx.

How much you pay one of these companies depends on a variety of factors, including the number of user accounts your company requires, the level of tech support you want available, and the other services you want or need.

The good news is that there is a lot of competition among independent Microsoft Hosting Providers, so be sure to shop around for a service that offers all of the value-added services you need that go above and beyond the Microsoft Exchange email hosting service and access to Office 365 applications and tools.

Chapter | **13**

Bringing Teams Together with Salesforce

This chapter covers the following:

- An introduction to Customer Relationship Management (CRM) applications
- The benefits of a cloud-based CRM platform
- An overview of Salesforce, how it can be used to improve sales and service, and how it can help with a company's marketing and social media efforts

All of the other cloud-based services and platforms covered within *Working in the Cloud* are designed to be used by virtually any type of business or individual users who need to store, sync, share, and collaborate using cloud-based tools. This chapter, which covers the Salesforce platform, is a bit different because it's focused on some specific tasks that CRM applications can do. Salesforce can be used effectively by many types of businesses of all sizes, but it offers specialized functionality for creating, managing, and expanding professional relationships, particularly when it comes to sales, service, and marketing. The focus of this chapter is on Salesforce Sales Cloud, which has become the most popular cloud-based CRM platform in the world.

Overview of CRM Applications

Most business professionals are accustomed to using software or a mobile app to maintain an easily accessible, personal database of their contacts. At the same time, they use different applications that are designed for time management and scheduling, email management, and project management. In some cases, these applications work together, but more often than not, the user must jump between applications to manage their overall workday activities.

The concept behind customer relationship management (CRM) applications is to allow individuals or teams to create and share information within one application that has capabilities far beyond simply storing a contact's name, address, phone number, and email address.

When it comes to sales, for example, a CRM application allows someone to manage a vast database of prospective and existing customers and clients, store customized information about each contact, and maintain a detailed log of every interaction. All activities related to each prospect or account are kept in one easily accessible place, and relevant files from other applications (such as Word, Excel, Power-Point, or PDF documents) also can be stored.

In Practice

Use Document Protection When Storing Sensitive Files

If you're storing Microsoft Office-related files that contain sensitive information within Salesforce's Files module, consider using the Protect Document feature built into Word, Excel, and PowerPoint to add a password to each document before storing it in the cloud. You'll provide the people you're sharing with the necessary password for opening the file.

FYI: CRM Cross Departments

Sales isn't the only department that can make use of a CRM application. Any department within your company that interacts with customers, clients, prospects, vendors, suppliers, or any other individuals or companies, can benefit from a CRM application (as opposed to a contact manager) to help manage all of the information that allows a company to build and maintain positive business relationships.

The goal of CRM applications is to help businesses of all sizes use technology to streamline the process of finding, establishing, and then building and maintaining long-term relationships with customers and clients. A CRM application makes pertinent, contact-specific information readily available to the people within an organization who can best use it.

When a CRM application is cloud-based, a company's entire database of leads and established accounts is kept in one centralized and secure location. Individuals in many different departments that interact with customers or clients can all access detailed and up-to-date information. The information can then be used in the most efficient way possible to build and maintain strong relationships between your organization and the people your business interacts with.

When a business only has a few people working within the organization, customer relationship management can be handled with a spreadsheet, basic contact management software, or even a paper-based system. As a company grows, those simple record-keeping solutions wind up becoming unwieldy and impractical. This is when it becomes time to adopt a CRM solution that's customizable to meet your organization's needs and easily scalable so that it can handle your company's growth. In fact, some CRM solutions, such as SalesforceIQ, cater to businesses with just a handful of employees and can grow along with a company.

Benefits of a Cloud-Based CRM Solution

Simply collecting and manually entering the vast amounts of information related to leads, customers, clients, vendors, and other suppliers can become a time-consuming and convoluted process. However, a cloud-based CRM platform automates many aspects of this process because it helps automatically track and log the activities of people within an organization that relate to finding and building relationships.

When a sales team adopts a CRM solution, individual salespeople spend a lot less time finding and pursuing leads, so they can spend more time actually selling to the most qualified leads. The software enables salespeople to spend less time doing busywork and spend more time selling. However, in some cases, the CRM solution can also help discover qualified sales leads or gather and organize information about leads.

After a sale is made, everything that anyone in your company needs to know about a new client or customer, as well as every interaction with them, is documented and easily accessible. This includes detailed client information, the client's history, client preferences, and information about past interactions and purchases. All of this information can be made available in a customized format that can be securely accessed from any type of computer or mobile device from virtually anywhere. Information can cross departmental lines so that everyone who interacts with the account has the same knowledge.

> ### FYI: CRM Offers a Great ROI
>
> CRM solutions that are available today offer tools that automate many aspects of a company's interactions with each of its prospects and customers. According to Salesforce, the average ROI (return on investment) for companies that invest in CRM is $5.60 for every single dollar spent.

Of course, simply adopting a CRM solution doesn't magically transform your business or increase sales and improve customer service overnight. However, it does provide your team with the tools needed to work and communicate more efficiently; automates what were previously time-consuming and repetitive activities related to sales and gathering information; gives your team access to the information it needs, when it's needed; and simultaneously allows management to analyze activities and measures results in real time.

Before any company can efficiently adopt a CRM application, the company's leaders need to define a clear vision for their company and then define a sales strategy and business objectives that will be followed by everyone within the organization. When a CRM application is adopted, everyone who will be using it needs to be on board, understand what's possible, and learn how to become proficient using the new tools at their disposal. Proper training should be as big of a priority as adopting the CRM solution, or else the potential benefits of utilizing a CRM application will be lost.

Benefits of a Cloud-Based Solution

By adopting a cloud-based CRM solution, a company doesn't need to acquire or manage any new hardware (such as servers), install and manage software on every user's equipment, or take steps to continuously update specific software. All access to a cloud-based CRM platform is handled via any web browser on any Internet-connected computer or with a proprietary mobile app on a smartphone or tablet. Most cloud-based CRM solutions also integrate with third-party software or mobile apps, which makes it easier to access, collect, modify, store, and share pertinent information in the most efficient ways possible.

When used correctly, the information gathered, managed, and stored by a CRM platform enables companies to build relationships with customers and clients that last, because more personalized attention can be provided during every interaction, whether it happens on the phone, via email, through social media, or in person.

Available CRM Solutions

If you believe a CRM solution would be viable for your business, first determine what's possible based on the various tools the CRM solutions currently offer. Next, identify the needs within your organization. Figure out exactly how this type of tool can best be used, which departments within your organization should use it, and then shop around for the most cost effective and powerful CRM solution that will meet your needs today and be scalable in the future.

You need to evaluate the tools, features, functions, support, and training that are provided in a variety of CRM solutions. In addition to Salesforce, six other CRM solutions that are cloud-based, or that fully integrate with the cloud, include

- Accelo's Capterra (http://grow.accelo.com/capterra-crm)
- Act! (www.act.com)
- Insightly (www.insightly.com)
- NetSuite CRM (www.netsuite.com/portal/products/crm.shtml)
- Pipedrive (www.pipedrive.com)
- ZoHo CRM (www.zoho.com/crm)

> **In Practice**
>
> ## Take Each CRM Solution for a Test Drive
>
> As with any cloud-based service, first assign a small team within your organization to participate in the training required to become proficient in using the tool. Then have those individuals test the selected platform in their real-world environment to ensure it can work effectively for your company.
>
> Most cloud-based CRM solutions offer a free trial period, so you can gain full access to an application and test it out on a small scale before paying for it and fully adopting it within your organization.

Overview of Salesforce

Salesforce is a comprehensive, cloud-based CRM solution that was originally designed to increase the productivity of salespeople. Salesforce allows salespeople to spend more time actually making sales and building relationships than in doing the time-consuming paperwork associated with collecting, researching, organizing, finding, and managing details and information related to prospects, customers, and clients. What started as a powerful database management tool to handle contact information has grown into a highly interactive and powerful toolset that can improve efficiency and communication in every aspect of the sales and customer/client management process.

Salesforce's core functionality can be used by one person or simultaneously by an entire sales team. The same toolset can be used by a company's customer relations, technical support, and marketing teams. Salesforce provides a seamless, cloud-based platform that enables each person within a company to access the up-to-date information they need for communicating between departments or communicating directly with prospects, customers, or clients.

Salesforce allows a vast amount of useful information to be collected and stored in one centralized location, so the information can be accessed, managed, and utilized in a variety of different ways. Most importantly, it provides a company with the tools needed to more cost efficiently find sales leads and prospects, close sales, and then build long-term and successful relationships with customers and clients.

The tools offered by Salesforce are highly customizable, yet allow companies to keep their information secure. Because Salesforce is entirely in the cloud, users can access their accounts from any Internet-connected computer or mobile device, making it cross-platform compatible and ensuring that all users have access to the same set of tools regardless of how they're accessing the platform.

Salesforce's offerings can be customized to meet the CRM needs of start-ups, small businesses, organizations of any size, and companies working in specific industries (such as financial services, banking, insurance, healthcare, retail, manufacturing, communications, media, government, automotive, higher education, or non-profit). Salesforce is also scalable, so an organization can adopt it to accommodate the needs of a small team but scale use as it's needed.

Salesforce Subscription Plans and Pricing

The tools offered by Salesforce cater to the needs of the sales, customer service, technical support, marketing, and commerce teams within an organization. Additional services, like Community Cloud, Chatter, and Quip, focus on providing cloud-based communications, collaboration, and productivity tools across an entire company.

CAUTION

An Internet Connection Is Required

In order for someone to access the Salesforce account, their computer or mobile device must have continuous Internet access because Salesforce is an entirely cloud-based platform.

The most popular of Salesforce's offerings is Sales Cloud, which provides a cloud-based platform for managing all sales-related activities within a company of any size. Salesforce offers four subscription-based plans for its Sales Cloud platform, ranging in price from $25.00 per month, per user to $300.00 per month, per user. (See the following sections for specifics about what's offered with each plan.) However, special bundled packages are offered to companies that want to simultaneously use other Salesforce applications and services, across multiple divisions or companywide.

FYI: A Detailed Subscription Plan Comparison

To download a detailed overview of all current Salesforce Sales Cloud subscription plans, visit www.salesforce.com/content/dam/web/en_us/www/documents/datasheets/DS_SalesCloud_EdCompare.pdf.

SalesforceIQ CRM Starter

Priced at $25.00 per month, per user, this plan is ideal for small sales teams of up to five users. Some of the key features offered by this plan include

- **One List:** An integrated to-do list manager

- **Automatic data capture:** Tool for automatically logging emails, phone calls, meetings, and other interactions

- **Customizable sales tracking:** Customizable tracking for specific information related to the sales process

- **Follow-up reminders:** Automatic reminders for follow-up calls, emails, or appointments

- **Contact auto-complete:** A tool that obtains additional information from the Internet (or other applications) and adds it to a contact's record after you've filled in basic information

- **Shared address book:** A comprehensive contact list that's shared across an entire team

- **Sent email notifications:** History of when emails are sent to prospects, customers, or clients; also includes read receipts for sent messages

- **Collaboration tools:** Tools that enable team members and management to stay in contact with each other

- **Mobile app access:** Mobile apps for iOS or Android smartphones and tablets

- **Chrome extension:** Extension for the Chrome web browser that enables you to access certain Salesforce tools directly from the browser without having to first access the Salesforce platform

- **Salesforce training:** Webinars and live training sessions that facilitate training

Sales Cloud Lightning Professional

Priced at $75.00 per user, per month, this subscription plan is designed to be adopted by a sales team of any size. It includes all the tools offered by the SalesforceIQ CRM Starter plan and has additional tools and features that enable larger teams to work together and share information.

This plan also includes a more robust account and contact management tool, opportunity tracking, lead management, task and event tracking, customizable reports, email integration, quote and order tracking, and tools for administrators to oversee the Salesforce service and manage individual accounts.

Sales Cloud Lightning Enterprise

The Lightning Enterprise plan builds on what's offered by the Lightning Professional plan and is priced at $150.00 per month, per user. The Lightning Enterprise plan offers much more customizability into every element of the application. It's designed to be used by large teams and includes more powerful automation, account management, security, and administration tools.

Sales Cloud Lightning Unlimited

The Lightning Unlimited plan is $300.00 per month, per user and includes everything the Salesforce Sales Cloud platform has to offer, including additional online data storage, expanded sandbox environments, access to more than 100 admin services, unlimited online training, unlimited 24/7 tech support, and full integration with optional tools and services offered by Salesforce. Before committing to this plan, it's recommended that you determine that the Lightning Professional or Lighting Enterprise plan is beneficial to your organization.

FYI: Optional Account Add-Ons

Depending on which type of Sales Force subscription plan team members utilize, you can add a la carte tools to your implementation. Some examples are Salesforce Inbox (email integration), Salesforce Quote-to-Cash (a tool for automating a company's price, quote, and billing processes), and Salesforce Engage (the addition of B2B marketing tools). These add-ons have additional monthly fees.

In Practice

The Einstein AI Add-on Gives Salesforce Artificial Intelligence

In 2016, Salesforce introduced an add-on component called Einstein AI, which is a series of additional tools that offer predictive lead scoring, activity capture, and an integrated dialer.

The lead scoring element helps salespeople choose which leads to pursue first, so the most time possible is spent focusing on the most qualified leads. The activity capture element automatically syncs calendar and email data with a prospect's record, which reduces the busy work associated with keeping information within the CRM application up to date. The integrated dialer enables a user to click a phone number to initiate a call from within the Salesforce platform. Salesforce automatically logs the call and stores any notes entered by the sales rep during the call.

The goal of Einstein AI is to save users time by collecting data automatically and anticipating the need for information that can be provided faster and displayed more efficiently. Some Salesforce Sales Cloud subscription plans come with Einstein AI bundled in. Other plans require users to pay an additional monthly fee for this functionality.

You can find more information about Einstein AI and how it works at https://www.salesforce.com/products/einstein/overview.

Getting Started with Salesforce

Salesforce Sales Cloud is a vast online platform with many components and modules. The easiest way to familiarize yourself with what you can do is to visit the Salesforce website (www.salesforce.com) and create a free trial account by clicking the Try For Free button.

The first step involves creating a single user (Admin) account. From the account creation screen (see Figure 13.1), you can import your personal information from a Google, LinkedIn, or Facebook account, or you can manually enter account details in the fields provided.

FIGURE 13.1   Salesforce's new account creation screen.

After you complete the new account information, you receive an email prompting you to verify your account. You're also prompted to verify the account using a code sent via text message to your smartphone. In the future, Salesforce keeps a detailed log of what each user does while using Salesforce and records from where they logged in to the system and what equipment was used to log in.

In Practice

The Initial Account Creator Becomes the Administrator

The person who creates a Salesforce account becomes the administrator. That person sets account-wide security settings and adds, deletes, oversees, and manages user accounts for all other employees. To access a comprehensive Admin menu, click the account Profile icon in the top-right corner of the screen, and then click the Settings option. The Administrator menu is displayed along the left margin of the screen. Before additional user accounts are set up, it's important for the administrator to establish and set security settings and permissions that will apply to all users.

Salesforce offers to take you on an interactive tour of the platform (see Figure 13.2). This tour can help you get acquainted with Salesforce's user interface.

FIGURE 13.2 After creating a new account, take the virtual tour, which helps you become acquainted with Salesforce's intuitive user interface and menu structure.

At its core, Salesforce is a contact management application, so one of the first tasks you need to take care of is manually entering information for all of your individual contacts or importing your existing contact database from another contact manager or CRM application. To manually create a contact, click the Create (+) icon at the top right of the window and then click New Contact (see Figure 13.3). The Create Contact screen (see Figure 13.4) opens so you can enter the contact's information.

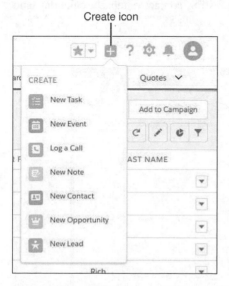

FIGURE 13.3 Click the Create (+) icon to access the menu that allows you to create new contacts and other types of entries within Salesforce.

Create Contact

Contact Information

*Name

Salutation

--None--   ▼

First Name

Middle Name

*Last Name

Suffix

*Account Name

Search Accounts...

Contact Owner

Jason Rich

Reports To

Search Contacts...

Cancel   Save & New   Save

FIGURE 13.4 The Create Contact screen.

Figure 13.5 shows the main screen of the Data Import Wizard, which allows you to import content from a wide range of other sources. If you're already a Microsoft Outlook user, for example, Salesforce has a separate edition that fully integrates with Outlook (see Figure 13.6) so that you can access Salesforce's features and functionality and combine it with your existing contact database, calendar, and email account that's managed via Outlook.

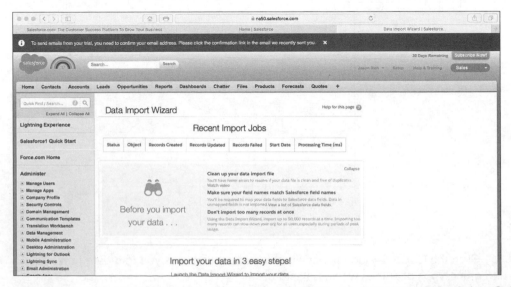

FIGURE 13.5 You can import your entire contact database or a listing of new leads into Salesforce.

FIGURE 13.6 Salesforce's integration with Microsoft Outlook allows you to use Salesforce functionality from within Outlook.

The More Information Salesforce Collects, the More Helpful It Becomes

It's worth the time investment to manually enter or import all your existing contacts and details about your current leads. After Salesforce is populated with your data and you've completed your user profile within the application, you're ready to take advantage of the platform's functionality for managing your sales efforts.

It's essential that all users keep Salesforce up to date regarding their interactions (calls, emails, meetings, etc.) related to each contact and lead. This way, anyone else within your organization can access a specific contact and see all notes and information related to that contact to date so that they can quickly get up to speed on everything that's transpired in the past. New follow-up calls or meetings should be added to Salesforce. Figure 13.7 shows what the Log a Call screen looks like. This is used to add details about a phone conversation with a contact or lead. In some cases, information is automatically collected and logged on your behalf.

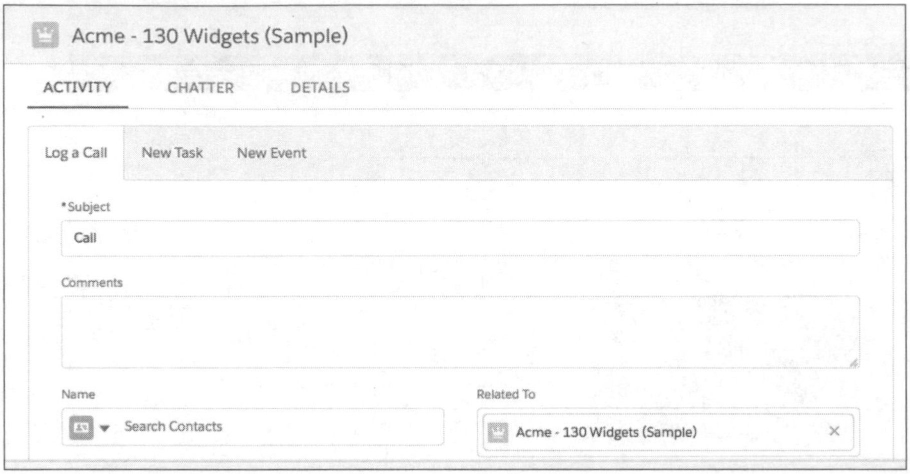

FIGURE 13.7   As new interactions take place with contacts or leads, enter details within the appropriate record.

As details about follow up phone calls, to-do list items, meetings, and other events are added to Salesforce as part of each contact entry, a centralized calendar is maintained (see Figure 13.8). Individuals can select the Calendar viewing options, so they can manage their own schedules or see scheduling information for an entire sales team. This is one of the places within Salesforce where you'll be reminded about account or lead-specific tasks that need to be accomplished on any given day.

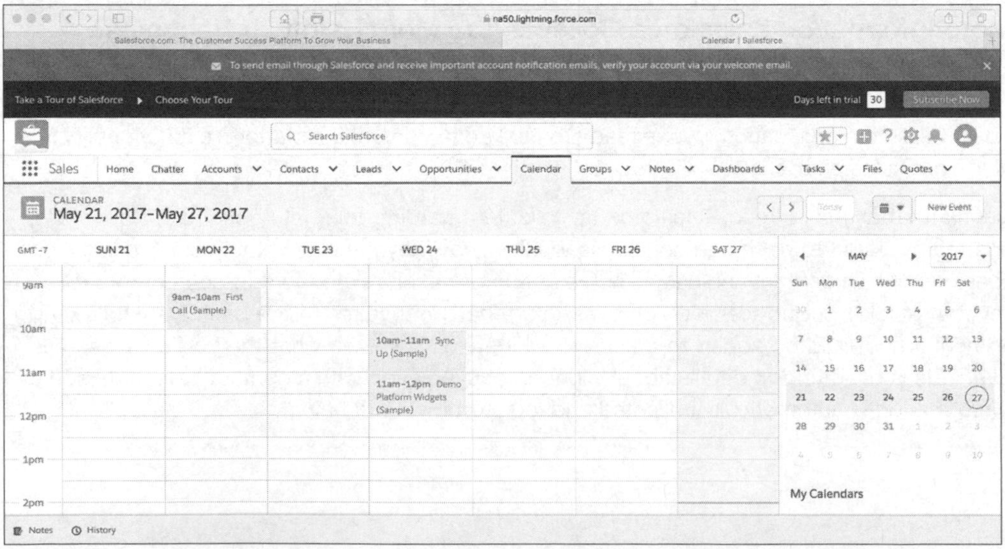

FIGURE 13.8   Salesforce includes a full-featured calendar function that can help you manage your time, track appointments and to-do lists, schedule meetings, and share scheduling information with co-workers.

In addition to collecting and storing a vast amount of information about individual contacts, and keeping a detailed log of all interactions with each contact, Salesforce offers a cloud-based file-storage and file-sharing service that enables you to store files in the cloud and then share them with co-workers or embed them into outgoing communications.

Figure 13.9 shows what the cloud-based file storage and sharing screen looks like. The functionality offered by this module of Salesforce works very much like other cloud-based file-storage and file-sharing services, such as Dropbox or Box.com. Each file listing indicates the type of file it is. Click the menu icon associated with each listing to reveal a submenu for managing each file. Click the listing itself to see a preview of the file within a browser window.

File Type icon

Menu icon

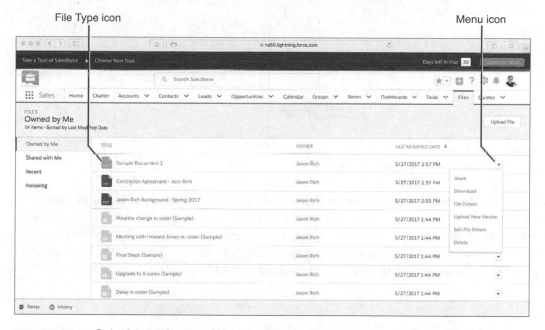

FIGURE 13.9   Salesforce offers cloud-based file storage that includes the ability to easily preview and manage stored files and share files with others.

To add new information to a record, click the Create (+) icon (refer to Figure 13.3) and then choose what type of content you want to add. Options include New Task, New Event, Log a Call, New Note, New Contact, New Opportunity, or New Lead. Based on which option you select, the appropriate add content fields are displayed, and if relevant, you can link the new information with an existing contact or lead.

For example, if you want to add a new lead, click the New Lead option on the Create menu and then fill in the empty fields in the New Lead pop-up window (see Figure 13.10). As with any content you add to Salesforce as part of an entry, the more detailed you are with the information you provide, the more helpful the Salesforce platform can be moving forward.

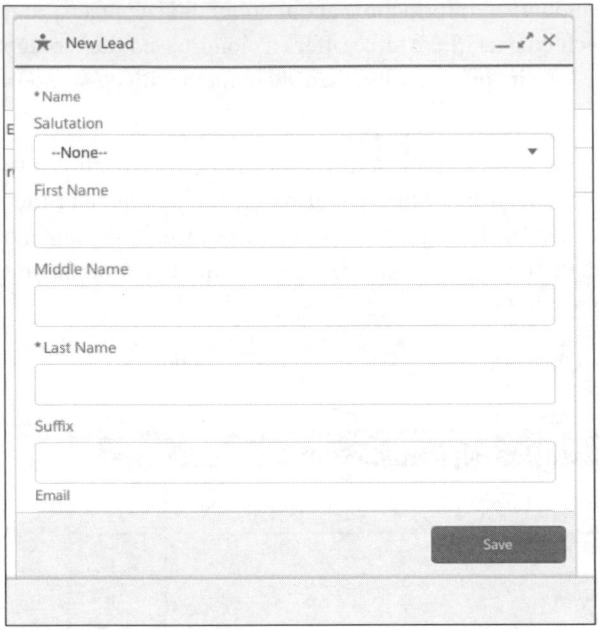

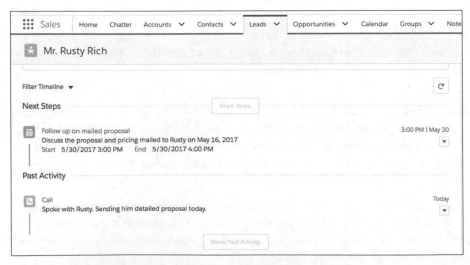

FIGURE 13.10   The New Lead entry window.

When you view individual records, Salesforce provides a detailed, chronological log of all communications and activities related to that record (see Figure 13.11). Not only is this information useful to you, but if you're not around and a client, customer, or prospect calls your company, someone else who answers the phone can access the appropriate record within Salesforce and quickly get up to speed on everything that's already transpired between you and that contact.

FIGURE 13.11   Select a particular record and then scroll down within the browser window to see a chronological listing of all interactions and communications to date.

As new information is added to a record by other people, the time, date, and name of the Salesforce user who did the updating is recorded along with whatever changes or additions he or she made to the record.

Throughout your day, you can click the Tasks option menu (see Figure 13.12) to see a detailed listing of what you need to accomplish. This includes a list of follow-up calls and actions as well as other responsibilities that are also listed as part of your schedule. Click an item in the task list to view details about that item in the right side of the browser window.

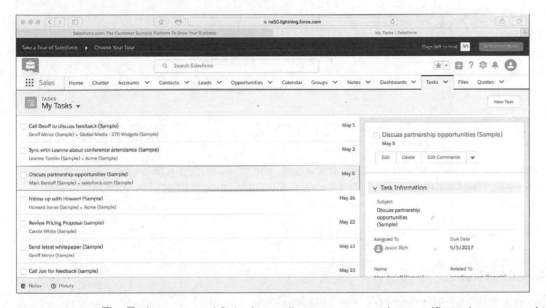

FIGURE 13.12 The Tasks screen of Salesforce allows you to see the specific tasks you need to accomplish on any given day.

Click the Dashboard tab in the top navigation to see a graphical representation of specific types of information related to a user's or team's performance. Figure 13.13 shows the Sales Manager Dashboard. Salesforce allows users and managers to create custom Dashboards.

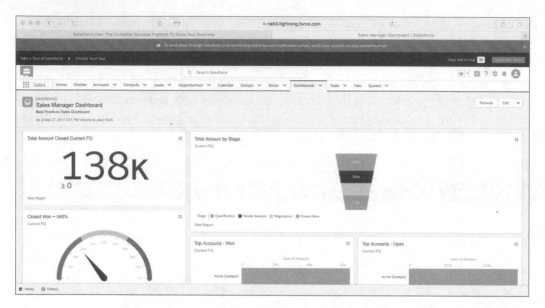

FIGURE 13.13 Salesforce allows users, managers, and administrators to create customized, graphic-intensive Dashboards that showcase user actions, progress, and successful sales during a period of time.

In Practice

Salesforce's Chatter Keeps You Up-To-Date

Chatter is a continuously updated log of everything you've recently done using Salesforce. It also provides a summary of items and tasks that still require your attention. To access Chatter, click the Chatter tab in the Salesforce main menu. You can also set up your account to have a daily Chatter summary emailed to you.

One of the great things about Salesforce is that the user interface is intuitive and easy to navigate. Regardless of which web browser you're using, all of the same tools are available. However, when you use the Chrome web browser, you can add functionality for accessing Salesforce tools.

The Salesforce App Marketplace (see Figure 13.14) enables you to browse through the hundreds of third-party apps and add-ons that have been designed to integrate with Salesforce. Options include integration with Office 365, DocuSign, MailChimp, Slack, Box.com, Dropbox.com, and countless other applications and cloud-based services.

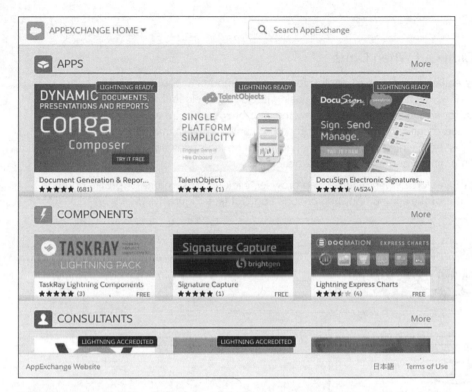

FIGURE 13.14 Use the Salesforce App Marketplace to find hundreds of third-party applications, mobile apps, and cloud-based services that work with Salesforce.

In Practice

Salesforce Mobile Apps

Not only can you access Salesforce via your web browser, but you can download and install the Salesforce mobile app on your smartphone or tablet. You need only one account to access Salesforce using either the web browser or the app. Check the app store for your devices to find the Salesforce app.

> **CAUTION**
>
> ### Be Sure To Sign Out When Done
>
> When using any entirely cloud-based application from a computer's web browser, be sure to sign out from your account when you're done using it. Don't just close the browser window and walk away. Also, for added security, don't allow the web browser you're working with to store your Salesforce username and password (or any other service's username and password). If you allow the browser to store that information, anyone who later uses that same web browser could easily gain unauthorized access to your account.
>
> To sign out from Salesforce when using a web browser, click your username or profile photo in the top-right corner of the screen and then choose Log Out (see Figure 13.15).

FIGURE 13.15 Be sure to sign out from your Salesforce account when you're done using it from any computer's web browser.

Chapter 14

Communicating via Skype

This chapter covers the following:

- Using Skype to make and receive voice calls
- Using Skype to participate in video conferences
- Understanding text messaging and other communication tools offered by Skype and Skype for Business

This chapter focuses on the core features and functions offered by Skype and Skype for Business, which are standalone services that can be used for making and receiving voice calls or participating in conference calls via the Internet. You can also use these tools for participating in video conferences, instant messaging, and group messaging conversations between two or more other Skype users. The Skype for Business service is ideal for groups of up to 250 people, whereas the basic Skype service is suitable for individual users or smaller teams or companies.

Skype for Business offers a more robust set of communications tools than Microsoft's core Skype service, and it also integrates directly with Microsoft's other cloud-based services, including Office 365 and Microsoft Exchange Online.

Skype Overview

On their own, Skype and Skype for Business are tools that allow computer users to make and receive voice calls anywhere in the world—either with other Skype users or with any mobile phone or landline. In addition to handling calls between two parties, Skype offers phone conference or group calling capabilities and many of the standard calling services available when using a traditional phone line, such as Caller ID, call waiting, call forwarding, and group voice calling.

Skype and Skype for Business are inexpensive and easy to implement, whether your team or organization has just a handful of people or hundreds of people. The learning curve tends to be very short, which allows users to become productive and proficient using this communications tool very quickly.

FYI: Skype Is a Voice-Over-IP Phone Service and More

One of the core functions of Skype and Skype for Business is to serve as a voice-over-IP (VoIP) calling service, which means that calls can be initiated or received from a computer or mobile device that's connected to the Internet. No traditional phone line or a connection to a cellular voice service is required. Calls between Skype users that use only the Internet are always free. Calls that originate from a Skype user's account (while connected to the Internet) that are made to a mobile phone or landline incur a fee. As long as a decent Internet connection is available, voice calls are typically crystal clear, and the other party can't tell the incoming call originated from a computer or Internet-enabled mobile device.

In Practice

The Cost of Voice Calls

When Skype or Skype for Business is used to communicate with another Skype user via the Internet, all voice calls are free. When a call is made to a mobile phone or traditional landline from Skype, a low per-minute charge is incurred, unless the Skype user pays for a separate Skype domestic or international calling plan. The per-minute charge is just pennies per minute. This is much less expensive than international calling rates from a phone company or international roaming rates from a cellular service provider.

Skype's Unlimited World calling plan is priced at $13.00 per month for voice calls to mobile phones and landlines in eight countries, and landlines only to 63 additional countries. If there's one country or region you plan to call often, per-minute voice calling plans and country/region-specific unlimited voice calling plans for calling mobile phones and landlines are available. To learn more about voice calling rates, visit https://secure.skype.com/en/calling-rates.

When a Skype user sets up any type of account, one of the first steps is to create a unique username. This is how you are identified on the service, and it serves the same purpose as having a traditional phone number. When one Skype user calls another, this username is used to make the call. Skype also offers the option (available for a small fee) for you to acquire a unique phone number that's associated with your Skype account. Callers can use this phone number from any mobile phone or landline anywhere in the world to call you. As long as your computer or mobile device is connected to the Internet and has the Skype software or mobile app installed, you will receive the call on your computer or mobile device without needing to connect directly to a phone line.

Unanswered incoming calls are forwarded to the Skype voicemail service. However, you also have the option to set up your account with call forwarding, so any calls coming in to your Skype account's phone number can be forwarded to a traditional phone number, such as an office phone, home phone, or cellular phone.

Beyond serving as a full-featured VoIP service for making and receiving voice calls, Skype and Skype for Business offer the ability to host Internet-based video conferences between two or more users. A video call utilizes a computer or mobile device's camera, built-in microphone, and built-in speaker. You can also use a wireless or corded telephone headset that connects to the computer or mobile device (with a microphone and headphone speaker built in).

A third major component of the Skype and Skype for Business service is unlimited instant messaging and group messaging. Messaging can be between two or more people, and a Skype account can accommodate any number of messaging conversations happening simultaneously. For a fee, messages from Skype can be sent to the smartphone via their cellular service provider's text messaging service.

In Practice

File Sharing

Built into the instant messaging and group messaging service of Skype is a file-sharing tool. It enables you to attach a document or file and send it directly to the other participants in a messaging conversation. You can also share files via Skype directly from the Share menu built into Microsoft Word, Excel, PowerPoint, or OneNote, but you have to set up this feature from System Preferences on a Mac or Control Panel on a Windows 10 PC.

Because Skype is owned and operated by Microsoft, it completely integrates with Office 365 and Microsoft Exchange Online. As a result, Office 365 subscribers have access to a variety of additional (and secure) virtual meeting and collaboration features.

For example, Office 365 users can schedule voice or video calls or virtual meetings using Outlook. During a phone conference, video conference, or virtual meeting, participants can share and collaborate using Office applications, such as Word, Excel, PowerPoint and OneNote. In fact, when a virtual meeting is conducted using Skype for Business, up to 250 people take advantage of screen sharing, a virtual white board, interactive polling, viewing and annotating a PowerPoint presentation, and/or participating in a Q&A session. All calls, video conferences, and virtual meetings can be stored and saved in the cloud along with any Office files that are created, reviewed, or used during a virtual gathering.

In Practice

No Cost Virtual Meetings

When Skype or Skype for Business is used with Office 365, unlimited virtual meetings for up to 10 people can be held without incurring additional costs. Meeting participants can join the meeting using Skype from their PCs, Macs, smartphones, or tablets.

Skype Pricing

The price for using Skype or Skype for Business varies based on the type of account you have, the calling plan you use, and the add-on services you get. Some Skype functionality is free for everyone. Some features require a paid Office 365 subscription, and some require a Skype for Business subscription. In some instances, the number of people who can participate in a group call, video conference, or virtual meeting is also capped, based on the type of Office 365 or Skype for Business account you have.

CAUTION

Determine What You're Already Paying For

Many Office 365 subscription plans for individuals, businesses, and enterprise include Skype for Business. Meanwhile, some Skype services are offered freely to individuals. Before purchasing a subscription plan, determine your needs and figure out the best subscription plan for you based on the number of users in your group, company, or organization.

For rates related to Skype for Business Online plans (that offer only Skype functionality), visit https://products.office.com/en/skype-for-business/online. For other Skype for Business plans that include an Office 365 subscription, visit https://products.office.com/en/skype-for-business/compare-plans.

You can find an entirely different set of subscription plans for Office 365 Business (that includes Skype) at https://products.office.com/en/business/compare-office-365-for-business-plans. For Office 365 Enterprise plans, visit https://products.office.com/en/business/compare-more-office-365-for-business-plans.

For individual users, Office 365 subscription plans that include Skype are at https://products.office.com/en/buy/compare-microsoft-office-products. Be sure to click the Office for PC or Office for Mac button near the top of the webpage to obtain accurate pricing for the equipment you'll be using.

In Practice

One Skype Account Per User

Even if you plan to use Skype on several computers and mobile devices, you need only one Skype account. Each time you begin using Skype on a particular computer or mobile device, sign in to the software or mobile app using your unique Skype username and password. Based on the type of account you have, only the Skype functionality you're entitled to is active within the software or mobile app. If you need to upgrade your account to utilize certain functionality, you can do so from within the software or mobile app.

Getting Started Using Skype for Business

Most small business users benefit greatly by taking advantage of an Office 365 subscription plan that includes Skype or Skype for Business. More information about the collaboration and file-sharing tools offered by Office 365 is in Chapter 11, "Using Microsoft Office 365 for Collaboration and File Sharing."

Whether you opt to take advantage of Office 365 integration or just Skype or Skype for Business' communications features, the first thing you must do is download and install the Skype software or mobile app onto the equipment you'll be using. To do this from a PC or Mac, visit www.skype.com/en/download-skype/skype-for-computer, and click the Get Skype for Windows or Get Skype for Mac button. The appropriate software automatically downloads. Double-click the downloaded file to install it.

FYI: Getting Help

The Skype software and mobile app have a built-in Help feature that provides assistance to new users who are setting up and personalizing their accounts. Skype's online support (https://support.skype.com) offers how-to articles, instructional videos, and interactive tutorials related to using each of Skype's features and functions.

To get Skype for your smartphone, visit www.skype.com/en/download-skype/skype-for-mobile to access specific links for the Skype mobile app for your smartphone. To get Skype for your tablet, visit www.skype.com/en/download-skype/skype-for-tablet to access specific links for the Skype mobile app for their device. You can also visit the app store for your smartphone or tablet and use the search field to find the Skype mobile application.

> **FYI: The Skype Smart Watch App**
>
> A special Skype app is also available for the Apple Watch and Android Wear smartwatches. Visit the app store for your smartwatch to find the Skype app or visit www.skype.com/en/download-skype/skype-for-wearables.

When you have the Skype application on the computers and mobile devices you plan to use the service with, launch the software or app and sign in to Skype using your Skype username and password (see Figure 14.1). If this is your first time using the service, click or tap the Create Account option on the Skype opening screen. You can also sign in using an existing Facebook or Microsoft account.

FIGURE 14.1 Sign in to your Skype account from your Internet-connected computer or mobile device to begin using this service.

You can customize a wide range of options in the Skype software. To do this on a Windows 10 PC, launch the Skype software, access the Tools pull-down menu, choose Options, and then click on the option icons displayed along the left margin of the screen, which include General Settings, Audio Settings, Sounds, Video Settings, Skype Translator, Privacy, Notifications, Calls, IMs & SMS, and Advanced.

On a Mac, launch the Skype software, access the Skype pull-down menu from the top-left corner of the screen, and choose Preferences. Click each of the tabs at the top of the Preferences window to customize the General, Privacy, Calls, Messaging, Contacts, Notifications, Audio/Video, and Advanced options.

Personalizing Your Skype Account

After you establish your Skype account and unique Skype username, personalize your profile to make it easier for other Skype users to find you, and to make yourself more easily identifiable when you're engaged in group voice or video calls. All of these customization options are optional. Ultimately, you determine what profile information other Skype users can see.

The following are some of the personalization you can make:

- Add a photo of yourself to your profile

- Associate your cellular phone, work phone, and/or home phone with your account, which makes it easier for people to find you through Skype

- Fill in the About Me field with a short profile about yourself

- Include your full address, or at least your city, state, and country within your profile, which makes it easier for people to find you through Skype

- Associate your personal and work-related email addresses with your Skype account, which makes it easier for people to find you through Skype

- Add your gender, birthday, and native language, webpage, and time zone details to your account

To personalize your Skype account, launch the Skype software or mobile app and click or tap your username. Click the available fields or options (see Figure 14.2). In the area below the Manage Account heading, you can purchase Skype Credit for making fee-based calls, acquire a Skype calling plan, or upgrade/downgrade your Skype account.

In Practice

Choose Who Can See Your Profile

While editing your profile, click on the Visible To Everyone option (refer to Figure 14.2) to adjust who is able to view your Skype profile in the future. If you select the Visible to My Contacts option, only people you establish as a contact within Skype are able to see your full profile. Everyone else sees only your Skype username. Be sure to adjust your account's privacy options to determine who can see your photo, who you will accept calls from, and what calling features can be used when you're engaged in conversations with specific people. For example, you can block specific Skype users, block anyone who is not an established Skype contact, or turn on or off the Save Chat History feature.

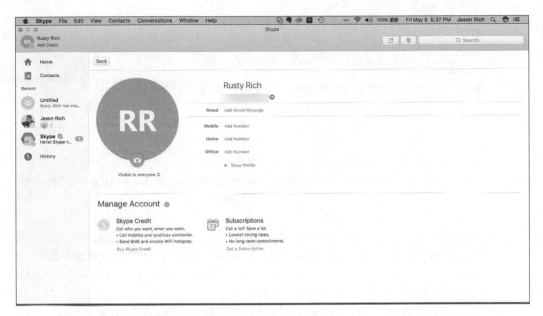

FIGURE 14.2 Add information to your Skype profile and then adjust the Privacy settings associated with your account.

Making and Receiving Voice Calls

Making a call with Skype is easy. Either click or tap one of the contacts already stored within the software or mobile app, or click or tap the numeric telephone keypad icon, and then type the phone number you want to call. You can also use the calling options from the Call and Conversation pull-down menus in the Windows or Mac version of Skype.

In Practice

Locate Other Skype Users

To try to find someone else on Skype, click the Add Contact icon and then enter their Skype username, email address, or phone number (see Figure 14.3). To narrow your search results, also include the person's city, state, and country in the Search field—for example, enter *John Doe, New York, New York, USA.*

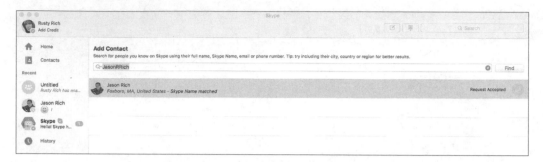

FIGURE 14.3 Quickly locate and establish contact with other Skype users by using the Search field.

When you've selected a contact, click or tap the Call or Call Phone icon to initiate a call. The Call icon initiates the call to a fellow Skype user, whereas the Call Phone icon allows you to place a call to a mobile phone or landline. Some versions of Skype use a single Call icon. Only icons applicable to your available communications options for each contact are displayed.

When you have the Skype application running on your Internet-connected computer or mobile device, and you receive an incoming call, simply click or tap the Answer icon when details about the caller are displayed. You see the appropriate call management options based on whether someone has initiated a Skype-to-Skype call or is calling from a mobile phone or landline. For Skype-to-Skype calls, you can accept a voice or video call request. If you do not answer the incoming call, it is either forwarded to your Skype voicemail, forwarded to the phone number that you've set up using the Call Forwarding feature, or it simply goes unanswered. Skype's call log indicates the missed call.

From the call-in-progress screen (see Figure 14.4), you have a wide range of options for managing the call. For example, click or tap the Mute icon (the microphone) to keep the call connected but turn off your computer or mobile device's microphone. Click or tap the Add Call (+) icon to establish a conference call or to use the screen-sharing feature with another Skype user. Click the End icon (the red phone handset) to end a voice or video call.

During a voice conversation, you can click the messaging icon to simultaneously conduct a text-based conversation—either with the person you're speaking to or any other Skype user. This is a useful tool if you want to send the person you're speaking with a file during the conversation or if you need to communicate with someone else altogether during a voice conversation.

FIGURE 14.4 Skype's call-in-progress screen.

FYI: Skype Keeps Track of Your Communications

Skype automatically maintains a detailed call log. It tracks incoming and outgoing calls, the length of calls, and other related information. To quickly re-establish a call with someone, look under the Recent heading or the History heading.

Understanding Voice Call Features

For making and receiving voice calls and/or group (conference) calls, the following functions are available:

- **Call forwarding:** Have incoming calls to your Skype account forwarded to any other phone number that you choose.

- **Caller ID:** When you initiate a call, your name and/or Skype phone number will be displayed on the receiver's Caller ID display, so they'll know exactly who's calling. In addition, if you receive a call, you see details for the person calling you.

- **Calls to mobile phones and landlines:** Enables you to call a mobile phone or landline; a small per-minute charge applies but there are also optional calling plans that make this type of calling less expensive.

- **Group calls:** Allows you to initiate a voice call with two or more people. Most Skype plans allow for up to 25 people to participate in a call, but some Skype Business plans (as well as Enterprise plans) allow for even more parties to participate in a single call.

- **Skype phone number:** Assigns you a unique Skype phone number, which allows anyone to call this number and reach you anywhere in the world as long as your computer or mobile device has Internet access. No per-minute international calling fees apply for the caller, even if you're traveling abroad when you receive the call via Skype.

- **Skype to Go:** This option allows you to make calls to international phone numbers using any phone, at low calling rates.

- **Skype-to-Skype voice calls:** Calls that are always free and unlimited.

- **Voice mail:** Assigned voice mailbox where missed incoming calls are forwarded so the caller can leave you a recorded message.

FYI: Save Money When Making Calls

Even if Skype voice calling is the only feature you use, you can save a fortune on international calling charges when calling overseas, or when you're abroad and calling home to the United States. All you need is an Internet connection for your computer or mobile device.

You can also use Skype to transform your tablet into a full-featured speakerphone for making and receiving calls (via the Internet) directly from your tablet. This works using the Wi-Fi or cellular data connection offered by your tablet. Unless you have an unlimited cellular data plan (or don't mind using up a lot of your monthly cellular data allocation to make or receive important calls), consider using Skype exclusively with a Wi-Fi Internet connection.

FYI: Learn About All Skype Features

The Skype communications platform is always evolving, and new features are frequently added. To learn about all of the current features through Skype, visit www.skype.com/en/features. Depending on which version of Skype you're using and the type of Skype account you have, all features described on this webpage might not be available to you.

Initiating or Answering a Video Call

Skype video calls or video conferences are available only between you and other Skype users. When this feature is available, you see a Video Call icon (a video camera) next to a contact's listing. When you initiate a call, or answer an incoming call, a Video Call icon is displayed along with a Voice Call icon (a telephone handset).

Video calling with Skype works almost exactly like voice calling except that you can see the other caller in addition to hearing the person or people you're communicating with (see Figure 14.5). During a call, it's possible to mute the microphone, switch to just a voice call, add one or more additional Skype users to the call, or use Skype's messaging or screen sharing capabilities.

FIGURE 14.5 The video call screen in Skype for Business.

FYI: Declining Video Calls

You can turn off the video calling option in Skype's Preferences menu. Alternatively, when an incoming video call is received, you have the option to answer it as a voice call and keep your camera turned off.

During a video call, you see a video window that shows your image in the corner of the main video window. You can move this small window around within the larger video window, so it's a good idea to position the Skype video window as close to your computer or mobile device's camera as possible. Doing so helps you remember to look into the camera during the call. Ideally, you want to position the camera so that you're centered in the tiny video window, which depicts exactly what the other party is seeing.

In Practice

Tips for Successful Calls

When you're preparing for a video call, try to position yourself so that the primary light source is in front of you and is shining as evenly as possible onto your face. In other words, don't be sitting or standing in front of a window or bright lamp (that's behind you). When the primary light source is behind you, you will appear as a silhouette during the video call. To counteract this, some people place a lamp next to or behind their computer to light up their face, which is facing the computer screen. In some cases, light from the computer screen will brighten your face, but this depends on what's being displayed on your screen.

Skype works best for voice or video calls if you have a strong Internet connection, and there is little or no ambient noise in the room. Your computer or mobile device's built-in microphone picks up all of the nearby sound, not just your voice, which can make it very difficult for other people to hear you. If the computer's microphone is too sensitive, you can adjust it within the Skype app. Another easy fix is to use a wireless or corded telephone headset with a built-in microphone.

If you're engaged in a group video call, consider having everyone mute their microphone when they're not speaking to eliminate as much excess noise as possible.

When you're engaged in a video call from a PC or Mac, you can click the Full Screen icon in the top-right corner of the screen to toggle full-screen mode on and off.

FYI: The Main Features of Skype Video Calling

The following are the main options for Skype's video calling:

- **One-to-one video calls:** Initiate or receive a video call from another Skype user.
- **Group video conferencing:** Manage a video call for a group of people who are all at different locations. How many people can engage in a group video call varies based on the type of Skype account you have.
- **Screen sharing:** Share what's on your computer screen with other call participants.

CAUTION

Some Restrictions Apply

If you're using a free Skype account for an individual, for Skype's video-calling feature, you're limited to 100 hours per month with a maximum of 10 hours per day and a limit of 4 hours per individual video call. Once you've used this monthly allocation, you can either upgrade your Skype account or revert to unlimited audio calls. Based on the type of paid Skype account you have, different maximum usage restrictions may also apply.

Using the Skype Messaging

If you're already accustomed to using Facebook Messenger, Apple's iMessage, and/or the text messaging capabilities built into your smartphone or tablet, for example, you'll have no trouble using Skype's messaging capabilities while you're engaged in either a voice or video call—or anytime you want to participate in text-based conversations with one or more other Skype users (see Figure 14.6).

FIGURE 14.6 Skype messaging can be used alone or while you're simultaneously engaged in a voice (shown) or video call.

After you open a messaging window with one or more people, type the message you want to send. (The field where you typed is labeled Type Here in some versions of Skype but is a blank field in others.)

Some versions of Skype enable you to attach additional content to an outgoing message. After entering the information, press the Enter/Return key on the keyboard or tap the Send icon. Within a fraction of a second, the message will be displayed for the other person or people you're communicating with to see and respond to. You can do more than type an outgoing message. To send additional types of content, follow these directions:

- ■ To attach a file or photo to the outgoing message, click the File Attachment icon. It's located to the right of the Type Here field. This icon looks like a photo with a document on a Mac. On a PC, the Photo and File Attachment icons are separate. Select the file you want to attach and send and then click or tap the Send button.

■ To share your current location with other people in the messaging conversation (when using some versions of Skype, including the mobile app), click the location icon. To use this feature from a computer, Wi-Fi must be turned on.

■ To share contact information, click the Contact icon (which looks like a business card), and then select which contact that's stored within the Skype app you want to share.

■ To include an emoji, music, or a sticker within the text-based message, click the Emoji icon, which looks like a smiley face, and then choose what type of content you want to send by clicking or tapping an icon in the scrolling menu. Next, select the specific item, such as an emoji, that you want to include within the message. What you select will be placed in the Type Here field.

FYI: The Main Features of Skype Messaging

When using Skype's group messaging and instant messaging features, the following options are available:

■ **Emojis:** Incorporate a variety of graphic-oriented emojis into your text-based conversations.

■ **GroupMe:** A separate app that provides group messaging for Skype's instant messaging service. The Skype GroupMe mobile app allows users to use one-on-one or group messaging and includes the ability to include text, photos, and a user's current location within a message. The regular Skype app offers limited functionality for establishing multi-party phone calls or text messaging sessions.

■ **Instant messaging:** Type text messages that the recipients can read and respond to in real time through Skype's instant messaging service. Identify people you want to communicate with using their unique Skype username.

■ **Send Texts (SMS):** Send text messages from Skype to any smartphone, anywhere in the world, using the recipient's cellular phone number rather than a Skype username. An additional per-message fee applies for using this feature.

■ **Video messaging:** Attach and send a short video clip as part of an instant message. (This option is not available from all versions of Skype.)

Sharing Files and Using Screen Sharing via Skype

When you share your screen, the contents of your screen will be displayed within the other party's main Skype video window. To make your screen visible to others while you're engaged in a voice or video call, click the + icon in the calling window (see Figure 14.7) and then select the Screen Sharing option, which is available in most, but not all versions of Skype. Then select the Share Entire Screen or Share Window option, and click or tap the Start button.

After you click on the Screen Sharing's Start button, everything you do on your computer will be seen in real time by the call's other participants (see Figure 14.8). This feature only works when communicating with other Skype users.

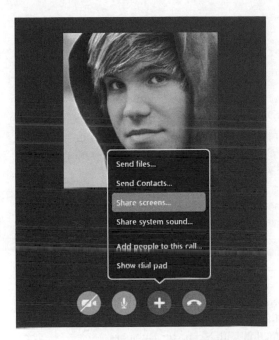

FIGURE 14.7 Initiating the Screen Sharing feature.

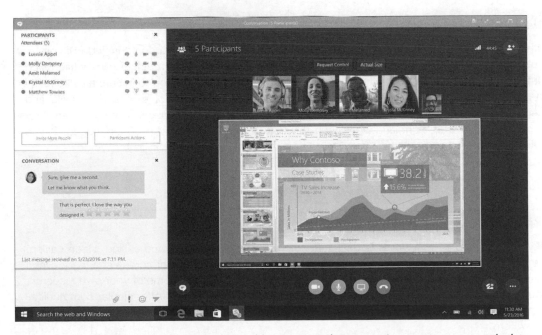

FIGURE 14.8 With screen sharing, share either your entire computer screen or one window running an application.

> **CAUTION**
>
> ## Be Careful What You Share
>
> When you use the Share Entire Screen option, other people in your call see everything that's displayed on your computer screen. Before activating this option, be sure to close any windows or shut down any applications that might reveal private or sensitive information.
>
> To keep attention focused on a specific application, open only that application and then opt to share only that program window. If you choose to share just an application window and you have more than one application open, Skype asks you to select which open and active window you want to share.
>
> While you use the Screen Sharing feature, you can switch between full screen sharing, window sharing, or switch the feature off altogether and revert back to a normal video or voice call.

When you're on a video or voice call and watching a screen that someone else is sharing, you'll see more detail if you switch to full-screen mode. Remember that when someone else is sharing their screen with you, you're not able to manipulate any content that you're seeing. If you want to have a virtual white board experience, where people can collaborate in an interactive environment, you need to use tools that are bundled with Office 365 in conjunction with Skype for Business.

> ### FYI: Other Useful Skype for Business Features
>
> Other useful features Skype for Business offers with most types of accounts include Skype for Outlook.com (an interactive tool that allows you to initiate calls with a single click while using Outlook), Share Button (which allows people visiting your website or blog to initiate a call directly to you via Skype), and Skype Translate (which automatically translates voice calls, video calls, and instant messages between two languages as a conversation is taking place). The voice translator currently works with eight languages, and the text translator works with 50 languages. Skype Translator currently only works with certain versions of Skype, such as Skype for Windows.

> ### FYI: Skype Isn't Your Only Option
>
> Skype and Skype for Business is definitely not your only option for voice calling, video calling, instant messaging, group messaging, participating in virtual meetings, or screen sharing. Several other tools mentioned in this book offer the same services. By doing some of your own research, you'll easily be able to find other competing cloud-based services that offer similar communications tools. Do your due diligence and you might find more viable and cost-effective solutions elsewhere.

Chapter | **15**

Discovering Slack

This chapter covers the following:

- An overview of Slack and what it can be used for
- Communication strategies when using Slack
- An explanation of Slack integrates with other cloud-based services and why this is important

Slack was designed by computer programmers. The initial intent was a tool for programmers to use to collaborate when working on the same project from different locations. Since its origin, Slack has become more user friendly with more business-oriented tools, such as drag-and-drop file sharing and Internet-based voice and video calling. The primary goal of Slack is to reduce internal email and make communications between team members and co-workers more productive but less time-consuming.

Slack communication tools make it particularly useful. In addition to being able to establish text conversations with different individuals or groups of people (as you can with any group messaging service), you can create separate Channels to handle specific topics of conversation. All messages are logged and stored by Slack and can be searched by any participants.

Slack is a cloud-based service that can be accessed using any Internet-connected computer's web browser by visiting www.slack.com. A user simply needs to sign in to his account to gain access to.

You can also use the free Windows PC or Mac application. Visit https://slack.com/downloads to get the appropriate version of the software.

If you prefer to use a mobile device, you can get the Slack mobile app for your iOS or Android devices. The iOS edition of the mobile app is available from the App Store (https://itunes.apple.com/app/slack-app/id618783545). The Android edition of the mobile app is available from the Google Play Store (https://play.google.com/store/apps/details?id=com.Slack).

Each Team Member needs only one active Slack account, which she can use to sign in to her account from any number of computers and/or mobile devices.

Slack Overview

Within a business environment, people can be more productive when they can easily communicate and share files with each other in a way that's fast and convenient. Slack provides a slick messaging solution that helps you avoid playing phone tag, relying on voicemail, or adding more clutter to your email inbox. Slack combines the features of instant messaging, group messaging, and direct messaging from popular social media services with additional tools targeted to the needs of business users.

Slack is all about making it easier for team members to communicate in topic-specific group message forums, referred to as Channels, as well as using one-to-one Direct Messages. Messages in Channels are searchable, and you can share files with one or more people. Plus, two or more users can quickly establish an Internet-based voice or video call (with screen sharing functionality) to further facilitate efficient communication.

> ### FYI: Channels Are Virtual Workspaces
>
> A Slack Channel is a virtual workspace in which two or more people can communicate about a specific topic. The Team Owner or Admin (read more about these roles later in the chapter) can set ground rules for what should or should not be discussed within specific Channels. Each Channel is given a name (using the #*channelname* format). Any number of Channels can be created and maintained. Each Channel can be open to all Team Members or specific groups of two or more Team Members.
>
> By default, when a new Slack Team is created, two Channels, called #General and #Random, are automatically created. It's then up to the Team Owner, Admin(s), and Team Members to create and work within separate Channels, which can be topic-specific or created around departments, office locations, teams, or specific projects. Team Members can become active in as many separate Channels as needed and can quickly switch between Channels.
>
> Once a Channel is created, only the Team Owner or an Admin has the ability to rename, delete, or archive a Channel, or adjust the Channel Message Retention settings, and customize or alter a wide range of Channel-specific settings.

Most of the communication that happens using Slack takes place in Channels. All messages are automatically time stamped, which means the Slack service records the date and time every message is published, as well as when individual files are uploaded and shared.

When two or more people need to converse privately, they use Direct Messages (DMs). A group of up to eight users can participate in a DM conversation, but any number of users can participate within a Channel.

Although Slack is designed to make communicating faster and more efficient because users can post short messages, it's also possible to compose and publish a Post within a Channel or DM conversation. A Post is simply a long-form message that contains formatting, so it's easy to read.

FYI: Learn Slack Quickly from Free Slack Guides

Available for free from the Slack website (https://get.slack.help/hc/en-us/categories/202622877-Slack-Guides) is a series of online guides that help Team Owners and Admins establish and manage a Slack account. The guides also help individual users quickly learn how to use this service and become more efficient communicators.

Separate Department Playbooks are available to help companies use Slack for specific tasks. This series of guides includes *Slack for Software Developers, Slack for Project Management, Slack for Human Resources, Slack for Executives,* and *Slack for Sales.*

Slack Subscription Plans and Pricing

Originally, Slack was an entirely free service for all users and for teams of all sizes. For small- to medium-sized teams or companies, a free plan is still available, but some of the more advanced features of the service remain locked unless you have a paid subscription.

FYI: Who's Using Slack?

According to a report issued by DMR (http://expandedramblings.com/index.php/slack-statistics), as of March 2017, Slack had more than five million users, hosted more than 60,000 Teams, and hosted in excess of 1.5 million paid accounts. (The majority of users and Teams are taking advantage of free accounts.) As of May 2016, approximately 77 percent of Fortune 100 companies used Slack.

The Slack Free Plan

The Free plan is ideal for a team that wants to get started with Slack. After the service has proven itself to be a viable and efficient way to communicate within your organization, the Team Leader can upgrade the account (and all of the Team Member accounts) to paid accounts.

A Free plan offers the following functionality:

- Access to Slack from the Slack website (www.slack.com) or through the free Windows PC or Mac software and the official Slack mobile apps

- Searchable message archive that holds up to 10,000 messages sent and received by a Team

- Storage space of 5GB for the entire Team

- Two-factor authentication for individual user accounts

- Up to 10 different integrations with third-party software, mobile apps, and cloud services

- Only two participants for voice and video calls hosted by Slack

All of the Slack plans allow for an unlimited number of Channels to be created and for any number of Team Members to participate within each Channel. Any number of Direct Messages can be sent or received as well, although only the most recent 10,000 messages are searchable.

The Slack Standard Plan

Designed specifically with small- to medium-sized businesses in mind, the Standard plan offers a more robust collection of features and functions that expand the way Team Members can communicate while also enhancing security. This plan is priced at $8.00 per month, per user, when billed monthly. Alternatively, you can be billed annually, which breaks down to $6.67 per month, per user.

The Standard plan includes everything the Free plan offers plus the following:

- More than two participants allowable for Slack-hosted voice or video

- Screen sharing during voice and video calls

- Detailed profiles for each Team Member that include the Slack username (*@username*), full name, photo, and details about themselves

- Online storage space of 10GB for each Team Member

- Guests access to participate in one or more Channels (as well as send/receive DMs with Team Members active within those Channels) without having a paid Slack account

- Capability for users to search all Channels for relevant people and/or content

- Additional security features that the Team Owner or an Admin can manage (Mandatory Two-Factor Authentication for all Team Members and requirement that guest users sign in using Google account credentials)

- Unlimited integrations with third-party software, mobile apps, and cloud services can be activated

- Unlimited searchable message archives

The Slack Plus Plan

The Slack Plus plan is $15.00 per month, per user, when billed monthly. Alternatively, you can be billed annually, which breaks down to $12.50 per month, per user. The Slack Plus plan includes all of the features and functionality offered by the Free and Standard plans, but it includes more emphasis on account security and provides additional security for all content that's stored online.

This plan also offers a 99.99 percent guaranteed uptime for access to the Slack service, as well as 24/7 support with a four-hour response time. The Team Owner or Admins are given more control over individual user accounts, and 20GB of online storage space is provided for each user.

The Slack Enterprise Grid Plan

Pricing for the Slack Enterprise Grid plan is based on a number of factors, including the number of Team Members who will be using the service. This plan is designed for large companies, and the added functionality that's offered to this type of account is mainly about adhering to industry-specific compliance regulations and providing additional security.

This plan includes additional tools for data loss prevention, eDiscovery, and offline backups, and each user gets 1TB of online storage space. Support is available 24/7, with a two-hour response time. You can find additional information about Slack Enterprise plans at https://slack.com/enterprise.

In Practice

Productivity Tips from Other Slack Users

The Slack community of users is diverse and ever-growing; in many cases, users are passionate about this platform. To help companies and Teams exchange ideas and strategies for using the service to increase productivity and improve internal communication, free Slack Meetups are held in major cities throughout the year.

In addition, Slack hosts Slack Frontiers events, which are two-day, hosted conferences that include seminars and workshops. They also provide networking opportunities for Slack users to exchange ideas about teamwork and collaboration using the cloud. The admission fee is between $399.00 and $999.00 per person, depending on how far in advance you book your ticket(s).

To learn about Slack Meetups and Slack Frontiers Events, visit https://slack.com/events.

FYI: Slack Proficiency Is a Marketable Skill

The skillset and knowledge associated with being a proficient Slack user has become a sought after and marketable skill for job seekers, especially when applying for jobs at companies that have already adopted Slack. To make it easier for job seekers to find jobs where Slack proficiency is in high demand, Slack offers a free job search tool, which you can access at https://slackatwork.com.

Getting Started with Slack

When a group of people or an entire company want to begin using Slack, the first step is for one person (known as the Team Owner) to create a Team by visiting www.slack.com and clicking the Create a Team option or the Get Started button (See Figure 15.1). A Team comprises any number of people: include a small group, an entire department, or all employees within a company. By default, new Slack accounts are set up as Free accounts, but the Team Owner can upgrade at any time.

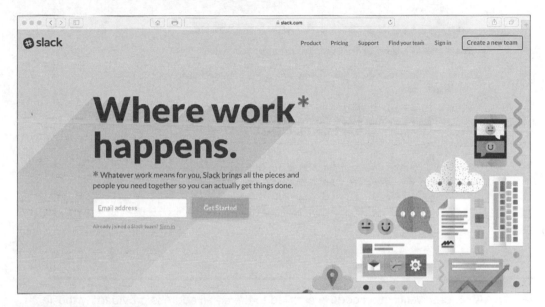

FIGURE 15.1 The Slack homepage, from where you can start a new account.

> ### FYI: Team Management
>
> The Team Owner can opt to handle all management aspects of the account or delegate certain account management tasks to Admins. An Admin is able to manage members, Channels, and account maintenance tools. The Team Owner controls payments and billing, Team authentication, message and file retention, and security tools.

The Team Owner is prompted to provide his email address. Within a minute after an email address is provided, Slack sends a confirmation email to that address, so the Team Owner can verify the account. Enter the six-digit verification code (see Figure 15.2) from the email on the Check Your Email screen (see Figure 15.3).

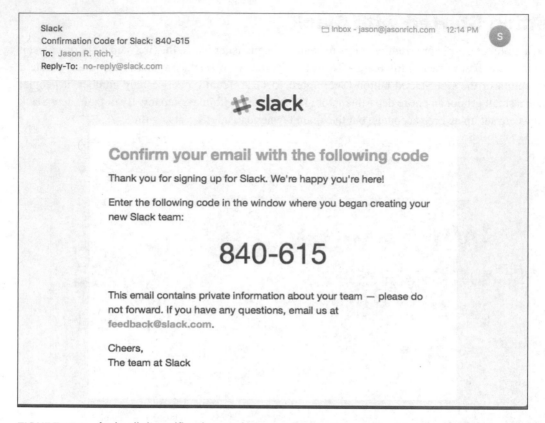

FIGURE 15.2   A six-digit verification code is emailed to the email address provided by the Team Owner.

FIGURE 15.3   Enter the verification code when prompted.

Provide your first and last names in the fields provided and then choose a unique, personal Slack username. This username is always displayed using all lowercase letters (for example, @jasonrich).

A username can include letters, numbers, periods, underscores, or hyphens. Click the Continue to Proceed button to continue.

FYI: Getting Help with Slackbots

Slackbot is a tool built into Slack that helps users get started using this service by explaining key features and functions. You also can create custom Slackbots to generate automated and customized responses related to specific actions by Team Members. For example, if you ask a question related to how Slack is used, the Slackbot either provides an immediate answer or provides a link to an article within Slack's Help Center.

When prompted, enter a unique password for the Team Owner account being created. The password must be at least six characters long. Click the Continue to Team Info button to proceed.

Answer the five questions on the Tell Us About Your Team screen (see Figure 15.4). Choose the most appropriate answer to each question from each respective pull-down menu. After responding to these five questions, click the Continue to Company Name button.

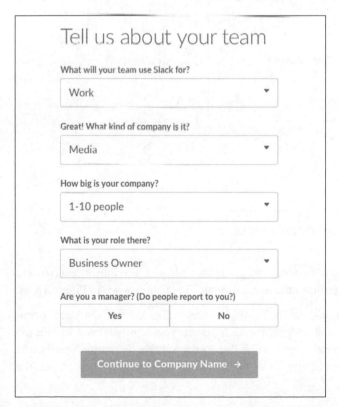

FIGURE 15.4   Answer these five questions to provide Slack with basic details about your team.

When prompted, enter the name of your Company, which is also your Slack Team Name. So, if you represent just one division or team within a large company, choose a name that's descriptive and appropriate, such as "The Sample Company Marketing." The Team Owner can always change the Team Name later. Click the Continue to Team URL button to proceed.

Every Team is assigned a unique Slack URL. Based on the Team Name you just created, Slack recommends a Slack Team URL. You can accept this URL by clicking the Create Team button, or make up your own alternative (see Figure 15.5). The Slack URL must be unique and previously unused. If you try using a Slack URL that's been taken, you're notified and asked to create a different Slack URL. After clicking the Create Team button, agree to Slack's Terms of Service by clicking the I Agree button.

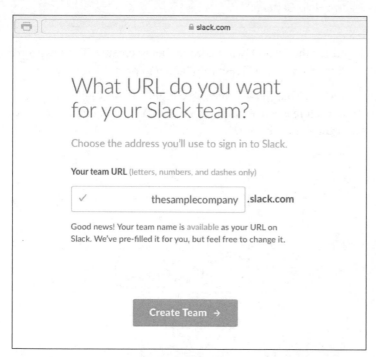

FIGURE 15.5   Confirm or edit the proposed Slack Team URL.

Once again, you'll be prompted to provide the six-digit verification code you previously received via email. You'll then receive an email which outlines the terms of your Free plan (shown in Figure 15.6).

Now that the Team has been created, it's time to invite Team Members to Slack. From the Send Invitations screen (see Figure 15.6) enter the email address for each person you want to invite to join the team. (If you need to invite more than three people, click the +Add Another Invitation option.) At anytime in the future, the Team Owner or Admin(s) can invite additional Team members. Click the Send Invitations button to continue.

In Practice

People Can Join Your Team Based On Your Email Domain

If all of your employees or team members have an email address with the domain name as the Team Owner, you can click the Let People on Your Team Sign Up with Their Verified *@YourCompanyName.com* Email Address check box so that anyone with a qualifying email address is able to access the Slack website and join your team, even without having received an invitation.

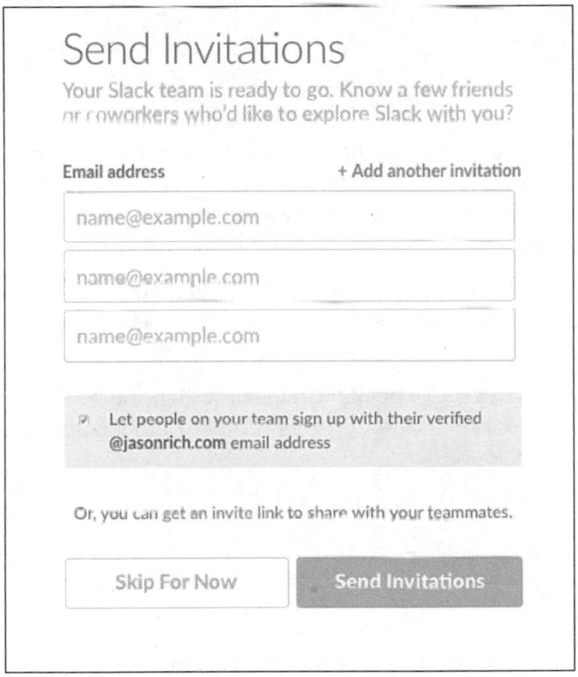

FIGURE 15.6 Invite individual users to your team from this Send Invitations screen.

When the Welcome screen appears, you and your team members are ready to begin using Slack. As the Team Owner, click the Explore Slack button to continue. In the meantime, the people you've invited to the team can accept their respective emailed invitations and begin using Slack after they register their account as a Team Member.

In Practice

Adjusting Team Members' Permissions

The Team Owner is responsible for adjusting the permissions for each Team Member. This task should be handled as soon as a Team is established. For example, the Team Owner can transfer management responsibilities to another user or give specific Team Members Admin authority. The Team Owner can also revoke permissions, shut down user accounts, and establish Guest Accounts and associate permissions to those accounts. See the "Adjusting Slack's Security Features" section later in this chapter for information on where to make these changes.

FYI: Guest Accounts

The Team Owner or Admin for a Team with a paid account can set up two types of guest accounts so that a guest can access data in Slack without having to have an account. These guest accounts are helpful for people who need to temporarily communicate with Team Members on a particular Channel but are not permanent members of the team:

- **Single-Channel Guests:** A Single-Channel Guest can be invited to access just one Channel established by a Team. The guest is allowed to send and receive direct messages only with other participants of that single Channel.

- **Multi-Channel Guests:** A user is given access to only specific Channels within the Team's account. The guest can send and receive direct messages only with other participants in those Channels.

FYI: Upgrade a Slack Account Anytime

After a Team Owner has established a Slack Team account, the Team Owner can upgrade the accounts of all Team Members by clicking the Team name in the top-left corner of the browser window, selecting the Upgrade Slack option, and then clicking the Upgrade Now button for the desired type of account.

You see the main Slack screen (see Figure 15.7). Along the left margin is a list of Channels that are already established for the Team. The defaults are #general and #random. Below that is the Direct Messages (DM) menu that displays the name of all current Team Members. Click a Team Member name to send that person a DM. Click the + Invite People option to invite additional Team Members to the Team.

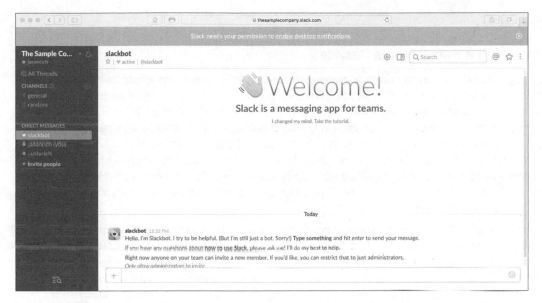

FIGURE 15.7   From this main screen, you can jump between Channels, initiate or respond to DMs, and initiate or answer voice/video calls.

Within the main area of the browser window is the open Channel's chat window. Here, you can view all of the text-based messages (in chronological order) published by Team Members. To compose and post a new message, type the message in the Compose Message field at the bottom of the browser window. All messages within a Channel can be seen by all Team Members who are active in that Channel, along with the Team Owner and Admin(s).

In Practice

Getting Someone's Attention

When you're communicating in a Channel or having a group DM conversation, you can address one specific user by name by using the @ symbol followed by his or her username. Doing this calls that person's attention to the message and also generates a Notification to that user. When someone is referred to by name (@username) within a Channel or DM, this is referred to as a *Mention*.

CAUTION

Slack Isn't a Social Media Service

Although Slack's communications features resemble the text messaging, group messaging, direct messaging, and instant messaging features in Facebook Messenger, iMessage, Twitter, Instagram, Google+, and other social media services, remember that Slack is meant to be a business communication tool. Consequently, you should use only professional language (suitable for a workspace). In other words, you should avoid the use of abbreviations, sentence fragments, emojis, and slang, which are commonplace on social media. Watercooler chitchat should also be limited to specific Slack Channels, or prohibited altogether. If you wouldn't say something out loud during an in-person meeting or during a conference call with everyone listening, don't type it within a message via Slack.

Channels created to host work-related conversation should be used only for information/file/content exchange purposes. Stick to the topic(s) that the specific Channel was created to host, and remember that in addition to Team Members, the Team Owner and Admin(s) will be able to see anything and everything that's discussed using Slack, and everything is saved and logged.

To attach a file or other content to a message, click on the + icon and then choose the file or type of content from the menu (see Figure 15.8). The added file or content is stored online and made available to all Team Members participating in that Channel. If the file was sent as part of a DM, only the recipients of that DM will have access to the file. You can also insert emojis in a message by clicking the emoji icon at the right of the Compose Message field.

In Practice

Emoji Etiquette

Keep in mind, some teams frown on using emojis within messages because they're "unprofessional." This is a decision that the Team Owner needs to make and enforce. If you believe emojis should not be used within a specific Channel, or at all by Team Members using Slack, make this clear upfront. You might find it beneficial to create a customized Slack style guide or policy guide to help people use this tool properly.

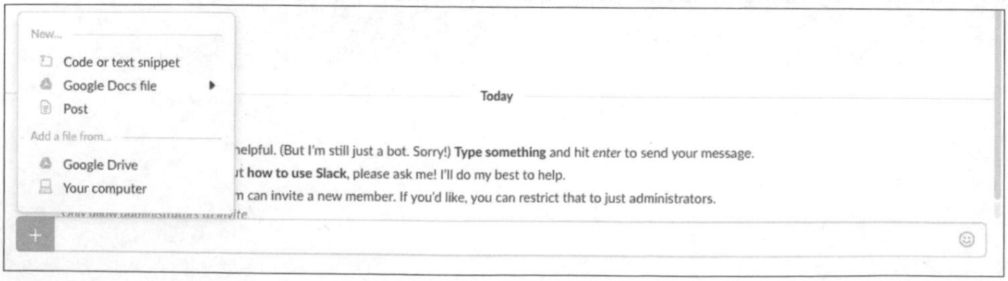

FIGURE 15.8   Click on the + icon to add a file or content to a message.

You can navigate a long conversation by clicking the gear-shaped icon in the top-right corner of the browser window and then choosing the Jump to Date, View Slackbot's Profile, or View Conversation Details option.

To view or hide Conversation Details, click the Conversation Details icon (see Figure 15.9). To quickly find any content within a specific Channel's conversation, type a keyword, date, name, or phrase within the Search field.

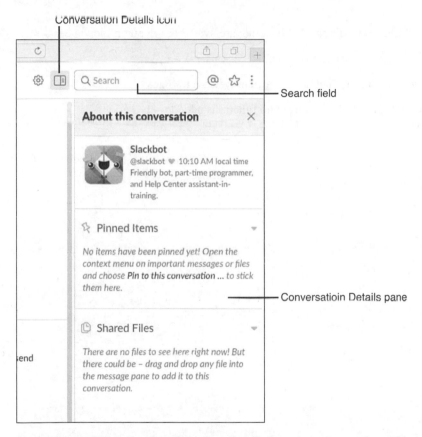

FIGURE 15.9   Click the Conversation Details icon to open or close this pane that includes details about the open Channel's conversation.

Pinning Messages

As you participate in a Channel or DM session, you have the ability to Pin individual messages that you deem important, which makes them easier to find and return to later.

Click on the @ icon to learn about and use Mentions (a way of referring to a specific Team Member) within a message. Click the star icon to add a star to a message to indicate that it's important. Starring a message is like bookmarking a website. It makes the message easier to find and access later. Click the Menu icon in the top-right corner of the browser window to access the following options (see Figure 15.10):

- **Your Files:** Access content that you've stored online that you've shared or plan to share with Team Members

- **All Files:** Access all files from all Team Members that are available to you online via Slack

- **Team Directory:** View a list of all Team Members (Slack users)

- **Help:** Access online-based tutorials and how-to articles related to Slack

- **What's New:** Learn about the newest features and functions added to the service

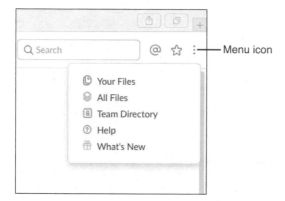

FIGURE 15.10   The Slack menu.

In Practice

Managing an Account

The Team Owner or Admin can manage aspects of the account by clicking the Team Name in the top-left corner of the browser window and then clicking the option for the function that needs to be managed (see Figure 15.11).

FIGURE 15.11   This menu offers tools for managing the entire Team and individual Team Member accounts.

In Practice

Managing Your Notifications

You can set up your account so you receive Notifications when something needs your attention when you're away from Slack. Click the bell-shaped Notifications icon next to the Team name and then select Your Notifications Preferences. Follow the on-screen prompts to adjust the settings for your account.

If there are specific times during the day or night that you do not want to be disturbed by Notifications, adjust the Do Not Disturb Schedule options, and select time periods each day when you don't want to receive Notifications in real time. Any Notifications you would have received are stored and presented to you after the Do Not Disturb period ends.

One of the useful features of Slack is that many different Channels can be created, and users can quickly switch between Channels and DM conversations. To switch between Channels, click the Quick Switcher icon in the bottom-left corner of the window, or click on a Channel name in the left margin (see Figure 15.12).

To switch between DM conversations, click a username in the left margin of the browser window (below the Direct Messages heading).

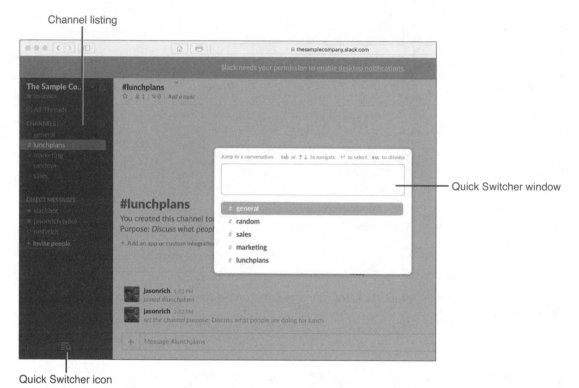

Channel listing

Quick Switcher window

Quick Switcher icon

FIGURE 15.12   Team Members can quickly switch between Channels and take part in numerous separate, topic-specific conversations.

To initiate a voice or video call with one other Team Member (with the Free plan) or with multiple people (with a paid plan), click the Call icon (see Figure 15.13). After a call is initiated, a new browser window opens that reveals the voice and video-calling features.

FYI: Calling Has Its Limitations

At the time of writing, the Calling feature didn't work with all web browsers. It did, however, work with both the Windows and Mac OS version of the Chrome web browser. Only one-to-one voice or video calls are available with a Free account. In addition, with a Free account calls can be initiated only from a DM conversation, not from within a Channel.

Call icon

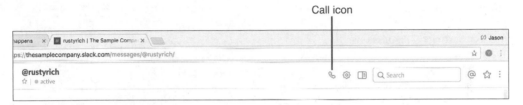

FIGURE 15.13   Click the Call icon to initiate an Internet-based voice or video call via Slack.

All of Slack's menu options and command icons are displayed within the main browser window, giving you access to the majority of this service's features and functions you need. The same functionality is also provided by the Slack Desktop software for Windows PCs and Macs, as well as in the Slack mobile app for smartphones and tablets.

Communicating More Efficiently Using Slack

The following are a collection of tips and strategies that will help you and your team communicate more efficiently using Slack.

Adjusting Slack's Security Features

The Team Owner or Admin should monitor Team invitations to ensure only the appropriate people have access to and the ability to participate in topic-specific conversations within Channels. To further protect against unauthorized access to Slack accounts, turn on the two-factor authentication feature for all Team Members to use this each time they log in to their account. Users also should refrain from allowing their web browsers to remember their account usernames and passwords.

The Team Owner or Admins should also make a point to review and adjust the Settings & Permissions options for the entire Team. Click the Team Name in the top-left corner of the web browser window and select the Team Settings option.

The Settings & Permissions menu screen (see Figure 15.14) displays four tabs near the top: Settings, Permissions, Authentication, and Attachments. Review each of these menus and adjust each setting based on company policy and the level of security that's required or desired. Some of these options are available only for paid accounts.

FYI: Adjusting Team Members' Roles

To make adjustments to the Team Member roles, from the Settings and Permissions menu screen, click the Manage Your Team Members and Roles option.

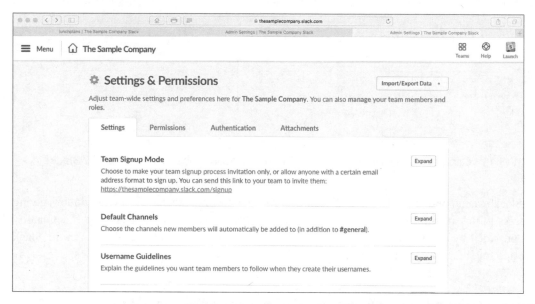

FIGURE 15.14   The Team Owner can adjust security and permissions-related settings related to all Team Members from the Settings & Permissions screen.

Creating Detailed Profiles

When you work with a large team, especially when not everyone knows each other well, companies should require all users to complete their Profiles to include their full names, usernames that include their full names, and job titles. Users should also add profile photos that are clear headshots that are easily identifiable.

In Practice

Keep a Business Tone

The Team Owner or Admin should instruct Team Members to avoid using nicknames and profile photos that show anything other than the face. In other words, no cute family photos, pet photos, or cartoon-like avatars.

It's also helpful if each user adds a phone number, time zone, and, if applicable, a Skype username. All of this information is displayed to all Team Members.

To update or edit your Profile, click your username in the top-left corner of the browser window, and then click Profile & Account. Next, click the Edit Profile button. After making the desired changes, click the Save Changes button.

During conversations, Team Members should be able to click someone's profile and easily be able to determine who they are and what they do within the company. A complete profile also makes it easy for Team Members to address specific questions or comments to the appropriate people within a company using a DM, if necessary.

Creating Topic-Specific Channels and General Channels

For Slack to be the most useful as a communications tool, Team Members need to get into the habit of using it to handle all conversations rather than also making voice calls, sending internal emails, or covering information that's of interest to the entire group during in-person meetings that all Team Members don't attend. After all, Slack can only make transcripts of conversations and files available to everyone when that information is actually collected and stored by the service.

To facilitate organized and focused conversations, use as many topic-specific Channels as are necessary. Create at least one or two general Channels, such as the default #general or #random channel, that can be used to facilitate conversations that are not directly related to the work at hand. For example, a #lunchplans Channel can be where people discuss where they're going or what they're doing for lunch, so this topic of conversation doesn't create distracting "noise" within a Channel created to discuss a more pressing topic or project.

Customizing Notification Settings

Slack should help facilitate convenient communication between people; it shouldn't become a distraction. Each user should customize the Notification Settings and Status so that they're not disturbed at inopportune times by messages and conversations that aren't time-sensitive or pressing.

You can set up the Notifications feature to email or text message you when you're mentioned by name within a Channel or when you receive a DM. You can adjust your real-time Status to display a message, such as Currently Available, In a Meeting, Commuting, Out Sick, Vacationing, or Working Remotely. You change your status by clicking your username and choosing Select a Status. Type a status in the What's Your Status field or choose from the available suggestions.

Customizing the Appearance of Channels

Each time you create a new Channel, you should give it a descriptive title so people clearly understand what the Channel should be used for. Create a handful of general channel topics, and then create more specialized Channels based on the needs of Team Members. It's the job of the Team Owner and Admin to keep everyone on topic within each Channel.

The person who creates the Channel also can customize the appearance by choosing a theme and color scheme. It's also possible to create motivational messages or announcement messages, which you can have displayed at designated times.

Making Communication More Efficient

The concept behind Slack is to create one centralized forum for people to communicate, so it's in your best interest to encourage Team Members to use Slack for as much communication as possible. Because Slack allows for group messaging within Channels as well as DMs, consider whether a topic needs a resolution urgently before you initiate a voice or video call with other users. If a simple question can be responded to with a short text-based message, don't call someone and chat for 20 minutes. Another goal you might have for Slack is to reduce email inbox clutter by encouraging Team Members to communicate via Slack instead of relying on internal email.

Figure out how your team works best and then set up guidelines for when other forms of communication (calls, emails, and in-person meetings) that take place outside of Slack can be used. When these alternative communication options are used, someone should be responsible for updating Slack with the appropriate information and files so that all team members always have access to the information.

Taking Advantage of Integrations

Your company probably already uses a handful of popular software applications, mobile apps, and other cloud services. To make sharing content from these applications easy and secure using Slack, install Integrations. For example, if your company already uses Dropbox or Box as a file-storage and -sharing solution, content stored on one of these services can be shared via Slack, when the appropriate Integration is installed and set up.

Slack offers more than 900 optional Integrations. The number of Integrations that can be installed at any given time depends on the type of account the team has. The Team Owner or an Admin can choose which Integrations are allowed and sets them up with specific Permissions to ensure the Team Members have access to content they need from third-party applications and services.

Visit https://slack.com/apps to explore the Integrations that are available.

In Practice

Take Advantage of Keyboard Shortcuts

As you become proficient using Slack, you can speed your navigation around the service by taking advantage of keyboard shortcuts. To view a complete list of keyboard shortcuts that work with Slack visit https://get.slack.help/hc/en-us/articles/201374536.

Chapter | **16**

Maximizing Communication Efficiency with Trello

This chapter covers the following:

- How Trello is different from other cloud-based collaboration tools
- How to get started using Trello
- How to share files
- How to integrate content from other applications with Trello

Trello is a unique online collaboration tool because it enables individuals and teams to compose, gather, organize, and share information in a format that's useful for brainstorming sessions, managing lists, and managing projects.

Trello Overview

Imagine a giant bulletin board or whiteboard in an office's conference room where people display color-coded index cards to facilitate creating and organizing ideas, lists, and any kind of project-related information. On each card, team members write or draw a separate item of information so that everyone can see it to collaborate and brainstorm together.

With this board, team members can write as many separate cards as needed; post them; rearrange them; and add, remove, or draw attention to specific cards as needed. When everyone gathers around the board, individuals can comment on ideas, raise questions, and freely discuss information displayed on specific cards.

Unfortunately, this scenario has a few rather significant drawbacks:

- At some point, the conference room would run out of bulletin board or whiteboard space.

- Everyone on your team needs to be in the same room, at the same time, to openly share their ideas, discuss them, and see the layout of the cards as they're being created or re-organized.

- If a document or other content is needed because it relates to a specific card, someone would need to make copies for everyone, and then distribute it.

- When the team leaves that room, all the information is left behind.

Well, think of Trello as a virtual room with a bulletin board that never runs out of space. You can create any number of computer-generated, color-coded cards, and then any number of team members can edit and move the cards from anywhere in the world as long as they can connect to the Trello service.

In addition, users have the ability attach files, documents, and content from other applications and mobile apps to individual cards to share information as needed. Team members can simultaneously create and manage lists and other project-related information that's securely stored in the cloud. When topic-specific questions or concerns arise that relate to content on a specific card, any team member can add comments and start a text-based discussion. If content is time-sensitive, users can assign due dates and alerts to individual cards. Users also can customize labels, so it's easy to determine what each individual card relates to.

A virtual team that uses Trello can include any number of people who view and collaborate on the board for free. Because team members can securely access the service from any Internet-connected computer or mobile device, everyone can work together from any location that's most convenient. Users can collaborate in real time from different locations or simply check in to the service at their convenience to see what information has been added or changed since their last visit.

Any information in Trello that's date or time related can be synced with the users' calendars or scheduling applications. In addition, users can configure Trello to send notifications via email, their web browser, or forwarded to their mobile device.

FYI: Trello History

Established in January 2011 by a company called Fog Creek Software, Trello was designed to provide an easy-to-use, cloud-based way for groups of people to create, gather, display, organize, and share almost any type of information in a visual way. In July 2014, the Trello service was spun off from Fog Creek Software and became Trello, Inc. At that time, the company had raised $10.3 million in Series A funding and had more than 4.75 million users.

In early 2017, with more than 19 million users, Trello was acquired by a company called Atlassian (www.atlassian.com), which at the time already operated multiple software applications and online platforms designed to help small businesses be more productive.

An individual user or team can create one or more boards within Trello. Each board can contain any number of cards and lists. One user can be a member of several different teams, and each team can have its own boards.

In Practice

Lists and Checklists

Individual cards within Trello can contain unlimited bulleted lists, numbered lists, or interactive checklists. You can assign alarms to lists or list items that have deadlines. As checklist items are completed, they are crossed off the list, and a graphic progress bar is updated in real time so team members can see the progress through the list.

FYI: Trello Compared to Evernote or OneNote

There are several popular note-taking and information-gathering applications that allow users to organize information and collaborate. The big difference between Trello and similar applications, such as Evernote or Microsoft OneNote, is that Trello users create virtual boards and then populate those boards with virtual cards that can each contain text, graphics, file attachments, and several types of lists or checklists.

Applications like Evernote or OneNote allow the same types of information and content to be created and managed, but content is organized within virtual notebooks. Within each notebook can be sections that are then populated with any number of virtual pages that contain a user or team's content.

Deciding which note-taking and information-gathering tool is most appropriate for you is mainly a matter of personal taste. Whatever your preferences, it's a good idea to research several tools and then choose just one service or application and stick with it. Otherwise, your content will wind up spread across multiple apps, stored on different cloud services, and ultimately be harder to find and manage later.

Trello Subscription Plans and Pricing

One of the great things about Trello is that any group, team, or company can begin using the service for free. A Free account allows you to create unlimited boards, and each board can have an unlimited number of cards, lists, file attachments, and members associated with it. You can attach files as large as 10MB each to cards.

When using a Free account, each board can only utilize one Power-Up (see the nearby FYI), and many of the security features and options that are built into Trello, such as two-factor authorization for accounts, are locked for the Free account.

FYI: What's a Trello Power-Up?

What Trello refers to as Power-Ups are really optional add-ons that provide seamless integration with other software applications, mobile apps, and cloud services, such as Google Drive, Dropbox, Box, Microsoft OneDrive, Slack, Evernote, Google Hangouts, and/or Salesforce. These Power-Ups make it easy for Trello users to attach, share, and distribute documents, files, and content from other sources by attaching them to virtual cards within the Trello virtual workspace.

Currently, hundreds of Power-Ups are available, although with a Free account you can use only one Power-Up with each board. A Trello Gold account entitles you to three Power-Ups per board. For even greater flexibility using Power-Ups, both the Trello Business and Trello Enterprise accounts allow unlimited Power-Ups.

To view the ever-expanding line-up of Power-Ups that work with Trello, visit https://trello.com/power-ups.

In Practice

Getting the Most out of a Free Account

The Trello Free plan offers plenty of tools to handle the needs of small- to mid-sized teams, assuming you don't need any additional security or integration functionality. Keep in mind, though, that you can always take advantage of file encryption and password protection tools offered by other applications to protect the data that you share via Trello. To compensate for the ability to only attach small-sized files to cards, you can use the Share Link feature to display URLs that lead directly to files, documents, or content that's stored on another cloud-based service, such as Dropbox, Box, Google Drive, or OneDrive. In other words, instead of attaching the actual file to a card, the card includes a link to a different file-storage service. Your teammates can use that link to easily access a large-sized file (or an entire folder containing multiple files) as needed.

The Trello Gold Plan

Priced at $5.00 per month, per user on a monthly basis (or $45.00 per year, per user for an annual subscription), the Trello Gold plan expands Trello's functionality and customizability by allowing users to add up to three Power-Ups per board and to customize each board with backgrounds and virtual stickers. You also can upload and attach files that are as large as 250MB. Attached files can originate from your computer or another cloud-based service. Frequently used searches are saved, so it's easier to locate content that's stored within Trello.

The Trello Business Class Plan

Priced at $9.99 per user, per month (when paid annually), the Trello Business Plan includes everything that a Trello Gold plan has, including the ability to add unlimited file attachments (as large as 250MB) to individual cards. The Business Class plan also adds unlimited Power-Ups and introduces a handful of features and functionality that cater more to business users, such as Admin tools for managing users and the ability to designate specific boards as public or private. You can also send restricted invitations to specific boards, which enables you to control which team members have access to which Trello boards.

The Trello Enterprise Plan

This plan is best suited to large companies or organizations that have many individual users who will be working with Trello. The Enterprise plan includes the additional security measures needed to protect data and adhere to industry-related compliance regulations. The Enterprise plan allows a company to manage many separate teams of people who work within an unlimited number of Trello boards.

The base price of this plan is $20.83 per month, per user (when paid annually), although discounts are offered to companies with more than 300 paid users. For example, the price of the Enterprise plan drops to just $4.17 per month, per user, when a company has more than 1,000 paid users.

Some of the additional features offered by the Enterprise plan include the following:

- More secure user sign-in options—including two-factor authentication—which are designed to keep all data and accounts more secure.

- The ability to assign an Account Executive (administrator) who can manage and oversee all user accounts and has the ability to add, delete, and adjust account-specific permissions as needed.

- Additional support for helping with the migration to Trello and training users.

- Priority customer service and tech support, with guaranteed responses in less than one business day.

- File encryption and other security features for protecting data, documents, and files stored within Trello. This includes intrusion detection with enhanced software monitoring.

Getting Started with Trello

To get started with Trello, use your computer's web browser to visit www.trello.com, and click the Sign Up button to create a free account using the form in Figure 16.1. Alternatively, download and install the official Trello mobile app on your smartphone or tablet. Upon launching the app, tap the Sign Up button.

The account creation process takes just a few minutes. You provide your name, email address, and some other basic information, and then verify the new account via email and your smartphone. Follow the on-screen prompts to accomplish this straightforward task.

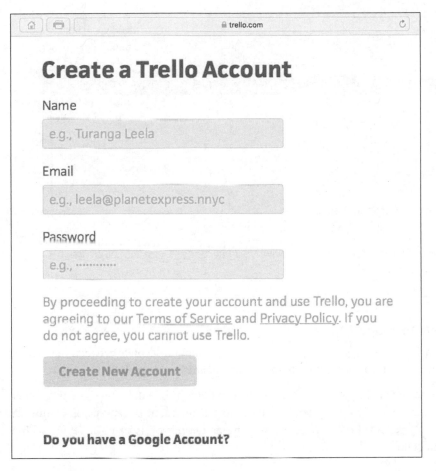

FIGURE 16.1   The Create a Trello Account screen.

In Practice

Use Trello on Multiple Devices

Some people opt to use Trello from all of their computer(s) and mobile device(s). After you set up a single Trello account, all your content automatically syncs with your account and is instantly accessible from any computer or mobile device you use to sign in to the service.

After you've verified your account and signed in to Trello, the main screen is displayed within your web browser (see Figure 16.2) or via the mobile app. The tasks you can handle from this screen are described in the following sections.

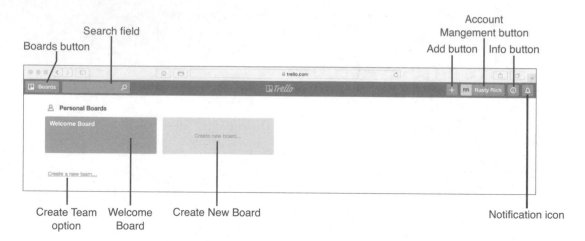

FIGURE 16.2   From this main Trello browser window, you can access virtually all of Trello's features, functions, and menus.

Switching Between Boards

Click the Boards button in the top-left corner of the browser window to switch between any Trello boards your account has access to. This includes both personal boards and team boards.

A personal board is one to which only you have access. A team board is one that you share with other people on your team. Changes made by any team member to a team board (or any cards within the board) are almost instantly reflected on your screen as long as the person is using a device with a continuous Internet connection.

> **FYI: Create as Many Separate Boards As You Need**
>
> A single Trello user can create as many separate boards as needed in order to manage her content. This can include a combination of personal boards and team boards. Subsequently, each board can include any number of separate cards or lists.
>
> A user can use Trello for her personal use, but she can be part of any number of separate Trello teams. Each team can have its own collection of boards and cards that are shared among that team's members. A user can switch between teams as easily as she can switch between boards when using Trello.

Creating a New Team and Inviting People to Collaborate

When you click the Create a New Team option, you have the opportunity to create a Team Name and then provide a description of the team (see Figure 16.3). Click the Create button to open the Team Management browser window.

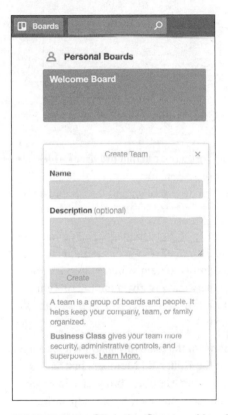

FIGURE 16.3 Click the Create a New Team option to set up a new team.

From the Team Management browser window, you have the following options:

- **Edit Team Profile:** Click this option to add more descriptive information to the Team Profile (see Figure 16.4). This can include a Profile photo or logo, and a website URL. After you start working with multiple teams, you'll definitely want to use these tools in order to make each team easier to identify and differentiate between from a visual standpoint.

FIGURE 16.4   Personalize each Team Profile to make it easier to identify.

- **Manage Team Boards:** Use the Boards tab to create new Trello boards that are accessible to all team members. Each board can be created to handle information and content related to a specific topic or subtopic. Click the Create New Board option to establish and then populate a shared team board.

- **Manage Team Members:** Click the Members tab (see Figure 16.5) to manage the admin duties for a team board and also to manage members. A Trello team can have two or more "members" who are able to view and collaborate on the creating and editing content stored within boards and individual cards. By default, the person who creates a new team is given the job of Team Admin. From the Manage Team Members browser window, however, the board creator can transfer the team management responsibilities to someone else.

  The Team Admin can also add or remove new individuals from the team. To send invites to new team members, click the Add by Name or Email button or the Bulk Add Members button. As members are added to a team, they're listed in the Manage Team Members browser window. When the Team Admin selects and highlights an individual team member, he can adjust that person's permissions. To remove a member, the Team Admin simply clicks the View Team option, clicks the Members tab, and then clicks the Remove button that's associated with a listed team member.

- **Adjust Team-Related Settings:** Click the Settings tab to adjust Trello-related settings pertaining to the team. (Only the Team Admin can make adjustments on this tab.) To access and use the majority of the features offered on this tab, you need to upgrade your Trello account to a paid Trello Business Class or Trello Enterprise account. To delete the team altogether, scroll to the bottom of this browser window and click the Delete This Team option.

- **Upgrade to Trello Business Class:** Click this tab to learn more about the benefits and additional features offered to Trello Business Class users.

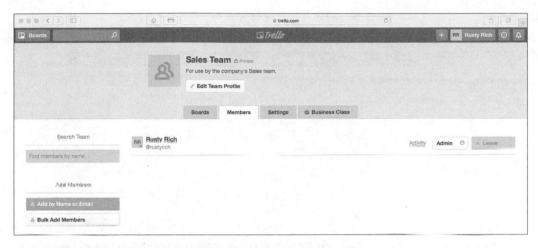

FIGURE 16.5   The Team Admin can add new team members, remove members from the team, and adjust the permissions for specific team members.

Exploring the Sample Welcome Board

By default, a Welcome Board is created for each new account. This board includes sample cards and lists, plus provides an overview of key Trello features and functions. As a first-time Trello user, explore the contents of this board to become familiar with how Trello works. You can also simply delete it and begin creating your own boards, cards, and lists.

Searching for Content

Within the Search field in the top-left corner of the browser window, type a keyword or search phrase that pertains to content you have stored within Trello. You see search results relating to the keyword or phrase that you entered. You can search for a name, date, subject, or any word that helps you locate the content you're looking for.

Creating a New Board

To create a new (empty) board within which you'll add cards that contain content or lists, click the Create New Board option that's displayed under the Personal Board or any Team heading (see Figure 16.6). Alternatively, you can click the Add icon near the top-right corner of the browser window to choose between adding a Personal or Team board.

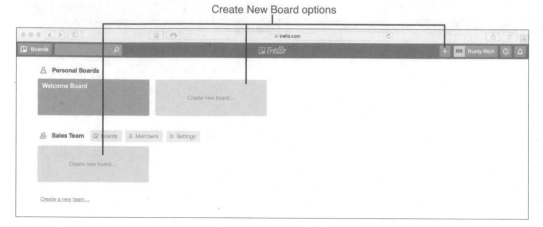

FIGURE 16.6 Create as many separate personal boards or team boards as you need by clicking the appropriate Create New Board option.

Each time you create a new board, you need to provide a Title for the board and then determine if it will be a Private board or a Team board. If it'll be a Team board, use the pull-down menu to select which Team the board should be associated with.

In Practice

Create Boards and Then Populate Them

After you've created a new board, click its listing to open the board and begin populating it with cards (that contain your content or lists).

Managing Your Trello Account

Click your Trello username in the top-right corner of the browser window to access a menu (see Figure 16.7) that gives you the ability to edit your personal profile, view cards you've created, and adjust settings related to your own account (as opposed to Team-related settings, if you're a Team Admin).

To sign out of your Trello account, click your username, and then choose the Log Out option from the menu. Although you're not required to log out each time you're done using Trello from your web browser, signing out is an extra security precaution that can help keep unauthorized people from accessing your account. It's also a good idea to avoid allowing your web browser to remember your Trello username and password. If you also want to turn on the Two-Factor Authentication feature for your account, click your username, select the Settings option, and then choose the Configure Two Factor Authentication option and follow the on-screen prompts.

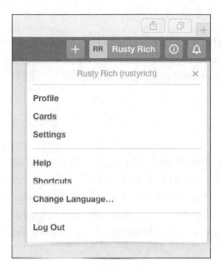

FIGURE 16.7   Access the Settings menu and other options by clicking your Trello username in the top-right corner of the browser window.

In Practice

Use Keyboard Shortcuts

To help you work with Trello faster and more efficiently, you're able to use keyboard shortcuts. To access a comprehensive list of shortcuts available to you, click your username and then choose the Shortcuts option.

CAUTION

Use Caution When Deleting Your Account

At any time after you create an account, you can permanently delete it. However, doing this automatically deletes all content you have stored within Trello, including all boards, cards, and lists. Access privileges to all Teams you're a part of are also revoked. There's no Undo option for deleting an account; everything is immediately deleted.

When you're certain you want to delete an account, click your username, select the Settings option, and scroll down to click the Delete Your Entire Account Forever option. Follow the on-screen prompts to confirm this request.

Keep in mind that you can delete individual boards and/or cards and remove yourself from one or more teams without deleting your account altogether.

Learning More About Trello

To access free, online Trello user's guides, tips, and details about paid Trello plans, click the Info ("i") icon that's near the top-right corner of the browser window. If you're new to Trello, click the Tour option, for example, to learn how to use key features and functions and learn about newly added features.

Reviewing Trello Notifications

Individual cards or lists that are added to boards can have a date/time alarm associated with them. The Notifications tool that's built into Trello keeps track of all alarms and notifications and displays them within a single window. From the account Settings menu, you can adjust Trello to send you important notifications and alerts via email and/or text message. To adjust Notification-related options, click your username and then click the Settings menu. From below the Notifications heading, choose either the Change Notification Email Frequency and/or Allow Desktop Notifications option.

Populating Trello Boards

Trello allows a user or team to create any number of separate boards. Each board can be custom named and then populated with any number of individual cards or lists. You can create a board to hold content related to a specific team, meeting, subject, or project, for example. After you've created a board and the privacy settings related to it have been set (making it accessible to just the creator, a team, or the public), it's then time to populate the board with cards or lists that contain content.

When you click or tap a board to open it, you have the opportunity to create your first card or list. The card is meant to resemble an index card, but in reality it can hold as much content as you want to add to it. Here's what you can do within the card field:

- **Add Stickers:** Drag and drop stickers that are bundled with Trello (see Figure 16.8) into a card. The majority of stickers aren't available until you unlock them by upgrading to a Trello Gold or Trello Business Class account.

- **Attach a file:** Attach a file to the card. A file attachment can be any type of file.

- **Create a list:** Compose a bulleted, numbered, or interactive checklist.

- **Type text:** Use Trello like a text editor, and type text content into the card. You can type sentences, paragraphs, or even several pages of text. It's also possible to cut and paste content into this field from other applications or from the Web.

Sticker added to card   Sticker menu

FIGURE 16.8   Add stickers to your content as a visual communication or organization tool—or just for fun.

Adding Members, Labels, Checklists, Due Dates and Attachments to Cards

Once you've populated a card with content, click or tap the card to work with it. A new window opens to show two text fields (see Figure 16.9). In the top field where it says "Add a more detailed description…," you can add a lengthier description for the card. Click the Formatting Help option to find out how to format the text in this field.

The Add Comment field is especially useful if you're working with other people. When necessary, you can create a conversation string that specifically relates to the topic of the card.

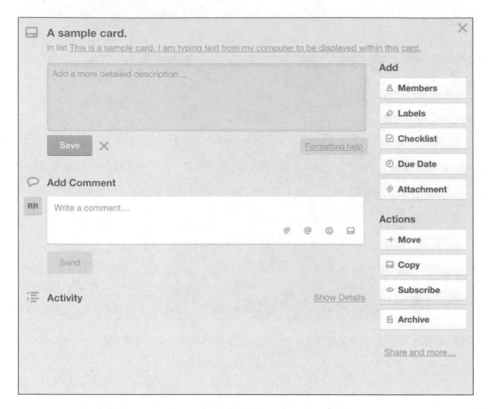

FIGURE 16.9   Add content to an individual card and use Trello's built-in features to manage that information.

In the lower-right corner of the Add Comment field are four icons:

- Click the Add File icon (which looks like a paperclip) to attach a file from another application to the card. You can share a file that's stored locally on your computer or mobile device, or one that's within another cloud-based service. If you use a Trello Power Up to link a service like Dropbox, Box, or Google Drive to your Trello account, attaching files to cards becomes even easier.

- Click the @ icon and then type a team member's username to address a comment or question to a specific team member. All team members can see the comment but know it is addressed to one or more people listed by name.

- Click the emoji icon to search for and add emojis to the card's content.

- Click the Search icon to locate content already stored within the card or within other cards.

Each time someone adds a comment to a card, the comment is identified with his username or initials, the time, and the date, so it's easy to follow a text-based conversation, and see a card's evolution.

Toward the bottom of the window is the Activity heading. This is an automatically created summary of each action taken by each team member as it relates to that specific card.

Under the Add heading on the right side of the card are five buttons that provide the following tools for managing the content of a list or card:

- **Members:** Click this button to add people (team members) who can access the card or its contents.

- **Labels:** Use this tool to create a list of one-word labels, and then associate one or more labels with each card or list item. You're also able to color-code content, so you can devise a visual system for organizing information based on what it's associated with or it's priority. For example, red items might be designated as extremely important, orange items designated as mildly important, and blue items designated as less important.

In Practice

Trello Maintains a Label Master List

Each time you create a new label, it's added to a master list that's stored within your account, which means you can easily re-use the same labels later without having to re-create them. For example, you can use a label to associate content with a particular topic, project, or client. Create and assign as many separate labels as you want with each card or item.

- **Checklist:** To associate an interactive checklist with a card or item, click the Checklist button. You name the checklist and then add individual items to it. Each item has a check box associated with it. When an item on the list is completed, you add a check mark to the box, and the item is changed to strikethrough text (see Figure 16.10). Each checklist has a progress to indicate how close the list is to completion. You can assign a due date to individual items on the list or to the list as a whole.

- **Due Date:** Associate a date and time when a checklist, a specific checklist item, or the contents of a card needs to be completed or needs further attention. This information is managed by Trello, but you can use a Power-Up to set up a sync with your Calendar application. When the due date approaches, Trello generates a notification to attract attention to it.

- **Attachment:** Attach a file from another application to the card or item by clicking the Attach button and then selecting where the file is currently located. The file can be stored locally on your computer or mobile device or in a compatible file-storage service, such as Google Drive, Dropbox, Box, or OneDrive (see Figure 16.11). You can also attach a URL link to other content or to a website within a card by typing the URL within the Attach a Link field. Click the Attach button after you've designated where the file should be attached from. A copy of the attached file is uploaded and stored within your Trello account so that you and other team members can get to the file from the card it's attached to.

Completed item   Checklist progress bar   Item being added

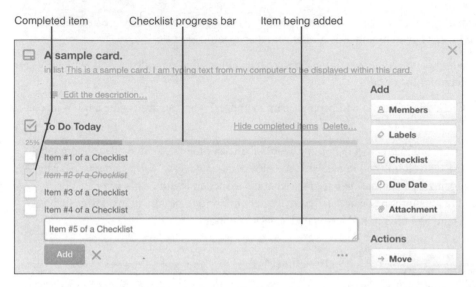

FIGURE 16.10   Add and manage interactive checklists to any card or item. You can add multiple lists to a single card, and each list can contain any number of items.

FIGURE 16.11   Attach one or more files from another source, or a website URL, to a specific card or item.

Reorganizing Your Cards

After opening a board and viewing all of the cards and lists that it contains, it's easy to reorganize and re-position the cards on the board by dragging and dropping them into place. For example, if each card represents one task associated with a project, as the project moves forward steps might need to be reassigned or reordered. Just drag the cards to their new positions, and all team members immediately can see how things have changed.

In Practice

List Items Can Be Re-Ordered As Well

It's as easy to re-order or re-organize list content as it is to rearrange cards. Simply drag list items up or down within a card. Click the pencil-shaped Manage icon in the top-right corner of a list item to access a menu that offers additional options for working with or managing that content (see Figure 16.12).

Click the Edit Labels option to add labels (individual keywords) to an item, which makes it easier to find and sort later. The Change Members option enables you to determine who can access the card item, and the Move option enables you to move the item from one card to another. Use the Copy command to copy an item from one card to another so that the item is displayed within two different cards. Click the Change Due Date option to associate an alert and due date with the item. This can be a date or a date and time. Each item within a card can have a separate Due Date associated with it.

When you're done working with an item, click the Archive option to store it and remove it from view. This tool can help eliminate clutter within cards and boards without actually deleting content.

Click the menu icon (the three horizontal dots) in the top-right corner of the card to access a separate menu (see Figure 16.13) for managing the card. From this menu, you can add a new card, copy a list, move a list, subscribe to a card, move all cards within a list, or archive all cards in the list you're working with. You can also archive only the selected list. Again, this stores the content but removes it from view.

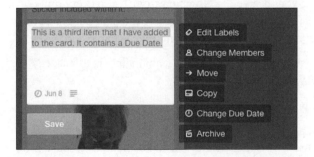

FIGURE 16.12   This menu offers options for managing specific items within a card.

Menu icon

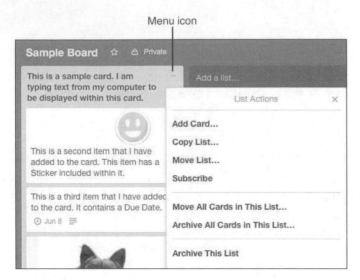

FIGURE 16.13   The options offered by this menu allow you to manage an entire card and its contents.

Using Actions to Organize and Manage Information

After opening a board, click one card or an item within a card to access the pop-up window that allows you to create additional content within the card, add or respond to comments pertaining to the card, or manage the card. Using the options under the Actions heading, you can do the following:

- **Move:** Move the content from one card to another. The content is removed from its original card and placed on the designated card. (Alternatively, you can drag and drop content from one card to another.)

- **Copy:** Copy the content from one card to another. The content remains within its original card but is also copied to the card or cards you designate.

- **Subscribe:** When you Subscribe to a card, you receive a notification from Trello every time something within the card changes, is deleted, or is archived. Customize the notifications option so you receive the Notifications from Trello for the actions you want to be aware of.

- **Vote:** When applicable, you can set up a voting option to allowing team members to make a decision. Trello tallies the votes and displays the results.

- **Archive:** Remove the content from view but have it stored within your Trello account.

- **Share:** Click the More option to access a pop-up window that allows you to print the content related to a specific card or item (see Figure 16.14), export the selected content, or create a Link to that content that you can share with others.

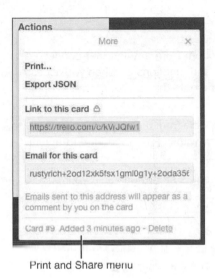

Print and Share menu

FIGURE 16.14 Content stored within a card can be shared with others or printed.

In Practice

Create Cards and Comment via Email

Every Trello board has a unique email address that you can use to create new cards, add comments, or respond to comments directly from the email application on your computer or mobile device. The subject of the email message becomes the card's title, and the body of the email message becomes the content added to the card that's created. File attachments added to the email you compose automatically become attachments to the Trello card.

CAUTION

Be Mindful of Board and Card Visibility

When creating a board, you have the option to adjust the visibility setting, which determines exactly who may access the content. If you use the Private setting, only you have access to the items you post to the board. If you select the Team option, you *and* your team members have access to the content. However, if you select the Public option, anyone with the URL for the board is able to access and view it. The content also potentially becomes searchable via Internet search engines, such as Google, although only board team members and Admins are able to change content on a public board.

Especially if you plan to store personal, confidential, or otherwise sensitive information within Trello, be sure to adjust the Privacy setting for each board separately and make sure it's set properly before adding or uploading any sensitive information to it.

> ### FYI: Trello Mobile App
>
> The Trello mobile app gives you full access to your Trello account from any Internet-connected smartphone or tablet. The app offers the same tools, features, and functions as when you access Trello using your computer's web browser. However, to accommodate the smaller screen size, the layout of the menus and content is a bit different.
>
> All of your boards, cards, lists, and related content become available from the mobile app, and any changes you make using the mobile app are instantly reflected within your account and appear when accessing Trello from your computer's web browser.
>
> Remember, Trello is a cloud-based service, so all of your content is stored online in your secure Trello account.

Adding Functionality with Third-Party Apps

Both the App Store for the iPhone and iPad and the Google Play Store for Android-based mobile devices offer a collection of third-party apps that work in conjunction with your Trello account and/ or the Trello mobile app. To find Trello-compatible mobile apps, launch the App Store app on your mobile device, and either enter the name of the app or the keyword *Trello* in the Search field. Click any of the search results to read an app's description or download the desired app. Most are available for free.

Some of these optional, third-party apps include the following:

- **Hillo for Trello:** The title of this app stands for "High Level Trello." It provides a bird's-eye view of your Trello boards, cards, lists, activity, and notifications and gives you added tools to help you stay up to date on due dates and the progress of multiple projects (even if they're spread across multiple boards) from a single screen.

- **L8r: Post Ideas to Trello:** Using your mobile device, you can write or draw content and then upload it directly to your Trello account. You're also able to use the camera built into your mobile app to take photos or scan documents and have that content added to a specific board.

- **Punchtime for Trello:** This app offers time-tracking capabilities to your Trello account, so you can determine how much time you're spending on specific tasks, projects, or clients, which helps you better analyze how you're using your time. Timers can be associated with an account, specific boards, or specific cards. You need to set up a free Punchtime account (www.punchti. me) and have an active Trello account to use this app.

- **Reminders for Trello:** With this simple application, you can view on a single screen all notifications and reminders generated by Trello. You can then tap a specific notification to go directly to relevant content within your Trello account.

- **TrePost-Trello:** This app enables you to collect information using your mobile device and send it directly to Trello with a single tap. Use this to add and manage to-do lists while you're on the go or to gather data from other mobile app sources and quickly send it to a board or specific card that you select.

FYI: Power-Ups are Different Than Third-Party Apps

Third-party apps are designed to function on their own using your mobile device. Power-Ups are available separately to allow popular software applications and cloud-based services that you use with your computer(s) to function more seamlessly with Trello. To learn more about available Power-Ups, visit https://trello.com/power-ups.

Chapter | **17**

Adapting to Quickly Evolving Technologies

This chapter covers the following:

- How technological innovations are causing cloud-based services to change

- Why it's important to take advantage of integration between services and applications

- How to avoid common cloud-based collaboration pitfalls

- Advice from cloud-computing experts

Every few weeks—not months or years—new technology or innovations related to the Internet, file storage, collaboration, data compression, encryption, mobile devices, cybersecurity, and computer hardware are making it possible for all of the cloud services to evolve. Because these services are based in the cloud and typically require no software to be installed on a user's computer, updates to these services can be created and released quickly.

These factors, combined with increased competition among cloud services, have led to each of these services continuously adding new features and functionality. The enhancements not only improve upon the toolsets already offered but also add new tools that enable the services to perform in cutting-edge new ways.

As a result, the lines have blurred between the features and functions offered by each cloud service. For example, Dropbox is no longer just a cloud-based file-storage and file-sharing service. Cisco WebEx has become much more than an Internet-based video-conferencing platform. And Evernote now does a lot more than serve as a text editor that syncs notes between a user's computers and mobile devices.

> ## FYI: An Expert's Thoughts on the Popularity of Cloud Computing
>
> Alex Miller, Senior Cloud Research Analyst at Clutch (http://clutch.co), explained, "Accessibility and functionality increases have led to a significant adoption rate for cloud-based tools. These will increasingly continue to grow in popularity amongst small businesses. Their unmatched ability to connect distant teams is now a necessity in business. In terms of accessibility, many cloud-based tools have made tasks that once required an IT department to now be completed without any complex computing skills. Whether it's simple tasks, such as joining in on a Google Doc, or a more complex endeavor, like firing up a virtual server, the barrier to entry has been significantly lowered."
>
> He added, "A large misconception is that the cloud is safe on its own. Some think that simply by trusting data with a powerhouse, like Google, the data will be safe. Working with cloud-based tools, whether it's for storage, backup, collaboration, communication, or any other productivity goal, also requires user commitment to security. Weak passwords, poor access control, and lack of training can lead to data breaches and losses from the user's side, an issue that providers often cannot prevent or correct. Especially in discussions of compliance, there is an equal share of responsibilities for safe document handling between the provider and the user."
>
> When asked about the biggest security-related drawbacks to working in the cloud, Miller responded, "Any time data is being transferred via the cloud, it has the potential of being compromised. It's a risk you take in exchange for an extraordinary level of connectedness. Using the cloud may open you up to security concerns that your hard drive wouldn't, but the benefits overwhelmingly outweigh these potential pitfalls. And, with just a little attention to security, these drawbacks can be significantly decreased."

In today's world of cloud computing, individual companies, like Microsoft and Google, are offering complete suites of online tools that can affordably handle all aspects of working in the cloud. Meanwhile, the cloud-computing tools offered by other companies are quickly expanding their respective toolsets, while providing secure integration with other popular applications and online platforms.

Thanks to well-established companies designing and building secure, cloud-computing platforms and infrastructures, companies of any size can now take full advantage of these tools and inexpensively migrate to the cloud without having to purchase and maintain their own servers or hire a team of in-house IT professionals. Instead, a single person (or several people), who might have minimal technical expertise, can be assigned the role of administrator to manage the user accounts that allow a company to take full advantage of the cloud while keeping all data, documents, and files secure. It's no longer a question of whether a company should use cloud computing; it's only a matter of which services a company should adopt.

Unfortunately, the answer to this second question has become somewhat of a moving target that's sometimes difficult to answer with any certainty. After all, as soon as a decision-maker within an organization does her research to choose what is currently the most suitable service to adopt, new innovations allow other platforms and services to offer similar, or even better, functionality, sometimes at a lower cost.

FYI: Expert Advice About Cybersecurity

Aaron Vick is the Chief Strategy Officer at a cloud-based analytics group, called Cicyda, which builds software for the legal space. When asked about the biggest drawbacks to using a cloud-based file-sharing service or online collaboration tool and how these potential security vulnerabilities can be overcome, he responded, "You have only the vendor's word on what they are doing from a security perspective and how. You don't know if they're implementing things properly, or if they are maintaining whatever defense mechanisms they put in place. By and large, however, the vendor is probably doing a better job than you would."

He added, "Too much is out of your control, and in the hands of the cloud provider. You can, however, reduce risk by using unique passwords for every cloud-based account. Don't sync or use the credentials of one service to log in to another. For example, don't use Google account credentials to log in to all compatible services. Also, use a password manager to create and store strong passwords or phrases. This will reduce the likelihood that someone will guess your password, and if somehow they compromise one account, they cannot compromise them all."

With regard to staying compliant while working in the cloud, Vick explained, "It depends on your threat model, and what you do for a living. If you deal with intellectual property, or things that are easily mobilized, you will want to be judicious about what you share. You might implement an additional layer of protection, like encrypting things before you upload them, so that if a cloud service is hacked, the files cannot be opened. When discussing sensitive data in a collaborative environment, consider using codenames for customers or projects, so that an outsider looking at your sensitive data might not fully understand what they're seeing.

"Also think about what kind of threat actor you're really concerned about. If you're in a cutthroat business that is international in scope, you have to consider threats that are very high end. If you're in a more mundane sort of line of work, the threat is typically much lower."

Vick stated that the biggest cybersecurity threat a company faces is often a disgruntled employee or former employee. He added, "The threat may not be from a hacker or a weakness in the service. It could be from an individual user or member of your team, or someone who is an ex-team member who does not appreciate the sensitivity of some data. This person downloads content that they shouldn't, shares it, or then gets their system compromised."

In terms of additional security measures that individual users can take when accessing cloud services, Vick stated, "Compromising public Wi-Fi is a trivial affair. Thus, you should be using a VPN of some type whenever you're using public Wi-Fi. You should also regularly scan your own systems for malware."

Because the probability that cloud computing advancements will slow down anytime soon is basically zero, a company looking to utilize these tools needs to do the following:

- Determine what's possible right now using the most popular cloud computing services and platforms.

- Clearly define how these tools can and will be used within their organization or by specific teams.

- Determine what compliance regulations and data security requirements your organization needs to adopt and adhere to.

- Choose one or more cloud computing platforms or services that currently meet the needs of the company.

- Set up the required integrations between the applications and cloud services you're already using with the new service or platform being adopted and be sure to test these integrations before deploying them.

- Train everyone on how to use the selected services to reduce human error as much as possible.

- Be prepared for, and be able to adopt change as it happens. This requires everyone to update to the latest tools as they become available. Ongoing training is necessary to ensure everyone remains proficient using the same tools. On the plus side, all services offer free online training videos, manuals, and interactive tutorials to keep users abreast of the latest advancements and how to use them.

FYI: User Error Causes the Most Problems

When you understand that user error causes more problems than any other issue when it comes to breaches in security to a cloud service, you'll understand that it's essential to provide your team or organization with the best training possible. Everyone needs to understand and be comfortable using the tools and services. Each individual needs to be taught how to employ basic security measures to protect their account password. Users should also double-check all account-related settings before sharing data or collaborating with others to ensure that only appropriate people are being invited to access sensitive information and that proprietary information isn't accidently misdirected to or placed in a more public cloud-based folder, for example.

FYI: Expert Advice About Online Collaboration

Calvin Wilder is the founder and CEO of Smartbooks Corporation (www.smartbookscorp.com). When asked what he believes individual users of cloud-based tools can do to help protect their content, he explained, "Know who you are collaborating with and understand the parameters of what they may share outside of the tool. Just as you would not click on odd links sent to you via email by someone you don't know, you also need to understand what is a normal or odd request or interaction using a cloud collaboration tool. Two-factor authentication is a huge safeguard for individual user accounts and should be used whenever available to prevent others from accessing your accounts."

He added, "Understand the basics of who can share the data, how it is backed up, and which users technically own the data and can edit or delete it. Most cloud collaboration tools are so simple to use, it can be easy to overlook these basics, only to discover too late that important files were owned by a departing employee under their personal Gmail account, or that you accidently deleted an important file in Google Drive that was not backed up.

"If you work with super sensitive or classified information, cloud collaboration is challenging. Understand that once you put your data in the cloud, copies of it will permeate, and you can never get it all back. The application service will have a backup service, and its backup service will have its own backup service. Their system administrators will have access to your data. For most small businesses, this is not a major concern, but for some, it is."

Taking Advantage of Integrations

At the same time as each cloud-based platform or service is striving to add features and functions to become all things to all users, there's also a strong focus being placed on creating secure integrations between applications and cloud services. For the end users, this means that two or more popular applications or online services can easily be set up to seamlessly sync and share information. When the cloud service you're using provides integration for specific applications, you know that the service's developers have worked to ensure seamless and secure exchange of information with the application. These integrations allow users to bridge the gaps caused by fast-evolving technologies.

> **CAUTION**
>
> ### Pay Attention to An Integration's Creator
>
> Integrations between applications and cloud-based services are often created and provided by the application developer or a cloud-based service. These integrations are typically secure and work well because the two companies have directly collaborated to ensure their products work in conjunction with each other.
>
> If you're interested in using third-party integrations to manipulate your data, documents, and files and allow them to sync or be shared between the applications and cloud-based services you're using, do the necessary research and testing to make sure the integrations work as expected and maintain the appropriate security measures.

As you begin using cloud-based services, you'll likely discover that there are features or functions that your services don't have but that do exist on other services or platforms. For example, if you've already adopted Dropbox or Office 365, you might want to make DocuSign's functionality available to your team. Perhaps you want to be able to communicate using Cisco WebEx's video-conferencing tools while also using the online collaboration tools offered by Slack or Trello. This is where integrations become extremely useful because you can bridge the gap between applications and cloud-based services without requiring any customized programming to be done on your behalf.

FYI: Expert Advice Related to Integrations

Jon Ferrara is the CEO and founder of Nimble, Inc., a social sales and marketing CRM platform. When asked how he thinks cloud-based services have evolved the most over the past few years, he explained that the biggest and best evolutions for users relate to integrations, and how content and information can more easily be shared across cloud-based platforms, software applications, and mobile apps.

He stated, "I think that the biggest change that occurred for cloud-based collaboration tools is their ability to work effectively together. In the past, you may have used Slack, which is a collaboration tool that worked well within itself but didn't talk well with other tools, like your email or contact management application. Ultimately, the evolution of these tools and services over the next few years will be that all of these tools will start playing much more effectively together.

"Today, there are still too many islands of information within a business, whether we are talking about their cloud productivity suites, email, contacts, scheduling, and collaboration tools; or their sales, marketing, customer service, or social media tools that they are using. There are walls between departments, and data is not shared. There's no unified record of relationships, and I see that changing over time because everyone in the company needs to work effectively together."

Ferrara added that it's important for individuals and companies alike to choose which services to subscribe to and pay for, otherwise you wind up having dozens of accounts across many different platforms and services. He said, "It's important to manage the subscriptions and the tools that you are using to make sure that you are effectively managing their usage." This also includes disabling integrations that are no longer required and closing accounts that are not being used.

In terms of integrations between applications and cloud services, one thing that Ferrara believes that many companies are missing is an integrated contact management, scheduling, and CRM application.

He stated, "One thing that is missing from most collections of programs is a tool that provides what Office 365 and Google G Suite are missing, which is a good contact manager. When you think about Office 365 and Google G Suite, email, contact, and calendar are in three separate tabs, and when you go to a contact record, you don't have context. By this, I mean you don't see the history of interactions that you and the team have had with your customers, and what the details about their companies are. A CRM program, like Nimble [www.nimble.com], layers intelligence on top of Office 365 or G Suite, and unifies all your contacts, calendars and communications into one easy-to-use solution. It allows you to manage and nurture your relationships, and for your sales and marketing departments to collaborate together, for example."

Expert Advice from Olivia Teich, Director of Products at Dropbox

Olivia Teich is a cloud computing expert who currently serves as Director of Products at Dropbox. During her interview for this book, she delved deeply into ways small businesses and teams can use all cloud computing services and platforms (not just Dropbox and Dropbox Paper) more effectively. She also discussed many of the trends that are causing businesses to rely heavily on these services in order to improve collaboration, communication, and the exchange of information.

Along with everything you've learned thus far within *Working in the Cloud*, the additional advice offered by Teich will help you more confidently make decisions about cloud computing that will directly impact your team or company—both now and in the future.

To begin, Teich explained what Dropbox actually is and the misconception people often have about the service. "What people think they know Dropbox for is only a piece of the story. The genesis of Dropbox was that people should be able to access their stuff from anywhere, from any device, and share it with anyone. The original focus of just keeping someone's own files in sync has evolved into being able to keep all content and your entire team in sync," said Teich. "This is where Dropbox Paper comes into play. This toolset allows for better collaboration above and beyond just file sharing."

As mentioned in Chapter 8, "Managing Collaboration with Dropbox," the focus of these two toolsets is to enable people to share content and work together in real time to create, compose, exchange, and review information and ideas, and in Teich's words, "to tell and share stories."

She explained, "Today, a lot of back and forth between people gets fragmented across several different tools and platforms. This creates a lot of friction. By combining file sharing and online storage with real-time collaboration tools, a team can now have one helm for keeping their content and team members in sync as they're trying to get work done."

In the process of learning about each of the popular cloud services and platforms, you probably noticed a lot of overlap in the tools being offered. "The biggest differentiator between Dropbox and other services is our philosophy about who we're building our platform for," stated Teich. "Dropbox has always been built for our end users to be the tool that they want to use, know how to use, and trust using. People share through Dropbox because they know that the people they're sharing with will receive the files being sent, for example. Other cloud-based platforms have been designed specifically for tech-savvy IT buyers, who then have to make end users adopt it, even though the service was not actually designed with non-technical end users in mind. This is a fundamental and philosophical difference between Dropbox and other platforms."

According to Teich, the mandates when designing and developing Dropbox and Dropbox Paper have always been on simplicity and ease of use. "Our service was built for the more than 500 million people who have chosen to adopt Dropbox because of this philosophy and because we are cross-platform compatible. Especially in a small business environment, there are a mix of PC and Mac users, as well as iPhone and iPad versus Android-based smartphone and tablet users. Dropbox accommodates everyone with the same tools. Plus, Dropbox is designed to handle all of your content, not just specific types of files," she added.

Ultimately, cloud-based collaboration and file sharing tools are also about building and maintaining interpersonal human relationships in a digital world. "So often, if you're not looking at someone face to face, it's easy to forget that they're a person. Dropbox is working hard to help people build and maintain an emotional connection as they're trying to get things done together," said Teich.

This trend toward humanizing cloud-based services will, no doubt, continue across all of the platforms, as each now realizes the need to be accepted and usable by non-tech-savvy people. "When you're not talking directly to a person, we're not always kind. Something as simple as bringing faces back into virtual interactions can make a huge difference," said Teich. "This can be accomplished in many ways, such as having team members include a photo of themselves within their profile and then having that profile photo appear in conjunction with messages and digital interactions that take place."

There are also what Teich refers to as "moments of awkwardness" that can often take place as a side effect of virtual interactions. For example, you send an important message to someone and then wind up stressing out about whether the recipient has seen it, and wonder how they feel about it, until they eventually respond. This causes anxiety.

"We all start to wonder what the other person's reaction will be, and then need to determine how to move forward. As the sender, you can nag the recipient, and ask, 'Hey, I haven't heard back from you, can you send me feedback?' or you can go down the path of, 'Oh, maybe they didn't like what I said,' which requires a whole different response. Of course, one reason for the lack of response could be that the recipient never actually saw the message to begin with. The sender needs to adjust their next step based on the reaction, or lack thereof, from the recipient. One way Dropbox overcomes some of this awkwardness is that we provide details about when information is sent, and when it's received and opened. As a result, the sender can have a much more appropriate and healthy response, based on knowing whether a message was unopened, or opened and read, but not responded to."

Teich believes that helping people have enough context, and the most current information, can go a long way toward better interpersonal communications in a virtual workspace. There's also the element of collaboration that includes getting and giving feedback. When the right tools are used, this can become a more humanized process, even when working in a virtual workspace.

"Using stickers or emojis in conjunction with text-based feedback can be a powerful communications tool. What we've found is that people love these tools as a way to give emotional validation and feedback, which is distinct from the words. For example, you can provide qualitative feedback in words, but when you end it with a smiley face, someone else will instantly know your comments are well intentioned. These are simple visual cues that can be anchoring in a relationship. Often, the intention can be lost in pure words. I recently saw a study demonstrating that everyone reads emails more negatively than they were intended. The way to combat this is to add the emotional cues offered by an emoji or sticker," said Teich. "When team members are able to build and maintain positive relationships even when they're working virtually, this makes accomplishing things so much easier."

Some people believe that using stickers and emojis is perfectly acceptable when communicating with friends on social media, or through smartphone text messaging, but that this lighter form of communication is not suitable for the workspace. This goes against the research that Dropbox has done when developing Dropbox Paper.

Teich explained, "For years, there's been debate about whether stickers and emojis belong in a collaborative workspace. Some believe that if the collaboration becomes too social, people will stop doing work. What we've found is that more often than not, people recognize that it's their job and are afraid of going too far when communicating using collaboration tools. Most people are able to determine for themselves what's appropriate versus what's too casual or inappropriate for a work setting. In general, the anxiety people have will prevent them from misusing stickers and emojis when collaborating with co-workers.

"The cultural norm of a company will come into play when it comes to users determining whether or not stickers and emojis are suitable within their work-related communications. If you work in a conservative environment, people won't use stickers or emojis anywhere near as much as if you're working in a super casual, young environment, where a group of friends are working together. Teams will establish their own ways of communicating with each other. The platform being used should, however, enable the culture and values of the company to come through."

When collaborating with others on the creation or review of content, Teich recommends that it be made clear as to what part of the process the team is in. For example, if you're in the brainstorming phase, it should be made clear that team members should share their ideas and opinions freely. However, if you're in the final review phase, this is when someone should be able to point out major errors but not start recommending new ideas or approaches. When everyone understands what type of feedback is needed and when, the team will be much more productive.

"Simply stating, 'Please provide feedback related to this document,' versus 'Please provide your approval for this document,' sends two very different messages about what is expected from team members during a collaboration process," said Teich. "Giving people the right context for what's expected makes the social interactions much more productive."

Whenever a company or team adopts new software or a cloud-based service, Teich believes in the importance of having an in-house champion or evangelist in place to oversee the transition or migration to the new tools. "This person needs to demonstrate to the team or other users how the software or service will be used and show some examples. People are very good at picking up on those examples and modeling their work habits after them. So, if the evangelist uses a smiley face emoji at the end of a message, this shows the team that this practice is acceptable. Even a very small amount of content shared by the evangelist can set the perfect example for how a new tool can be used and showcase what's acceptable," she said.

Another example is when the evangelist starts assigning names to files, folders, and subfolders within a cloud-based file-sharing service. People will pick up and adopt the methodology demonstrated to them without being told specifically to do so. "Practices like this tend to evolve and come together in a natural way, especially when something that doesn't feel right for the team is discussed and adjusted right away," explained Teich.

When asked about the fear people have of the various cloud-based services evolving so quickly, Teich stated, "We are forever seeing the pendulum swing between best of breed and the suite. A suite of applications may offer all forms of functionality that's needed, but each individual tool in the suite may not actually be good or powerful enough to meet the needs of the people using them. The alternative is to use a best of breed, and to choose a separate solution for each task that needs to be accomplished. Which methodology to adopt is a permanent source of anxiety. My advice is to figure out which tools work the best for you and your team, and go with that until something better comes along. Don't change for the sake of change. Find something that works now, but be able to identify when something is no longer working for you.

"If you're working around a tool more than using the tool, that's an indicator of a problem. This is when you should do more research and ask yourself if there's a better tool that will work for you. It comes down to really understanding the problem you're trying to solve using cloud computing and then choosing the tools that solve that problem."

Teich further explained, "More and more of these tools are now integrating together. People are working with all different systems, both cloud based and not. Being able to connect all of this together is critical. The integrations that are available allow you to use the best tools for the job. This is why we have seen the CRM apps and writing apps, for example, fully integrating with online file-storage, file-sharing, and online collaboration tools, and making the integrations work very well. Thanks to integrations, it does not have to be an either or choice when it comes to choosing which applications and cloud-based tools to adopt."

When looking to adopt new software or a new cloud-based tool, pay attention to how well it integrates with the software and online-based tools you're already using. If you find a set of tools that work together, any company or team can create a powerful ecosystem that works like a suite and that works very well to meet the unique needs of a team or company.

Dealing with integrations can be a confusing challenge onto itself. For example, you may know that Office 365 and Dropbox are secure and manage your files in the proper way, but what happens when you try to integrate these two services together?

Teich explained, "This is a valid concern, but it's rarely a real problem that users or companies encounter. My advice is to look at who built the integration. Does it come from one of the two companies whose software and services you're trying to integrate together? At Dropbox, we build many integrations ourselves, because they're so important for allowing our users to have a great experience. When a company puts their own name on an integration, you know that they're standing behind it and supporting it. One thing you don't want to do is build your business upon something that eventually goes away. Find tools that you can trust will be there moving forward and that will not ultimately lock up your data in the future."

Another thing to evaluate when choosing whether to adopt a new cloud-based application or service is how much training will be required to get everyone up to speed on using it. Because many users won't come from a technical background, you want the service to be as user-friendly and as intuitive as possible. The service also should offer the training tools and resources to help people easily acquire the skills needed to use the newly adopted tools. The decision-maker, however, needs to pay attention to ease of use and then be able to demonstrate to their team what can be done.

"In my experience, once you provide team members or users with an example or two of each feature being used in a real-world situation, they'll develop a faster understanding of what's possible and will catch up in terms of how to use each tool. It all comes down to building awareness of what's possible and then demonstrating how things can actually get done," said Teich.

Make sure that any service you choose has data security in place. As for compliance issues, you need to understand what's required for your business and then make sure the service adheres to those requirements. According to Teich, most of the cloud services publish whitepapers that focus on security and compliance.

"Security is there, and whatever you think you need, the major cloud-based services most likely already offer. When you have specialized needs—this is where a company needs to take a much closer look at what a cloud-based platform offers. Beyond that, don't worry.

"When you see a bunch of big-name companies listed on a cloud-based service's customer reference pages, this should eliminate much of your concern. If you see large companies that you respect and aspire to be like already using a specific service, you know those companies have already done a lot of vetting. Most likely, those companies have a lot more to lose then you do. Look for real case studies from major companies that have adopted a cloud-based service or platform, not just a listing of companies, which could mean that just one person at that company uses the service. Published case studies can be used as proof that certain platforms offer adequate security-related tools and resources," said Teich.

As for taking precautions to prevent user errors from causing data breaches or security problems down the road, Teich believes that companies can take two approaches—preventive and reactive.

She explained, "The cloud computing services typically offer security tools, like two-factor authentication for user accounts, that can help prevent problems from occurring. Using common sense when it comes to choosing with whom to share information and content is also a preventative measure that everyone can take. However, a company or team needs to be able to react properly if and when something does go wrong and be able to fix the problem and then recover from it quickly."

Be able to answer questions like the following:

- What actions need to be taken if someone sends the wrong file to the wrong person?

- What actions need to be taken if someone leaves the team, to prevent them from taking important files or data with them?

- What happens if someone deletes files that they shouldn't have?

Having a plan in place to deal with predictable mistakes will make them much easier to recover from.

One way to protect content that's stored online, as well as individual user accounts, is for the administrator and individual users to periodically review the adjustable default settings related to each account and make sure they're set appropriately for how the tool is being used. The administrator should also review the types of content being stored.

The final piece of advice that Teich offers is for people to seek out cloud-based tools that allow them to work and interact with people in a way that they want and need to. Users should not have to dramatically change their work habits or be forced to utilize impersonal interactions to accommodate the tools they adopt.

"I don't see a timeline where it will be mandatory for a company to be cloud-based. But right now, it's becoming less and less practical to not be working in the cloud," stated Teich. "The idea of a hard drive crash causing catastrophic data loss is foreign to most young people who have grown up storing their content in the cloud. By not working in the cloud, you're not taking advantage of all of the tools that are available and that can make your team or small business more productive. Yes, change can be scary. However, these days, when it comes to cloud computing, individuals and small business can get a ton of stuff for free, or at a very low cost, when they take advantage of the cloud-computing tools and services that are available to them today.

"When comparing cloud-based services available today, versus what was offered just a few years ago, it's important to understand that the experience is better, the quality is higher, and the costs are lower. So, unless you have a really, really good reason to avoid working in the cloud, you should err towards the side of taking full advantage of what cloud-computing technology offers today. Then you can focus on what you are uniquely great at in your business, because chances are, it's not running an IT infrastructure. The established cloud-based services provide the required IT infrastructure so individuals and small companies don't have to. Cloud computing makes it easier for you to run a much higher quality business, and you don't have to become a technology or cybersecurity expert to utilize these tools and truly benefit from them," she concluded.

Index

Symbols

A

O

REGISTER THIS PRODUCT
SAVE 35%*
ON YOUR NEXT PURCHASE!

How to Register Your Product

- Go to quepublishing.com/register
- Sign in or create an account
- Enter the 10- or 13-digit ISBN that appears on the back cover of your book or on the copyright page of your eBook

Benefits of Registering

- Ability to download product updates
- Access to bonus chapters and workshop files
- A 35% coupon to be used on your next purchase – valid for 30 days
  To obtain your coupon, click on "Manage Codes" in the right column of your Account page
- Receive special offers on new editions and related Que products

Please note that the benefits for registering may vary by product. Benefits will be listed on your Account page under Registered Products.

We value and respect your privacy. Your email address will not be sold to any third party company.

* 35% discount code presented after product registration is valid on most print books, eBooks, and full-course videos sold on QuePublishing.com. Discount may not be combined with any other offer and is not redeemable for cash. Discount code expires after 30 days from the time of product registration. Offer subject to change.